Poverty in Transition and
Transition in Poverty

Poverty in Transition and Transition in Poverty

Recent Developments in Hungary, Bulgaria, Romania, Georgia, Russia, Mongolia

Edited and with an Introduction by

Yogesh Atal

Berghahn Books
NEW YORK • OXFORD

UNESCO Publishing
PARIS

Published jointly by

the **United Nations Educational, Scientific and Cultural Organization**

and by

Berghahn Books

Library of Congress Cataloging-in-Publication Data

Poverty in transition and transition in poverty : studies of poverty
  in countries-in-transition : Hungary, Bulgaria, Romania, Georgia,
  Russia, Mongolia / edited and with an introduction by Yogesh Atal.
       p.   cm.
    Includes bibliographical references
       ISBN 1-57181-191-5 (hb : alk. paper). -- ISBN 1-57181-192-3 (pb :
  alk. paper)
       1. Poverty--Europe, Eastern.   2. Poverty--Georgia (Republic)
  3. Poverty--Mongolia.   4. Europe, Eastern--Economic conditions--1989-
  5. Georgia (Republic)--Economic conditions.   6. Mongolia--Economic
  conditions.   I. Atal, Yogesh.
    HC244.Z9P662   1998   98-47226
  339.4'6'0947--dc21   CIP

British Library Cataloguing in Publication Data

A catalogue record for this book is available from the British Library.

Printed in the United States on acid-free paper
ISBN 1-57181-191-5 hardback
ISBN 1-57181-192-3 paperback
UNESCO ISBN 92-3-103-575-3 paperback

CONTENTS

Introduction
Yogesh Atal   1

Chapter 1: **Recent Trends in Poverty in Hungary**
Julia Szalai   32

Chapter 2: **Emerging Poverty in Bulgaria**
Sasha Todorova   77

Chapter 3: **Poverty in Romania**
Traian Rotariu and Livia Popescu   102

Chapter 4: **Toward Poverty Eradication in Georgia**
Avtandil Sulaberidze   130

Chapter 5: **The Russian Case: Social Policy Concerns**
G. Pirogov and S. Pronin   177

Chapter 6: **Mongolia: In the Grip of Poverty**
Tsogt Nyamsuren   223

INTRODUCTION

Yogesh Atal
Coordinating Unit for Social Development, UNESCO

We commit ourselves to the goal of eradicating poverty in the world, through decisive national actions and international cooperation, as an ethical, social, political, and economic imperative of humankind.

Commitment # 2, *Declaration* by the
World Summit for Social Development

We have used our wealth and knowledge to explore space and reach the moon, while failing to reach poor neighbourhoods and ghettos. These people are reachable, but remain unreached.

We must commit ourselves to the geographically remote and socially distant … As we strive to build superhighways, we must not forget the streets and blind alleys where a vast segment of humanity lives in a constricted world, suffering from hunger, indignities, and neglect.

Federico Mayor
Director-General of UNESCO, 17 October 1995

Prologue

Preparing to enter the twenty-first century, and looking back at the gains of the past fifty years of developmental efforts, the world community has engaged itself in reprioritizing its agenda. There is certainly a feeling of satisfaction over the achievements made, but there is also a realization that much remains to be done. The development path pursued in the past five decades has not only failed to achieve some of its goals, but has also contributed to the inventory of problems. We need to attend to the unfinished agenda, and to address the newly emerging problems of global dimension. We have acknowledged the fact that despite growing modernization and gains in terms of economic growth, most countries of the world – both developing and developed – have faltered on the social front and have ignored environmental concerns while pursuing economic growth. Irrespective of the political system, and notwith-standing economic development, there are deficiencies in social devel-opment everywhere. All societies confront the problems of rising poverty, growing unemployment, and ruptures in social integration. The World Summit for Social Development (held in March 1995, in Copen-hagen) was convened to focus on these issues and to seek the commit-ment of world leadership to make a united effort to resolve them alongside the implementation of Agenda 21 adopted at the Rio Earth Summit. The road from Rio to Copenhagen helped expand the concept of sustainability by including social and cultural concerns; it was a move toward the integration of ecology and sociology.

"What if the environment is saved and cultures are lost?" was as im-portant a concern as "what if cultures are saved and the environment is deteriorated?" The two could not be seen apart from each other. Fusion of these twin concerns highlighted the need for a holistic approach to replace the economic orientation. The Copenhagen Summit called for an approach that would facilitate the search for solutions that are culturally rooted and ecologically sustainable. It endorsed the view that economic growth alone cannot ensure all-round development.

Traditional development strategies were based on the trickle-down theory and ignored the human factor. They failed to address the funda-mental imbalances in society and, thus, did not make any significant impact on poverty eradication. We have now realized that economic growth alone is not enough to ensure social development. Economic growth should be so planned that it serves the cause of social develop-ment rather than creating crises in the social sphere.

The Copenhagen message was loud and clear. There are common problems – problems that prevail in all societies, in the South or North, East or West; but there are no common solutions. The paradigm of development that was pursued in the Third World led to as much of frustration on the social front as the paradigm adopted by the socialist world. The collapse of communism, and the growing disenchantment with the development paradigm in the Third World, gave a clear signal that neither of these is appropriate for addressing the task of social devel-opment. Additionally, the presence of the problems of poverty, unem-ployment, and of tendencies toward social disintegration in the so-called developed world suggests that even these countries do not have an answer; they too are in search of solutions. Despite a high rating on all the indicators of development – economic growth, high industrializa-tion, total literacy, better health, and a democratic system – if these countries are also in deep social crisis then it is necessary to find out what else is needed to overcome these problems. We have reached a stage in which all countries are engulfed in social crises and in which there are no ready-made solutions for overcoming them. We live in a world of similar problems but of dissimilar opportunities.

Poverty is a problem with global dimensions. Reports on the world social situation hint at the rising numbers of the poor. It is generally believed that the number of the poor has already crossed the one billion mark. Standing at 1.3 billion, the number of poor today is greater than that of adult illiterates, which is around 800 million. In fact, the number of poor is much larger, as most of the figures regarding the size of the poor population, given in official publications, relate only to the developing world.[1] Poverty was officially denied in the socialist world until the collapse of the Soviet Union, and so data on poverty in those countries during that period are not available. Now that the existence of poverty is accepted even officially, statistics are being collected, but they are still not very satisfactory.[2]

Since most of the poor inhabit the so-called Third World – an appellation that has become redundant after the collapse of the socialist world – more statistics and better analyses of poverty in those countries are available. However, it must be said that most of these studies and reports are official accounts, or analyses carried out within the framework of macroeconomics. In-depth sociological studies of the poor in different socio-cultural settings are still scattered. There are several poverty groups that have not been studied, and there are several antipoverty measures

1. Replying to a question on the noninclusion of the industrialized countries on the Human Poverty Index, Richard Jolly, principal coordinator of UNDP's 1997 Human Development Report, said: "The measures are not the same. For instance, illiteracy is very low in most industrialized countries. We experimented behind the scenes on some measures such as people who didn't complete secondary schooling, lack of access to water and health services, and unemployment as another indicator. But we thought we would muddle the statistics." (See *Social Development Review*, 1997, vol. 1, no. 4:8).

2. For example, the United Nations *Report on the World Social Situation 1993* writes this about poverty: "Some 1,100 million people in developing countries – one in every five people in the world – lived in poverty in 1985. Some three-quarters of the poor, 57 percent of the world population, live in South Asia and East Asia. Sub-Saharan Africa has the second largest number living in poverty; 50 percent are below the poverty line. In West Asia, North Africa, and the developing countries of Europe, 60 million, almost one out of three, live in poverty. In Latin America and the Caribbean, poverty affects about 20 percent of the population, some 75 million people" (90-91). While there is no certainty about the exact number of the poor, as definitions differ, it is generally believed that today 1.5 billion people (out of a total world population of 5.7 billion people) are desperately poor, surviving on a daily income of less than U.S.$1. In 1960, the ratio between the richest 20 percent and the poorest 20 percent of the world's population was 30:1, which doubled in thirty years, standing at 61:1 in 1991. These figures give us an idea of the magnitude of the problem.

being taken without a proper empirical base. Application of set recipes is still the norm.

The designation of 1996 as the *International Year for the Eradication of Poverty* (IYEP), and the decade 1997-2006 as the *International Decade for the Eradication of Poverty* by the United Nations – following the recommendation of the Copenhagen World Summit – is a clear indication of the priority assigned to poverty by the world community. It is significant that the Copenhagen Summit preferred the word "eradication" to "alleviation," because it regarded the prevalence and growth of poverty as totally "unacceptable" and wanted the United Nations system, as well as member states, to make a concerted effort to erase this scourge by attacking its root causes, not just providing relief to those who live in poverty. There is, thus, an increase in governmental concern over poverty and a commitment on the part of the United Nations system to contribute to the eradication of poverty. But the academic research, particularly by domestic specialists, that is needed to support these initiatives is still very meager and not very dependable. The indigenous social science community has to undertake the tasks of developing suitable theoretical paradigms, of innovating new methodologies, and of coming up with policy-relevant findings and recommendations. So far, much of the impetus has come from outside agencies and foreign researchers. But external intervention, not based on a deeper understanding of the local situation, cannot substitute for insider insights. There is an urgent need to stimulate social scientific research on the phenomenon of poverty in different parts of the world, focusing primarily on those areas and groups that have not been studied. And in this task, the involvement of indigenous scholars must be secured so that they contribute both to the theory and methodology of poverty research, as well as to social policy in their respective countries. Such research, carried out by indigenous researchers, would ensure that culture-specific solutions will be found for the problems in place of borrowed solutions from abroad, which have generally ignored the cultural factor and thus failed to deliver.

Poverty is a multidimensional phenomenon and is caused by a variety of factors. Its manifestations also differ from context to context. There is no linear chain of cause and effect: an interrelated web of economic, social, psychological, cultural, and political factors influence the occurrence and persistence of poverty. Real poverty may not be apparent, and apparent poverty may not be real. Thus, there cannot be a single strategy to eradicate it in different societal contexts. In order to develop realistic national strategies for poverty eradication, it is of utmost importance that these be based on an objective appraisal of the etiology of poverty, its spread, and its pathology. For this, we need to take country-based stock of existing research and studies, including official reports and analyses, and to make an evaluation of the various antipoverty measures and policy initiatives. Such an exercise would help us to identify the research gaps that exist, and also to learn lessons from past experience about what went wrong and what should be prioritized. Toward this end, UNESCO is collaborating with the International Social Science Council, through its Program of Comparative Research on Poverty (CROP). UNESCO and CROP have jointly taken several initiatives to promote research on poverty in different parts of the world, and on different aspects of poverty. This collaboration has already resulted in two major publications: *Poverty: A Global Review – Handbook on International Poverty Research,* edited by Else Øyen, S.M. Miller, and Syed Abdus Samad; and *Poverty and Participation in Civil Society,* edited by Yogesh Atal and Else Øyen.

As a follow-up to the World Summit for Social Development, and as a contribution to the International Decade for the Eradication of Poverty, UNESCO decided to encourage a review of national strategies toward poverty eradication. For the Asia-Pacific region, it is supporting the initiative of the Association of Asia-Pacific Social Science Research Councils (AASSREC) for a regional cross-cultural project on environment and poverty. For the region of Eastern Europe, including other countries that formerly belonged to the Soviet bloc, it decided to invite national scholars from a select number of countries to prepare profiles of poverty and evaluate current social policies and programs on poverty eradication. This book has assembled these studies in order to provide a comparative perspective and to ensure a wider dissemination of this important research effort.

I. Countries-in-Transition : From No Poverty to Poverty

The focus on poverty in the countries-in-transition belonging to the former Soviet bloc is of particular importance. As mentioned earlier, during the socialist period these countries officially denied the existence of poverty. Making the transition from capitalism to socialism, they nourished the hope of completely terminating all oppression and all forms of social inequality to fulfill the Marxist dream. Feeling frustrated, these countries are now experiencing a reverse transition, from socialism to capitalism. Just as the entry into the era of socialism raised hopes amongst the masses of an emerging egalitarian society, the collapse of communism has caused a similar euphoria: people are hoping that all the troubles of the past will dissipate and sudden riches will appear. While there was an awareness of some of the social costs involved in this process of transition, the massive drops in output and income, which have caused large-scale unemployment and an upsurge in poverty were hardly anticipated.

Countries that denied the existence of poverty and unemployment in the past, and that boasted of high literacy rates and skilled manpower, are now acknowledging not only the prevalence of poverty but its sudden and rapid increase. "Eastern Europe and the countries of the Commonwealth of Independent States (CIS) have seen the greatest deterioration in the past decade. Income poverty has spread from a small part of their population to about a third – 120 million people below a poverty line of $4 a day," says the 1997 UNDP Human Development Report (9). "The transition from socialism to democracy and market economies has proved more difficult and costly than anyone imagined. The costs have been not only economic, from the dramatic decline in GDP. They have also been human, from falling wages, growing crime, and loss of social protection. In some countries life expectancy has fallen by five years or more" (UNDP 1997, 3). Such a situation challenges the existing theories on poverty and calls for a reexamination of the relationship between education, unemployment, and poverty. In poor countries, unemployment is usually the phenomenon of the middle class as the poor cannot afford to remain unemployed. It is a different matter, however, that in the long run the unemployed may become poor. In the countries-in-transition, most of the currently unemployed are those who have lost their jobs due to the restructuring of the economy. And these are people who are educated and mostly skilled. Furthermore, the reduction in state social assistance and benefits has caused difficulties both for pensioners and new job seekers.

Careful sociological investigation is needed to understand the phenomenon of poverty in these countries. Is it a new form of poverty that is emerging, or is it suppressed poverty that is resurfacing? During the socialist era, a distinction was made between the *capitalist poor* and the *socialist poor*. The capitalist poor were those who had been victims of the previous capitalist system and as such were given priority consideration in the new system for the amelioration of their situation. The socialist poor were the victims of the new system, such as the handicapped, the vagrants, and people with temporary jobs. The latter were never regarded as poor by communist ideologues; they were considered as mere "aberrations," To quote Milanovic, "Poverty was not only viewed as social pathology and an explicit denial of the 'perfectness' of the system but ... rather sinisterly, as an explicit *antisocial choice* by the poor" (Milanovic n.d. 4). That is the reason why poverty was never studied in that part of the world. To quote yet another author, Alastair McAuley, "In Soviet eyes, socialism was a progressive ideology ... Party propagandists liked to claim that, certainly by the 1960s, the USSR had made considerable strides toward the goal of creating a just and equal society. As a result, it was suggested that there could be no poverty. Furthermore, if there was no poverty, there could be no justification for the academic study of the phenomenon" (McAuley 1996, 355). However, the "growing economic crisis that preceded the collapse of state socialism and the breakup of the USSR was accompanied by a growth in poverty – and a belated recognition on the part of the Soviet government that poverty existed in the USSR. The transition to a market economy has been accompanied by an enormous further increase in poverty in Russia and, indeed, in most of the other successor states of the former Soviet Union (FSU)" (McAuley 1996, 354). The present effort at understanding the emerging phenomenon of poverty, thus, assumes special significance.

It would have been ideal to cover all the countries that once constituted the so-called Second World. However, neither the resources nor the time were available to launch such an ambitious project. Instead, it was decided to select some representative cases and have them studied by indigenous scholars rather than by "outsiders." The proposal was explained to eight regional UNESCO National Commissions, and their support was requested in identifying scholars who would carry out the studies, broadly following the outlines provided by UNESCO. Six of these countries responded promptly and identified scholars, who were then contacted. The countries covered by this study are: Bulgaria, Georgia, Hungary, Mongolia, Romania, and the Russian Federation. This is a rather fortunate composition as these countries represent different parts of the region that constituted the Soviet bloc, as shown below:

Central Europe	Hungary
Southeastern Europe	Bulgaria, Romania
Caucasian Republic	Georgia
Western part of the former Soviet Union	Russian Federation
Far Eastern	Mongolia

Together these six countries represent 197.4 million of the world's population. Their GNP per capita ranges from U.S.$310 (Mongolia) to U.S.$4,120 (Hungary). In all these countries the average annual growth rate during the decade 1985-95 has been negative, ranging between -1.1 percent (Hungary) and -17 percent (Georgia). In Romania, 17.7 percent of the population lives below the poverty line, having less than $1 a day, purchasing power parity (PPP), to live on. Table A provides a summary view of basic indicators culled from the World Bank Report in these six countries.

It should be stressed that the structure of poverty in Eastern Europe is radically different from that of the developing countries. In the latter, while the actual number of poor is still on the rise, their percentage compared to the total population is declining. As a result, the poverty gap is also being somewhat reduced. The situation in Eastern Europe is quite the opposite: an increase is registered on all three indicators. See Table B for these comparisons.

Table A   The Chosen Countries: A Comparative Profile

Indicators	Bulgaria	Georgia	Hungary	Mongolia	Romania	Russia
Population (millions)	8.4	5.4	10.2	2.5	22.7	148.2
Surface area (1,000 sq. kms.)	111	70	93	1,567	238	17,075
GNP per capita (1995 U.S.$)	1,330	440	4,120	310	1,480	2,240
Annual growth (%) 1985-95	-2.6	-17	-1.0	-3.8	-3.8	-5.1
PPP estimates of GNP per capita 1987 1995	23.4 16.6	28.1 5.5	28.9 23.8	10.6 7.2	22.2 16.2	30.9 16.6
Current int'l (1995 U.S.$)	4,480	1,574	6,410	1,950	4,360	4,480
Poverty (percent of people living on less than $1 a day [PPP])	2.6		0.7		17.7	1.1
Life expectancy at birth 1995	71	73	70	65	70	65

Table B   Growth of Poverty in Eastern Europe and the Developing Countries

Indicators	Years	Eastern Europe	Developing countries
Number of poor (in millions)	1987	2	1,225
	1990	n.a.	1,261
	1993	15	1,299
Head count index	1987	0.6%	33.3%
	1990	n.a.	32.9
	1993	3.5	31.8
Poverty gap	1987	0.2	10.8
	1990	n.a.	10.3
	1993	1.1	10.5

II. Measuring Poverty: Concepts and Methods

While there is a worldwide concern about the growth and spread of poverty, and an acknowledgment of its existence in practically all the countries – developed or developing, capitalist or former socialist – there is no unanimity as regards its definition. People regarded poor in a given country may be considered rich when measured by the yardstick of another country. The definition given by "outsiders" may not be acceptable to those who are being defined; and similarly, self-perception may contrast with outside observation, or even statistical indexing. Since poverty is said to be multidimensional, a monetary measure of poverty may not be a reliable way to determine poverty, or classify a person as poor. Moreover, all the poor cannot be classed in a single category. We already referred to a distinction made in the former socialist countries between the capitalist poor and the socialist poor – the latter regarded as a contradiction in terms, as an aberration. Differentiation is also made between those who are hereditarily poor, for whom poverty is an *ascribed* status, and those who are the "new poor," for whom poverty is an *achieved* status. Again, the new poor do not constitute a single homogeneous group. The political refugees and the environmental refugees have something in common – they both had to flee from their habitat and seek refuge elsewhere; but the amelioration of their situation would need different strategies. The new poor, in the countries-in-transition – the subject matter of the present study, are neither the illiterate, nor the continuing unemployed; they are mainly the job-dislocated people, those who are paid low wages, or those whose wages/salaries have been deferred, making it extremely difficult for the family to feed its members.

Difficulties in defining poverty have been aptly summed up in the 1997 UNDP Human Development Report thus:

> Concerns with identifying people affected by poverty and the desire to measure it have at times obscured the fact that poverty is too complex to be reduced to a single dimension of human life. It has become common for countries to establish an income-based or consumption-based poverty line. Although income focuses on an important dimension of poverty, it gives only a partial picture of the many ways human lives can be blighted. Someone can enjoy good health and live quite long but be illiterate and thus cut off from learning, from communication and from interactions with others. Another person may be literate and quite well educated but prone to premature death because of epidemiological characteristics or physical disposition. Yet a third may be excluded from participating in the important decision-making processes affecting her life. The deprivation of none of them can be fully captured by the level of their income (15-16).

Three distinct approaches are recognized by UNDP for the treatment of poverty. The *income perspective* focuses on the level of income of a person or family, and sets limits to draw a poverty line. The *basic needs perspective* views poverty from the angle of material deprivation rather than by income. A person or family is considered poor if it is not able to provide for minimally acceptable basic needs. The *capability perspective* focuses "on the functionings that a person can or cannot achieve, given the opportunities she has. Functionings refer to the various valuable things a person can do or be, such as living long, being healthy, being well-nourished, mixing well with others in the community and so on." The *human development approach* to poverty adopted in the UNDP Human Development Report "draws on each of these perspectives, but draws particularly on the capability perspective" (UNDP 1997, 15-16).

The Human Poverty Index (HPI), introduced by UNDP in its 1997 Human Development Report, "uses indicators of the most basic dimensions of deprivation: a short life, lack of basic education and lack of access to public and private resources"(UNDP 1997, 5). "The variables used are the percentage of people expected to die before age 40, the percentage of adults who are illiterate, and overall economic provisioning in terms of percentage of people without access to health services and safe water and the percentage of underweight children under five" (14). The UNDP has computed this index for only seventy-eight developing countries. It is obvious that computation of this index for the countries-in-transition is not possible due to the absence of adequate data, and also, perhaps due to the nonapplicability of these indicators in defining poverty in those regions, for the same reasons as advanced for the industrialized countries. Since Mongolia is classified as a developing country, however, its HPI is computed: its HPI value is shown as 15.7 percent, ranking sixteenth and implying that about one-sixth of its people suffer from human poverty. This ranking is incidentally higher than India (36.7 percent) or Indonesia (20.8 percent). At the bottom of the list are seven countries whose HPI exceeds 50 percent: Niger, Sierra Leone, Burkina Faso, Ethiopia, Mali, Cambodia, and Mozambique (21).

Since the measures of poverty employed in other developing countries are not suited to the situation prevalent in the countries-in-transition, the governments of these countries, as well as the scholars, employ the same standards that were used during the previous regimes – of course with some needed modifications. Rather than dividing people in terms of income – which is a measure for identifying relative poverty – the aim of these measures was to find out whether the income earned by the individual, or the family/household, was sufficient to meet basic needs. It may be recalled that in the socialist regimes, income inequality was minimized to the maximum, and minimum wages were fixed in terms of basic needs to ensure that nobody suffered from privation. With the arrival of differences in income due to the introduction of the market economy, the same measure is used to demarcate the poverty line.

The following is a list of some of the concepts employed in poverty research in these countries.

The concept of the *poverty line* is also used here, but in a somewhat different sense. We know that this line differs from country to country depending upon the definition and the criteria used to delineate it. For making international comparisons, the World Bank decided to use U.S.$1(PPP) a day as the demarcation line: families spending one U.S. dollar a day or less are regarded as living below the poverty line. However, for the countries-in-transition, U.S.$4 was considered to be the appropriate line by the UNDP.

In countries-in-transition, a different technique is used to draw the poverty line. It is drawn in relation to average income. For example, in Russia, all the people who receive less than the average income are regarded as living below the poverty line. However, these people are grouped into three categories depending on the distance between the average income and their own income. Immediately below them are the *indigents*, followed by the *poor,* and the *destitute.* The indigents are those whose income is between 50 and 75 percent of the average income; the poor are those whose income is between 25 and 50 percent of the average income; and the destitute, leading a life of misery, are those whose income is less than 25 percent of the average income. Some scholars also follow the OECD procedure for drawing the poverty line at 50, 60, or 70 percent of the average income level. In both cases, it is the money income which is the measure, irrespective of its PPP value.

A more refined method is the computation of the *subsistence minimum* – a concept of the old Soviet methodology. This is also calculated in different ways. Some determine it in terms of the *food basket.* For each member of the household, an appropriate number of calories are allocated depending on the person's age and sex, and then the cost of food items equivalent to those calories is calculated. Thus the total amount of money needed to buy food for the family, satisfying the calorie norm, is defined as the subsistence minimum. The standards set by the Food and Agricultural Organization (FAO) and the World Health Organization (WHO) are also employed for this purpose; these standards indicate the calorie value of each food item. This method is criticized on the grounds that people eat food not only for its calorific value but also for taste and cultural prescriptions. As such, the computation must be done on the basis of what people really eat, and not on what they should eat. However, people using this measure fix subsistence minimum differently for different regions because of the differences in the price of food items.

Using this technique, the subsistence minimum for the Soviet Union, before its collapse, was fixed at 190 rubles per capita per month, which was more than U.S.$220 at 1990 exchange rates. Accordingly, 11.4 percent of the population was identified as poor. This figure rose to 31 percent in 1993 at the 1990 price standard based on PPP.

In Hungary, the concept of subsistence minimum is further divided into two categories: *social minimum,* and *survival minimum.* "The *social minimum* is the income necessary to fulfill basic necessities, allowing for the consumption of goods and services desired by the general public, albeit of a modest but socially acceptable level and quality" (Szalai 1990, 297). The *survival minimum* is 80-85 percent of the social minimum. It is expressed as "an income which allows only a very modest fulfillment of basic necessities connected with a daily life routine"(297). The Hungarian author, however, warns that "the poverty line is not a 'neutral' form of measurement" in the Hungarian context. "In Hungary, the calculation determining the poverty line emerged, not in political debates, but by a decision of the Political Committee of the Communist Party in 1983." The poverty line was determined with an agreement on the extent to which poverty "should be admitted ... The poverty lines calculated for various social groups still do not serve as a legal basis to guaranteeing these groups the necessary welfare benefits" (297).

In Bulgaria, a distinction is made between the *social minimum* and the *living minimum,* much along the same lines as in Hungary. The social minimum in Bulgaria defines the "upper line of poverty," while the living minimum defines the lower line. Those who come under the first category are relatively better-off as they are able to spend something on 'comforts'; but the living minimum does not provide access to goods other than the bare necessities of life.

In Romania, three different measures are used, namely, *Subsistence Minimum* (SM), *Decent Minimum of Life* (DM), and *Minimum Determined by the Ministry of Labor and Social Protection* (MM). The subsistence minimum, in the Romanian context, is said to refer to "absolute" poverty, to draw the poverty line (but here absolute poverty is not synonymous with destitution). The DM, decent minimum, is equivalent to an average wage; it is used to define "relative" poverty. The MM is a value obtained for households whose income is below the SM and DM. Taking DM as a standard, SM is defined as 59.9 percent of the DM; those who get 31.5 percent of the DM, or 52.6 percent of the SM, are put in the category of MM. These people are considered to be suffering from severe poverty.

In Georgia, the subsistence minimum is calculated on the basis of a *consumer basket* – which is not the same thing as a *food basket.* Apart from the essential foodstuffs (thus excluding cigarettes, though they are a part of regular expenditure in most homes), this includes other services and utilities. Since these utilities are shared by all the members of the family, and the costs for each individual cannot be computed separately, the consumer basket is computed for the family as a whole. The basket varies with the size of the family and the age composition of its members.

The same method is used in Mongolia where a total of 508 primary necessary commodities and services are included in the basket. Here eight different types of consumer baskets are constructed for different groups, and the items included in them are valued at current prices. In Bulgaria, a consumer basket is constructed for a family of four since such families are larger in number.

These variations notwithstanding, all the countries included in this project employ the subsistence minimum as the yardstick to measure poverty. There are other measures used by scholars for assessing the extent of poverty in these countries. These are explained to below.

Gini Index. This index measures the extent to which the distribution of income, or consumption expenditure, among individuals/households deviates from a perfectly equal distribution. A Lorenz curve plots the cumulative percentages of total income received against the cumulative percentages of recipients, starting with the poorest. The Gini index measures the area between the Lorenz curve and a hypothetical line of absolute equality, expressed as a percentage of the maximum area under the line. Thus a Gini index of "0" shows perfect equality and an index of 100 represents maximum inequality. (See World Bank 1997, 261-62).

Decile Coefficient. This compares the average per capita income of the lowest 10 percent with the average per capita income of the highest 10 percent of the population. The greater the difference between them, the greater the gap between the rich and the poor. Similar comparisons are also made for the lowest 20 percent and the highest 20 percent of the population in terms of income and accumulation of wealth.

Engel Coefficient. This is the ratio of expenditure on food to the family's total general expenses. In 1992 the Russian government set the limit at 68 percent for households and 83 percent for pensioners. Households or pensioners spending more than this amount on food were treated as poor. Using this yardstick, the percentage of the poor in 1992 was estimated to be as high as 90.

Poverty Gap. This is used to measure the distance between the poverty line and the mean income of the poor. The formula used for this purpose is:

$$P_{gap} = \frac{\sum_{i=1}^{N} (y - x_i)}{N}$$

where *y* stands for the subsistence minimum, *x* for the income of the *i*-th observed household and *N* for the total number of households observed.

Head Count Index: This is the percentage of people who are below the poverty line. This index does not measure the depth of poverty, however. When the sum of all poverty gaps is multiplied by the head count index, the *Poverty Gap Index* is obtained.

PPP estimates of GNP per capita: This is calculated by converting GNP to U.S. dollars on the basis of purchasing power parity rather than the exchange rate. The calculation is made by converting one unit of the currency (the U.S. dollar, in this case) into the number of units of national currency required to buy specific goods and services in another country. The estimates are expressed in international dollars – a unit of account that has the same purchasing power over total GNP as the U.S. dollar (see World Bank 1997, 251).

III. Country Specificities of Poverty Profiles

We may now briefly review the situation of poverty in the six countries covered by this study.

Hungary

A country of 10.2 million people, Hungary has maintained a minus 0.3 percent population growth rate since 1980. The country has 7 million people in the age group 15-64, and 71 percent of them (5 million) are in the labor force – a constant figure between 1980-95. Between 1980-90, the annual growth rate of the labor force was minus 0.8 percent; it grew to 0.1 percent during 1990-95. In 1993, primary school enrollment was as high as 95 percent for both boys and girls; for the secondary school, the enrollment percentage for boys was lower than girls (79 percent for boys and 82 percent for the girls). Only 17 percent of the children, however, were enrolled in tertiary education. But what is more important is that no adult illiteracy is reported. The country is also growing more urban: from a 57 percent urban population in the year 1980 to 65 percent in 1995. With an average annual growth rate of minus 1.0 percent for the period 1985-1995, Hungary's GNP per capita stood at U.S.$4,120 in 1995, which in PPP terms is around $6,410. Measured in terms of the percentage of people living on $1 a day (PPP), the poor in Hungary constitute only 0.7 percent of the population according to the World Bank estimates. The average annual inflation rate is 19.9 percent.

Since the topic of poverty was taboo during the entire period of socialism, it is difficult to generalize about the growth of this phenomenon; however, several writers are now claiming that it existed during that time. In order to assess post-socialist poverty, Hungarian scholars employ three different approaches. These are: (1) the manifestation of income inequalities; (2) the manifestation of inadequate consumption; and (3) the manifestations of dropping below the minimally acceptable level of living. Using the third approach, Julia Szalai suggests in Chapter One that the ratio of persons living in households with a per capita income below 50 percent of the average income has been rising since 1992: from 10.1 percent in 1992, it has gone up to 14 percent in 1996. There is a high concentration of poverty in the Gypsy ethnic group (66.7 percent). Szalai also found that poverty is higher in villages (20.1 percent) than in small towns (13.3 percent); in the capital city of Budapest, it is the lowest (4.5 percent). Furthermore, there is a high occurrence of poverty among children: "… low schooling, loss of employment, several small children in the family, and the lack of rural agricultural support to compensate for the decline in cash income result in the frequent occurrence of poverty among young urban families."

Poverty in Hungary is caused by three sets of factors: the uneven socioeconomic impact of the economic crisis; the negative consequences of the systemic changes for employment; and the uneven repercussions of prevailing property dealings. The economic crisis is reflected in foreign indebtedness (which is 91 percent of the yearly gross per capita disposable income – U.S.$1,647 per head in 1995); the rise of consumer prices due to cuts in state subsidies; and the suspension of compulsory employment. In fact, the loss of employment has caused much poverty.

Szalai disagrees with the view that government "overspending" on social benefits and services is the root cause of the problem. She attributes it to the "low efficiency" of the government, which has not been able to develop coherent guidelines for welfare distribution. While "the principles and mechanisms of the socialist way of centrally distributing income" have been suspended in the new regime, no satisfactory alternatives have yet been found. "The still excessive presence of the state in the economy, as well as the understandably open aspiration of its bureaucracy to reinforce its own position of power, persuade the opinion of a broad strata of society against the creation of a private market, which is characterized as a 'foreign' prescription for the process of embourgeoisement in Hungary." The author believes that "the recent expansion of poverty is partly due to the prevailing dogmatic neo-liberal interpretation of a necessary economic transformation, and partly due to those legacies of the state-socialist past which have not yet been terminated." For the eradication of poverty, the author advocates for a wide range of well-targeted interventions, and not just interventions at the macroeconomic level resulting in the rise in personal income.

Bulgaria

Bulgaria is classed as a middle-income economy with a GNP per capita of U.S.$1,330, having a PPP value of $4,480 current international dollars. A small country of 8.4 million people, Bulgaria is said to have a poverty level of 2.6 percent – consisting of those people who live on less than a $1 (PPP) a day. Its population growth has been negative since 1980; for the decade 1980-90, the growth rate was minus 0.2 percent, and in the following five years (1990-95), it registered a further decline with an annual growth rate of minus 0.7 percent. Its labor force was reduced from 5 million in 1980 to 4 million in 1995. With an insignificant adult illiteracy rate, the country has had a shortfall in school enrollment ratios. In 1993, primary school enrollment was 84 percent for girls and 87 percent for boys; at the secondary school level, enrollment was 70 percent for girls and 66 percent for boys. Only 23 percent of the eligible children continued in tertiary education. With a 45.9 percent rate of inflation, the country is heavily indebted. The net present value of external debt is 87 percent of the GNP.

Prior to the political changes in 1989, the government did not acknowledge the existence of poverty, although it did refer to people with "low incomes," thus admitting income inequality. The Gini index, computed on the basis of a 1992 survey, stood at 30.8, suggesting an unequal distribution of income. But even today "there is no systematic mapping of poverty profiles." Sasha Todorova, the author of the chapter on Bulgaria, holds that various guarantees given to people during the previous regime did succeed in creating satisfactory living standards, but they also contributed to the decadence of society – as people became virtual parasites of the state and lost all motivation to work and earn. When there was a reduction in the protected incomes – salaries, pensions, indemnities, allowances, stipends, etc. – people were rendered poor. Furthermore, a drop in the purchasing power of income affected all citizens. Thus, in Bulgaria, there are people (1) who are " persistently poor," (2) who are in the process of impoverishment, and (3) who could become impoverished in the near future if the same trend continues. It must also be said that different people have different notions of poverty. In a sample survey carried out in 1992 and repeated in 1993, researchers found four different conceptions of poverty among the respondents:

1. incapable of meeting physiological needs (14.1 percent)
2. incapable of meeting daily needs (23.3 percent)
3. incapable of meeting physiological and daily needs without state assistance (40.1 percent)
4. unable to attain higher living standards (20.6 percent)

It is logical to collapse the first three sets of responses into a single category and conclude that poverty is defined as the inability to meet basic daily needs. The fourth category is indicative of *relative* poverty. What the survey data indicate is that while people were able to maintain conventional living standards during communist rule, it has become increasingly difficult to do so now with the withdrawal of state assistance. Bulgarian sociologists, Yossifov and Naoumov, have proposed a fourfold classification of poverty in terms of the behavior patterns of the poor. They regard these as different subcultures of poverty. Based on how the poor themselves perceive and rationalize their poverty, these authors have distinguished between normal, ideological, fatal, and pseudo poverty. Normal poverty is defined as income below the average level; ideological poverty is seen as a behavioral norm rejecting social standards and emphasizing austere living (as exemplified by hippies, for instance); fatal poverty characterizes those who accept their condition as "fate" and resign themselves to it; and pseudo poverty is a synonym for relative poverty, in which people treat the rich as a reference group and regard themselves as poor in comparison. In the absence of any other dependable statistics, Bulgarian scholars regard as "poor" all those who are entitled to social assistance. This number is much larger than the 2.6 percent identified by the World Bank as those who are living on less than $1 a day; in fact, their number is constantly rising. Poverty is said to be rampant among the farmers, Gypsies, intelligentsia, government employees, ethnic Turks, and those living in the border regions.

Post-communist poverty is said to have been caused by the inefficiency of structural reforms, foreign debt servicing, the high rate of inflation, an ineffective tax policy, and the lack of political consensus. The need to examine employment policy and to consider ways to manage the processes of the informal economy is particularly urgent. In Chapter Two, Todorova suggests a four-pronged strategy to arrest the growth of poverty: (1) by emphatically speeding up reforms; (2) by improving the social protection of the poorest strata; (3) by taking effective measures to reduce unemployment; and (4) by adequately updating the protected minimum incomes.

Romania

More than double the population of Hungary, and nearly thrice the population of Bulgaria, Romania is inhabited by 22.7 million people, half of whom are in the active labor force – a figure that has remained constant since 1980. The World Bank estimates 17.7 percent poverty in Romania in terms of the number of those who live on less than $1 (PPP) a day. This datum is significant in view of the fact that the country also has a middle-income economy with a U.S.$1,480 GNP per capita (or a

PPP of 4,360 current international dollars) – more or less similar to that of Bulgaria. However, its Gini index (25.5) is lower than Bulgaria's (30.8), which indicates that it has comparatively less income inequality.

Romania also has negligible adult illiteracy and a negative population growth rate (minus 0.4 percent per annum during 1990-95). It only has a 12 percent enrollment ratio at the tertiary level, while this ratio at the primary and secondary school levels is more than 80 percent with little gender difference. Experiencing an annual inflation rate of 68.7 percent, Romania's external debt is only 18 percent of the net value of its total GNP (compared to 72 percent in the case of Hungary and 87 percent in the case of Bulgaria).

The Romanian government has not been able to arrive at an official definition of poverty. As such, the only poverty prevention measure it has adopted is compensation for the unemployed. It is interesting to note that the 1996 Human Development Report for Romania, prepared by UNDP in collaboration with the National Commission of Statistics, has devoted only a small section to poverty under the heading "Social Equity and Stability: Limiting Social Tensions." The average income of U.S.\$86.63 per month certainly indicates poverty. In terms of expenditure, it has been found that an average of 65 percent of the total household expenses are spent on food, thus leaving only 35 percent for meeting other basic and social needs. The income gap between the lowest 10 percent and the highest 10 percent is constantly increasing – from 6.71 times in 1989 to 8.49 times in 1993. Only 33.6 percent of households are above the average income level. As opposed to this, 41.5 percent of households have an income below 60 percent of the average.

Such a situation is partly attributable to the slower pace of privatization and marketization. With the withdrawal of state support and delays in creating a newer system of administration, the growth of the "parallel" or "underground" economy has been encouraged. The privileged strata, including members of the ruling party, have taken advantage of the changing situation and have amassed wealth while the majority have been deprived of the former essential guarantees in the name of liberalization. State expenditure on social welfare has declined since 1991; in real terms, it is only 77.1 percent of the 1989 figure, although it constitutes 15.5 percent of GDP in 1993 compared to 14.1 percent of GDP in 1989.

In the post-communist regime, there has also been a deterioration of the health services. The government spends only 9 percent of its budget on medical services, which comes to a meager 2 percent of GDP. As a consequence, the people in the medical profession are forced to disregard contractual obligations and cater to the clients who can afford to pay them better consultation fees. The government is also having difficulty compensating the rising number of the unemployed, and providing shelter to the homeless, particularly during the severe winter season.

The growing feeling of relative deprivation, the deteriorating situation of government-supported social services, and the slower pace of economic development in Romania are indicative of the spread of poverty in that country. But in the absence of dependable data and carefully conducted studies, it is difficult to draw the contours of poverty and to map out appropriate strategies for its eradication. The authors have strongly advocated policy-oriented research. Two preconditions for such research are the training of indigenous social scientists in the methodology of survey research, and the strengthening of social science infrastructures.

Georgia

Inhabited in an area of 70 thousand square kilometers, Georgia has a population of 5.4 million people – smaller than the size of Moscow, the capital of the Russian Federation. With a negative growth rate of minus 17 percent during 1985-95, the country's GNP per capita is U.S.$440 or PPP 1,470 current international dollars. The World Bank Development Report for 1997 does not give any poverty figures (those living on less than $1 PPP a day) for this country, nor does it report its Gini index. The size of Georgia's labor force has held at a constant 3 million since 1980, with a minus 0.1 percent growth rate during 1990-95. It has an annual inflation rate of 310 percent with an external debt of U.S.$1,189 million, constituting 51.6 percent of the GNP.

An idea of the growing impoverishment in Georgia can be attained from the fact that while during the communist period, as a province of the former Soviet Union, the subsistence minimum constituted only 33 to 40 percent of the average wage; in the post-Soviet era the average wage itself has fallen to 37 percent of the subsistence minimum. Thus, the country draws the poverty line today at the subsistence minimum level (which is the monetary expression of basic minimum consumer goods needed to ensure the normal physiological and social needs of a citizen). Those receiving the average wage are described as suffering from physiological poverty, and those who have no monetary income whatsoever are identified as the absolute poor. However, the government focuses on poverty at the level of the household and not at the level of the individual, which is a very valid premise. Members of a household share common utilities, and therefore the costs for these should be computed at that level and the income of all the members of the family should be aggregated to find out the total resources available to the family. Additionally, Georgia tries to find out whether other resources help maintain the family. For example, households that have access to land and are able to produce food for their own consumption can compensate for a loss in their monetary income.

The informal economy has played a major role as a shock absorber in Georgia. The informal economy here is differentiated from the "shadow" economy: while the latter is somewhat illegal and also criminal, the former is not. Acknowledging the role of the informal economy, and thus hinting at the distorted interpretation of the situation based on official statistics, Avtandil Sulaberidze, the author of the Georgian chapter, writes: "Even today what baffles people most is the fact that while the formally registered income of many households is ten times less than the survival limit, they are not only surviving but enjoying a reasonably good life." But this observation may not apply to internally displaced persons (IDPs) and refugees who have been severely hit by ethnic conflicts that ensued soon after the birth of the new state. Coupled with the administrative infrastructure's inability to manage the transition to a market economy are the divisive factors within Georgian society that have created a crisis in the nation's cohesion and generated poverty among minority groups. The Georgian population suffers from malnutrition caused by a paucity of food, it lives in poor housing conditions, and it is deprived of adequate transportation and communication. The devastation of the Georgian economic base is attributed by some to the withdrawal of state support; in the Soviet era this poor region was able to maintain a standard of living similar to other regions through central aid. Now left to its own resources, the country is finding it hard to meet the demands of its population. That is the reason why 71.5 percent of the urban, and 42.7 percent of the rural respondents in a sample survey identified themselves as poor.

The Russian Federation

The largest of the six countries covered in this study, the Russian Federation is populated by 148.2 million people. Its per capita GNP is also quite high: U.S.$2,240 or PPP 4,480 current international dollars – higher than Bulgaria, Romania, Georgia, and Mongolia, but lower than Hungary. While its primary and secondary school enrollment ratios in 1993 were 107 and 87 percent respectively, and even tertiary enrollment was as high as 45 percent, the country has an adult illiteracy rate of 65 percent according to the 1997 World Bank Development Report. With 84.7 million people in the labor force, constituting 57.2 percent of the population, only 67.1 million of them were employed in 1995 compared to 75.3 million in 1990 – despite the fact that the size of the total population has remained constant during this period. This phenomenon is associated with the growth in the number of workers with two or more jobs. However, having two jobs does not imply having a higher income: those seeking second jobs are the people whose income from their primary job has been declining in recent years, thus causing a need for supplementary income. There is a good deal of hidden unemployment as large numbers of workers have been "laid off." These people are not social misfits, alcoholics, or work-shy; they are victims of economic factors of the post-Soviet era that are beyond their control. And they lack the social protection that they would have received had such a situation occurred during the previous regime.

The Gini index of 49.6 (in 1993) suggests that income disparity is growing fast. In that year, the lowest 10 percent had only a 1.2 percent share of the total GNP compared to 53.8 percent amongst the highest 20 percent, and 38.7 percent among the highest 10 percent. Russia's average inflation rate is 148.9 percent per annum, and the net present value of its external debt is 35 percent of its GNP.

During the Soviet era, while poverty was officially denied, there was a general acceptance of the fact that about 10 percent of the people were living below the poverty line. Since the entire Soviet Union pursued the Leninist strategy of the "decommodification of labor," money income constituted only a fraction of the total income of a worker. The money income figures of that era are not an accurate measure of total income. In addition to salaries, people received various other benefits – free services, entitlements, and earnings from secondary activities. In the post-Soviet era, labor has been commodified again, and money income is the sole compensation for work in most cases. This is why the country is witnessing massive increases in poverty. There has been a slump in production causing layoffs and nonpayment or delayed payment of wages, salaries, and state transfers. In addition, the high level of inflation has escalated the prices of all consumer goods.[3] It is said that between 1989 and 1996, the prices of consumer goods have increased by 10,000 percent. In 1989, the subsistence level was 140 rubles per month for an adult; with inflation, if the same subsistence level were maintained today, it would be as high as 14,00,000 rubles. In present-day Russia, only 10 percent of the people receive more than a million roubles per month, thereby implying a poverty rate of 90 percent! With very conservative price escalation figures and a reduction of the consumer basket items, the government has fixed the subsistence minimum at 368,200 rubles or U.S.$55 per month. Against this yardstick, the government has acknowledged the existence of 24.7 percent poverty. However, those people who have a higher official income on paper, but who are actually receiving much less due to the government's inability to pay salaries in time, must also be figured in this calculation.

3. A U.S. dollar today can buy as many as 6900 rubles; in the 1980s, a ruble was worth more than a dollar.

In the chapter on the Russian Federation, the authors Pirogov and Pronin have classified low-income people into four categories. At the bottom are the *paupers* whose income is less than the minimum wage; above them are the *destitutes* whose income is less than the cost of the minimum food basket. *Indigence* is experienced by those whose income is less than the official subsistence minimum. Those whose income is above the subsistence minimum but below the social norm for an adequate living standard are described as people with *low provision.* It should be mentioned that the subsistence minimum provides that 61.6 percent of income goes toward the cost for food for an able-bodied person, and 82.9 percent for a pensioner. Using this yardstick one finds a striking increase in the incidence of poverty among the "hitherto mainstream groups of society."

According to the 1996 UNDP Human Development Report on Russia, more than half the population had an income less than 150 percent of the subsistence minimum, indicating that they spent all their income on food alone. They could not even afford to buy a man's jacket as it was 60 percent of the official monthly subsistence income; in comparison, a woman's spring coat was 127 percent of the subsistence income! With a slump in housing construction, rental prices for houses have gone up and housing scarcity has become quite acute.

What is most striking in the case of Russia is the plight of the intellectual class. Educated and professional workers, and even the military personnel and doctors – all in the employ of the government – have suffered the most. In order to employ more people, the salaries of the already employed have been held down with the result that they receive only 62 percent of the average wage, and that too is in arrears for long periods of time. During the Soviet era, manual workers and people with mechanical skills were given more weight than intellectuals. And even now there is a continued deemphasis on their work in relation to technical and specialist skills. This has prompted people from academia to flee the country in search of better job opportunities and higher salaries. Such a flight has obviously generated frustration among less fortunate people who cannot leave the country and are not adequately paid for their services.

Mongolia

Of the six countries covered in this study, Mongolia is the smallest in terms of population (2.5 million), and it is not a part of the Eastern Europe. But as an important satellite of the former Soviet Union, and as a Far Eastern country in the process of transition, the Mongolian case is of special interest. It is the country with the lowest GNP per capita at U.S.$310 or PPP 1,950 current international dollars. It has a negative growth rate of minus 3.8 percent per annum. With an annual population growth rate of 2.1 percent, Mongolia has 1 million people in the age bracket 15-64. This is the same size as the country's labor force, of which 46 percent are female. Although recent statistics on school enrollment are not available, Mongolia had 107 percent primary school enrollment and 91 percent secondary school enrollment as early as 1980, suggesting a virtual absence of adult illiteracy in the country. The country is quickly becoming urbanized; from 52 percent in 1980, its urban population has reached 60 percent in 1995. Its external debt of U.S.$512 million equals 61.5 percent of its GNP. The country has an average annual inflation rate of around 51.6 percent.

Government estimates indicate that poverty has surfaced in the post-communist era. A total of 828,000 people – 478,000 from urban and 350,000 from rural areas – are identified as poor, constituting 36.3 percent of the total population. These people belong to 100,000 households, 43.2 percent of which are in the capital city of Ulan Bator alone. While the size of the labor force is enlarging there is no corresponding increase in the number of jobs. In December 1996, as many as 55,200 people registered with the labor bureaus as unemployed and looking for work. But the actual number of the unemployed is hard to guess. There are many unemployed who work in the informal sector, and there are many who do not have jobs but have not registered with the labor bureaus.

Mongolia faces the acute problem of street children who have left their families because of poverty or conflicts with their parents. Efforts to send them back to their families or to rehabilitate them at special centers created especially for them have not succeeded so far because they have been able to earn enough money on the streets to survive and even to support their parents clandestinely. With the halting growth of the private sector, inadequate legislation, and deficiencies in the administration, people are trying to improve their living conditions in several ways. Some even feel nostalgia for the previous regime in which the state provided support to all, irrespective of their qualifications or productivity. Critics attribute the lethargy of the people to the previous system, which made them parasites and quashed their motivation. The competitive character of the market economy makes demands for which neither the government nor the people are fully prepared.

IV. Concluding Observations

The decision to abandon socialism and central planning, and to embark upon the process of transition to a market economy and a democratic form of government has been a mixed blessing for the former socialist countries, now known as countries-in-transition. Suffering for years under totalitarian regimes, the people of these countries saw a ray of hope in the transition: better living conditions, greater freedoms, an invigoration of the stagnating economy. But the very process of transition caused shock and suffering. The rush to abandon prevailing practices in an almost revolutionary fashion did not allow the administration sufficient time to retool itself, and the exigencies of the emerging situation led it to take ad hoc measures. In the process, it was completely forgotten that changes created by a given social subsystem or cultural pattern have repercussions in the rest of the system. Not prepared to handle the unanticipated consequences – both functional and dysfunctional – the administrative systems in these countries are undergoing a period of stress. The people themselves are ambivalent about the changed situation. The sudden loss of a stable support system and the uncertainty of the future have extinguished their euphoria.

Societies that once claimed egalitarianism and full employment began to reveal their poverty profiles and felt the pangs of the swelling ranks of the unemployed. Contrary to expectations, the transition to a market economy resulted in a loss of jobs and sharp declines in industrial output. Economic collapse coupled with civil unrest has caused the escalation of poverty. Barring Poland (where growth resumed in 1992) and Hungary (where poverty could be relatively contained), all other countries of this region recorded steep increases in poverty. Some estimates indicate that between 1989-94, as many as 75 million people fell into the poverty trap in Central and Eastern Europe. In Bulgaria and Romania poverty increased from 1.5 percent in 1989 to around 27-35 percent in 1994. Added to this are those who have a "low income" – those receiving 40 to 45 percent of the average income. The poor are those who receive 60 percent of the low income.

The following table compares the growth of poverty in Hungary, Bulgaria, and Romania.

Table C: The Growth of Poverty in Hungary, Bulgaria, and Romania (in percentages)

Hungary			Bulgaria			Romania		
Year	Low income	Poor	Low income	Poor	Low income	Poor		
1989	10.1	1.1			28.2	7.0		
1990			13.8	2.0	21.8	3.5		
1991	15.6	2.3	52.1	12.7	28.7	8.6		
1992			55.5	21.8	46.2	16.4		
1993	22.5	4.5	59.4	25.3	59.9	25.3		

The situation of the former Soviet bloc countries can be described as a transition from *no-poverty* to poverty, and it is in the midst of prevailing and growing poverty that a transition to democratic governance and a market economy has to take place. Whether a successful transition will also mean a transition from the present poverty to no-poverty once again, or to a continuance of poverty, is a difficult question to answer since we know that even countries with market economies and democratic forms of government are not spared the scourge of poverty. For instance, a survey carried out in the countries of the European Union in March 1997 has suggested a surprising high level of poverty there – 57 million people, constituting 17 percent of the European population, are said to belong to poor households. This itself is a good reminder that mere economic growth, or the pursuit of a market economy with a liberal democratic polity cannot ensure the absence of poverty. It also serves to remind that the strategy to be worked out for the countries of the European Union cannot be the same as those for the countries-in-transition. The root causes of poverty in the two settings are very different.

In the case of the former socialist states, it is hard to generalize about poverty's recent emergence as no data regarding poverty during the socialist times exist. Moreover, the official statistics now available are deficient in many ways and cannot be fully relied upon. Neither the exact number of the poor nor their socio-economic background is known. Responses to poverty have also been different. And there is an additional point to be made: the recognition of the existence of poverty implies that there are also those who are nonpoor – in other words, a stratification that is supposed to be nonexistent in an "egalitarian" society has emerged. This could be the reason that when a protest was organized in Russia in March 1997 against unpaid wages, there was a poor turnout. Reporting on this event, the *International Herald Tribune* (28 March 1997) described the behavior of the nonpoor in these terms:

> … 20 yards from the crowd's rear fringe, under the watchful gaze of Lenin's statue, bustling shoppers in the packed central food market couldn't have been less interested. They were too busy inspecting pyramids of fresh sausage, glistening racks of fish and a cornucopia of cans, jars and bottles that might have caused a riot in Soviet times.

Quoting from a new survey conducted by the Russian Market Research Company among 4000 respondents, the paper said that "average household incomes, officially listed at $120 or so, are in fact at least 70 percent higher. Even the government has acknowledged its statistics may understate real incomes by a quarter or more."

Poverty in the context of the countries-in-transition has a different face than in other regions. During the socialist era, the countries themselves may have been poor in terms of their GDP or natural resource base, but their societies were characterized by a virtual absence of income inequality. The collapse of that system has generated income inequality in several ways: loss of jobs has caused a loss of income; differential payment for skills has now resulted in income stratification; the liquidation of wealth – through the sale of goods, land, and other hoards, even hidden stacks of foreign currency – by those who had a privileged position in the previous regime has made some richer; and wage arrears have impacted the salaried class and the pensioners. In such a situation, a money metric measure for poverty seems to be the only dependable measure. What is interesting is that the concepts of subsistence minimum and food basket that were evolved in socialist times continue to be relevant today, although in a different way. In previous times, computations of the subsistence minimum and food basket were made to fix salaries and wages to ensure that everyone was able to meet his or her basic and social needs. The same measures are used today to determine the gap between the income received and the money needed for the subsistence minimum. While the subsistence minimum was previously lower than the minimum wage, in the changed circumstances it is the minimum wage which has dropped below the subsistence minimum level, making it impossible for a growing number of families to provide for the satisfaction of their basic needs.

What has become clear in all cases is that, while during the socialist regime the costs of the subsistence minimum were lower than the minimum wage, the situation in the transition period has been reversed. Due to inflation, even the average income has become insufficient to meet the needs of the subsistence minimum. The local currencies of all these countries are sliding down on the purchasing power parity index. For example, the Russian ruble, which was more than the value of a U.S. dollar in the 1980s has been devalued so much that today a U.S. dollar can buy as many as 6900 rubles! It is the same story for other currencies. In 1990, just 2.97 Bulgarian leva could buy a U.S. dollar; today one needs 1800 leva for the same transaction.

It is also important to emphasize that, unlike in the countries of the "Third World,"[4] in the countries-in-transition, poverty has impacted those who are actually employed. The new poor in these countries, whose number is burgeoning, are neither all unemployed nor all illiterate – two characteristics often associated with poverty. Such a profile challenges the common theories on poverty which lead to the cherished prescriptions: educate the poor, generate employment. The poor in these

---

4. This euphemism has now lost its meaning with the collapse of the so-called Second World. And one is not certain where to place the countries-in-transition – in the First or the Third Worlds, or to keep them in a world of their own.

countries are educated – in fact, poverty is greater among those who are more educated, and they are employed. Fostering education and employment do not seem to be the solutions to poverty. Something else has to be done. This is not to deny the importance of education. It would be wrong to say that they are poor because they are educated. The findings from these countries simply challenge the imputed linkage between poverty and education, between poverty and unemployment, and between education and unemployment. These relationships can no longer be taken for granted.

While accepting the importance of education, we are called upon to ponder the kind of education needed in these countries to help them overcome the poverty syndrome. The high enrollment ratios at the primary and secondary schools in all these countries indicate that intervention at that level – in terms of increasing the ratio – is not needed because access to schools already exists. What is perhaps needed is to ensure that these ratios do not drop in the future because of poverty. Secondly, there may be a need to closely examine the content of the curricula and redesign them to meet the new exigencies. Reeducation and retraining of the adult population in the new skills needed to operate modern factories, or new office technologies, is another major challenge for education. Initiation of the social scientists from these countries into the methodology of empirical research and the theories of management and administration is yet another aspect to tackle.

On the employment front, actions are perhaps needed both for the creation of new jobs to accommodate youth in search of their first employment, and for the creation of better working conditions for those who are already employed. Here it may be noted that the relationship between employment and a person's well-being is not disputed. However, the evidence from these countries invites us to rethink this association. Generally, poverty is associated with unemployment: people who remain unemployed for longer periods are bound to become poor, and the poor are those who are jobless. In the countries studied here, a new pattern is found. The employed people are also growing poor during the period of transition – whether such a phenomenon is transitional or not is a matter of speculation. Transition to a market economy has changed the employment scenario completely. Previously, the government was the sole employer and pledged to provide full employment to all; now this responsibility is shared by both the government and the private sector. Having ceded most of the units of production to private entrepreneurs, the government's only remaining source of revenue is taxation, and the number of state employees has been drastically reduced. This has resulted in employee layoffs and delays in the payment of salaries on the part of the government – additionally, the financial departments of the government have managed to protect the salaries of their staff and have ignored the claims of other nonfinancial departments and ministries. Those who lost their jobs in government were not all able to get jobs in the private sector because of changing demands for skills. In such a situation, governments have the responsibility to not only find jobs for those who are seeking employment for the first time; they also have to "relocate" those who have lost their jobs, either through early retirement, or because they were laid off (on one pretext or another). In addition, there is the problem of those employees whose salaries have not been adjusted to rising inflation; they have suffered because of arrears in the payment of their salaries.

The new situation has changed the very structure of the employment market. There has been a massive transfer of employees from the government-run enterprises to the private sector. A serious mismatch between demands for skills and the availability of skills has occurred. The private sector cannot afford the luxury of paying for unwanted skills, or for "slow" and "lazy" workers. Improved coordination between the government and the private sector is needed to protect the interests of employees and to develop a better labor policy. A new relationship will have to be forged between the education system and the world of work to ensure fuller employment and increased productivity. The sudden transition has created a hiatus and jeopardized the interest of the employees.

Pension reforms are equally necessary. Some countries – such as Hungary and Romania – have taken steps to gradually increase the retirement age. Another concern is to protect the minimum pension levels so that pensioners are able to meet the requirements of the subsistence minimum.

The role of the informal sector in the countries-in-transition also needs careful review. Some authors have distinguished between the "black" or "underground" economy and the informal sector. The role played by the informal sector in providing relief to those hit by the transition and the resulting loss of income has generally been appreciated. It is, in fact, viewed as the society's hidden capacity to respond to the crisis and provide protection for its members (a virtual safety net). In its absence, there would have been a total chaos, a collapse. Such cultural homeostasis, as revealed by these countries, needs to be documented with carefully planned and executed case studies so that the process can be properly understood and institutionalized. At the same time, there is room to examine the way in which underground economies operate – both nationally and internationally.

These cases also invite a careful examination of the newly proposed paradigms of development. The emerging consensus on the failure of the previous paradigms – the modernization paradigm of the West and the socialist paradigm of the East – taught us that methods of promoting development through state intervention have varied from culture to culture, and that the homogenization model has been rejected by all.[5] A new development paradigm cannot, therefore, be yet another variant of the homogenization recipe. The new formula that is now gaining international currency – referred to by some as the "Washington Consensus" – suggests a mix of liberal capitalism, democratic polity, and good governance. As it is presented, it also seems to be a single recipe for all situations. If the past is any guide, one would doubt its universal applicability. Already the evidence of these country case studies challenges the idea that this formula can be replicated in the context of former socialist countries. If we looked at the developing countries, we would find at least three different patterns: (1) the "tiger" model – represented by the Republic of Korea, Taiwan, and Singapore – suggests the pursuit of liberal economic growth with an authoritarian rule; (2) the "democratic" model, as in India, where democracy was introduced without waiting for economic development, and the economy is now being liberalized after a decade and a half of successful democratic rule; and (3) the "transitional" model of the East European countries, which have given up both centralized planning and totalitarian regime in favor of a liberal market orientation and a democratic form of government. All three sets of countries are now engulfed in the process of economic globalization, but the polities in all of them have distinctive features. They may all be called democracies, but they do not correspond to any single model of democracy; and their economies are also responding differently to the global trends. The experiences of all the three sets of countries have been widely different, and all seem to challenge the applicability of a common prescription.

For the countries-in-transition, there cannot be a single prescription as their problem profiles in the present state of transition are vastly different, notwithstanding a common ideological past. The countries-in-transition offer us an opportunity to "take a positive step towards constructing explanations of diversity in the outcomes of liberalization and democratization processes" (Gills and Philip 1996, 589).

Whether simultaneous liberalization of economy and polity leads to more stability and prosperity, or produces both economic and political

---

5. I made this point in one of my earlier essays thus: "the phenomenon of cultural continuity has challenged the *homogenization* hypothesis. While individual cultures are experiencing vast changes, they are not becoming similar, not even look-alike. Even their own homogeneity has suffered; they are becoming heterogeneous both in terms of their demographic composition and cultural constitution. The so-called World Culture's monocultural stance is no longer tenable. The plausible perspective is to view both culture and future in their plurality. No single future can be imposed on all cultures" (Atal 1993, 21).

destabilization is a question that remains unanswered. "Though Chile, for example, seemingly represents a successful model of undertaking both strategies simultaneously and remaining stable and prosperous, it is nevertheless questionable to what extent Chile's economic structure is truly comparable to the advanced industrial economies of East Asia"(Gills and Philip 1996, 589) or to the former socialist states covered in this study. "It is … because of the historicity of national development and because cultural and regionally specific factors remain very important, perhaps even central, that diverse patterns of development trajectory will continue to emerge. Particular localities, particular countries, and particular regions will continue to evolve and develop in particular ways …"(589).

From the studies presented in this book an idea can be had of the poverty crisis. But the evidence is not sufficient to suggest concrete actions to remedy the situation. Piecemeal solutions to immediately respond to a pressing need may be helpful in the shorter run, but cannot become part of an overall strategy without properly investigating their repercussions in the wider social system. Similarly, borrowed solutions may not work; what may have been an ideal strategy in a given country may simply be inappropriate in another context because of baseline differences. What is needed, therefore, is a program of research to study various facets of poverty in different regions and different population groups. Careful analyses of existing policies and the evaluation of programs of social assistance are a sine qua non for developing a proper policy and a plan for the eradication of poverty.

The analysis presented in this book is just the beginning. It provides a good base on which to mount full-length empirical surveys that go beyond the analyses of secondary data. And the time for this is now.

Bibliography

Atal, Yogesh. 1971. "The Role of Values and Institutions." In *The Challenge of Poverty in India,* ed. A.J. Fonseca. Delhi: Vikas Publications.

———. 1993. "Asian Cultures: What Destination?" In *The Futures of Asian Cultures,* ed. Eleonora B. Masini and Yogesh Atal. RUSHSAP Series # 38. Bangkok: UNESCO.

Atal, Yogesh, ed. 1997. *Perspectives on Educating the Poor.* New Delhi: Abhinav Publications.

Atal, Yogesh, and Else Øyen, eds. 1997. *Poverty and Participation in Civil Society.* New Delhi: Abhinav Publications; Paris: UNESCO.

Gills, Barry, and George Philip. 1996. "Editorial. Towards Convergence in Development Policy? Challenging the 'Washington Consensus' and Restoring the Historicity of Divergent Development Trajectories." *Third World Quarterly* 17, no. 4: 585-91.

McAuley, Alastair. 1996. "Russia and the Baltics: Poverty and Poverty Research in a Changing World." In *Poverty: A Global Review – Handbook on International Poverty Research,* ed. Else Øyen, S.M. Miller, and Abdus Samad. Paris: UNESCO.

Milanovic, Branko. n.d. *Poverty, Inequality, and Social Policy in Transition Economies.* Washington, D.C.: The World Bank.

Øyen, Else, S.M. Miller, and Syed Abdus Samad, eds. 1996. *Poverty: A Global Review – Handbook on International Poverty Research.* Paris: UNESCO.

Szalai, Julia. 1990. "Some Thoughts on Poverty and the Concept of Subsistence Minimum." In *Social Report, 1990,* ed. Rudolf Andorka, Tamás Kolosi, and György Vukovich. Budapest: TÁRKI, 296-304.

Tabatabai, Hamid. 1996. *Statistics on Poverty and Income Distribution – An ILO Compendium of Data.* Geneva: ILO.

UNDP. 1996a. *Human Development Report — BULGARIA.*

———. 1996b. *Human Development Report — GEORGIA.*

———. 1996c. *Human Development Report — RUSSIAN FEDERATION.*

———. 1997. *Human Development Report — 1997.* New York: Oxford University Press.

UNICEF. 1995. *Poverty, Children, and Policy: Responses for a Brighter Future.* Economies in Transition Studies. Regional Monitoring Report No. 3. Florence: UNICEF International Child Development Centre.

United Nations. 1993. *Report on the World Social Situation 1993.* New York.

The World Bank. 1997. *World Development Report 1997.*

Chapter One

RECENT TRENDS IN POVERTY IN HUNGARY

Julia Szalai
Institute of Sociology, Hungarian Academy of Sciences

Introduction: The Politics of Poverty

Poverty is never and nowhere a self-evident and self-explaining phenomenon. Its conceptualization, measurement, and the actions taken for its alleviation are determined by the political culture of a given society. In the context of Hungary, the political character of the problem needs to be specially underlined for the following reasons. First, there is considerable confusion concerning the causation and recent growth of poverty; this has led to controversies surrounding policies for its alleviation. Second, the rise in poverty has raised questions regarding those political and social rights guaranteed by the newly introduced legal regulations. Because of serious loopholes in the prevailing system of social policy, many of the guarantees given to people have remained on paper. Third, the poverty question has become a heavily politicized subject because of the rivalry of competing social groups for the diminishing resources in the chronic economic crisis of the past decade. And finally, poverty has become a "hot" political issue in the context of the division of responsibilities and duties between the central and local administrations within the new democratic system of governance.

Because of their importance for the discussion below, let me introduce these four aspects of the "politics" of poverty at some length.

1. Confusion in the interpretation of poverty

The open acknowledgment of the existence of poverty coincided with the change in the political system of the country around 1989-90. There is no unanimity of opinion regarding its causes and consequently there is no consensus on a strategy to eradicate it. Different groups of experts and policymakers suggest different interventions depending upon their understanding of what has caused poverty. There are some who would argue that poverty is an utterly new phenomenon in Hungary, one which has been generated by the new economic processes of marketization. Poverty is perceived by these people mainly as a problem of inequalities in income and wealth, and its existence is taken as a "natural" price for economic advancement. Therefore, they opt for policies that are target oriented, and remain neutral toward the forces of the market.

Others hold an opposite view and emphasize that poverty is nothing new – that it was a traditional feature of Hungarian society and continued to exist even during the decades of socialism. General ignorance about the phenomenon was due to political factors: it was the ideological and political order of the totalitarian system that did not allow the problem to be exposed publicly. However, with the changes of 1989-90, the hidden face of poverty has surfaced. Thus, what is new is the shock of its sudden emergence and its acknowledgment by all quarters. Holders of this view do not attribute the eruption of poverty to the recently introduced market forces, as it would, in their opinion, be rather misleading. Instead, they propose comprehensive policies of social integration both on the part of civil society and the state.

A third set of arguments focus on the negative effects of the withdrawal of the state, and relate the jump in the number of the poor mainly to the drastic cuts in state spending on social benefits and services. They argue for clearer definitions of the responsibilities of the state and want to see legal and financial guarantees for their fulfillment. There is yet another interpretation based on an individualistic approach. According to this line of reasoning, poverty is caused due to a lack of adaptation by certain social groups to the changing conditions. It is a behavioral problem which should be corrected through discipline and education.

Given these controversial (in some ways, contradictory) interpretations of the phenomenon, there is no consensus in Hungarian society in regard to the measures and policies that should be applied to combat poverty.

2. Inconsistency between political and social rights

Much of the manifestation of poverty is closely related to the political changes that occurred around 1989-90. The first acts of the newly elected parliament were aimed at disowning the totalitarian heritage of socialism and reaffirming basic human and political rights. However, the newly founded legal guarantees of the universal rights of the citizenry have not been accompanied with sufficient provisions for the fulfillment of basic daily needs for all. In fact, there is an opposite trend: social programs that once covered the entire population have now been limited to those who qualify in means testing; access to many of the social services has become market regulated, and the poor get only marginal subsidies. Due to discrepancies between the political and social components of daily living, the issue of "social rights" has become one of the most debated aspects of the "essence" of democracy in the process of formulating a new constitution with the broadest possible social and political support.

3. The rivalry between impoverished social groups

The increased transparency of inequalities of income and wealth has generated a certain "competition" among those hit by impoverishment: the fight for maintaining previously acquired social positions on the part of the lower middle class of late socialist Hungary has intensified the marginalization of those in deep poverty. This fight can be seen as well in the labor market, as in education or health care. However, it is particularly affecting areas of social welfare: the distribution of funds in social security and payments in welfare assistance are subject to open rivalry for the status of being "most in need." Heated competition for the decreasing funds has created rivalries among various groups who suffer from deprivation. The revitalization of the concept of the "deserving poor" has made it difficult to conceptualize universal programs. When government help is restricted to certain categories of people, it encourages arbitrariness on the part of the officials and may even lead to unfair practices.

4. The "decentralization" of social tensions accompanying the increase of poverty

The decomposition of the omnipotent institutions of the central state (otherwise one of the major preconditions of the success of the ongoing transformation from a command economy to a market-based one) has strongly affected the entire sphere of social policy. The old, centrally administered provisions and benefit schemes have been terminated, while new substitutes have just partially been introduced at the local level. Thus, the issue of poverty is one of the core problems for local democracy and the cohesion of the communities.

The issue of poverty is closely bound to essential aspects of the post-communist transformation. Therefore, the presentation of basic facts about the changing number and socio-economic composition of the poor has to be viewed in light of an overview of broader political, social, and economic development. This overview will be of an historical character: it aims at reconstructing the "story" of the (re)discovery of poverty in Hungary in the 1980s. The methods of conceptualization and measurement in those years have greatly affected the general discourse since 1989-90, and have had their manifold direct and indirect impacts on alternative ways of thinking about policies that should be applied when dealing with poverty.

I. Measurements and Definitions of Poverty

When describing the major strands in thinking about poverty in Hungary, it should be said at the outset that the term "poverty" was taboo throughout the entire period of socialism. The denial of the existence of poverty followed from the ideological and political commitments of the regime. In concrete terms, the socialist regime promised to get rid of hopelessly immobile, backward social positions, and the subordination and defenselessness of the great masses of prewar agricultural laborers, unskilled workers, and the chronically unemployed. Its commitment to equality and justice was to be fulfilled through compulsory full employment and an exceptionally high concentration of the nation's wealth for "more equitable" redistribution under the close control of the Party. Admitting the existence of poverty would have caused serious harm to this policy. It would have questioned both the communist ideology and the daily politics of the Party to acknowledge that, despite all measures and direct interventions into people's daily life, poverty remained there – even if it changed its appearance over time.

Nevertheless, it was impossible even then to completely ignore the problem. With the turn in politics from the exclusive priority of forced industrialization toward attempts to raise the general level of living, the Communist Party became concerned with increasing income inequalities around the late 1960s. By admitting the "necessity" of cutting incomes for economic advancement, satisfactory explanations had to be given for the growth of income inequalities. Thus, while maintaining the taboo on "poverty," the problem of those with "low incomes" slowly came to the surface in public discourse. Statistical surveys and scientific research of the time reflected the shifts in the main emphases of party politics: from the late 1960s onward, rich empirical data provided information on changes in the living standards of different types of urban and rural households, on their sources of income and patterns of consumption, and also on the varying magnitude of the measurable income inequalities over time. Theoretical explanations of the findings began to concentrate on the issue of inequalities. However, theories of the "culture of poverty," social equity, or approaches focusing on problems of social exclusion, marginalization, segregation, etc. were less influential in the public representation of poverty, though they had great impact on the activities of various dissident groups. Still, in the official political discourse of those days, poverty appeared mainly as a problem of redistribution: scientific research strengthened the case of those wanting higher social security benefits and more equality in access to fundamental social services. In fact, follow-up research provided feedback to these claims and attempts. The sociological and statistical literature of the 1970s and early 1980s is rich in analyses of the impact of various social security and service delivery programs on the living standards in different regions of the country, in different social settings, age groups, and occupational groups.

The multifarious investigations into the conditions of daily living contributed to the development of another concept which substituted for "poverty": from the 1970s onward, politicians and responsible officers in public administration began to speak with increased emphasis about "the disadvantaged population" or about those "suffering multifarious disadvantages." In this approach, poverty was not reduced to the lack of adequate income alone; educational, regional, health, and occupational aspects of the problem were also taken into consideration. It has to be admitted that the new concept was certainly richer in its approach than the simplified one of inadequate finances. However, its application was rather problematic from at least three perspectives. First, it suggested the individual character of the social problem: "disadvantages" can occur to anybody at any time, and it is rather difficult to show that there would be any systematic processes causing their (re)production. Second, the new concept implied that poverty would just be a transitory phenomenon – if it were merely a "disadvantage," then it could be overcome by well-designed actions. Third, the concept of "disadvantage" combined poverty with other types of "difficulties," hiding its structural character and creating false equations between being poor, belonging to an ethnic minority, living in a single-parent family, or having a small dwelling. In other words, the coining of the new term oriented action from general and universal programs toward individual casework and ad hoc help.

It was this sharply individualistic approach on the part of those in power and administration which generated research and action. It encouraged social scientists to search for alternative interpretations of poverty and effective support for those affected by it. In response to the unclear concept of "disadvantages," the material side of poverty was repeatedly emphasized – though with a different perspective than before. Inadequacies in the living conditions of the poor were put into the focus, and claims for the introduction of a subsistence minimum driven from the normative concept of "decent living" were articulated. Thus, research to support the claims focused more on the characteristics of consumption and the constraints in the household budget of the poor than simply on their inadequate level of income. The arguments put forward by these investigations had clear policy implications: the goal was not only to reduce inequalities, but to formulate programs driven by positive discrimination in favor of the poor. Further, the new, consumption-oriented approach helped discover the ways and mechanisms by which the poor were excluded from access to certain basic social, health, and educational services. It assisted in drawing the map of poverty across regions and settlements, and, last but not least, it led to the articulation of alternative programs for assistance which were run and provided by a group of dissident intellectuals in the collective of SZETA (Fund for Aid for the Poor). SZETA-related activists concentrated their work in the most remote parts of the country. Besides offering financial help to those most in need in a given community, they tried to mobilize broader groups for self-defending actions. On the intellectual level, the famous and well-attended seminars of SZETA helped conceptualize the specific cultural features of modern poverty, and assisted in developing a more comprehensive understanding of the transmission of backward social positions to the microlevels of families and communities.

The slowly evolving dissident movements around the turn of the 1970s and 1980s greatly influenced the competing interpretations of the cause of poverty. Thanks partly to the literature analyzing power relations in the socialist states, and partly to the accumulation of substantial knowledge about people's self-defense against the totalitarian oppression through increased participation in the informal economy, analytical descriptions of poverty gradually moved toward a complex understanding of the problem as a certain manifestation of powerlessness. The implicit power relations in people's daily life were demonstrated through a rich set of sociological investigations which pointed out that the most effective means for self-defense was the building up of a way of life based on simultaneous participation in the formal and informal economies and social relations; that the poor were mainly those whose lives were dependent exclusively on the formal spheres of production and who usually suffered from the lack of a supportive family network to construct a second pillar in informal settings; that the better or worse bargaining positions of the different social groups were closely related to their strength in the markets of the informal economy – thus, an important aspect of poverty was the weak position of the disadvantaged in this hidden process of articulating common interests; that the weak representation of common interests was a self-sustaining factor in the atomization of poverty and in individualizing the socially determined defenselessness of the poor. In short, increased emphasis on the understanding of the roles and functioning of the informal economy gradually led to a coherent social critique of the socialist system, where poverty demonstrated in the original programs of equality and justice on the one hand, and pointed to the malfunctioning of institutions of centralized redistribution, on the other.

These traditions of social critique had a great deal of influence on the comprehensive reform programs which the newly organized parties formulated prior to the first free parliamentary elections in 1990. There was consensus among the various political actors that a rapid decomposition of the legacy of the omnipotent socialist party-state was the most important precondition for the systemic transformation from totalitarianism to democracy, and also for the move from a centrally regulated to a market-based economy. State-run social security, centrally administered price subsidies, and social services were among the first targets of reconstruction. Social services and welfare provisions were essentially decentralized, the price system was liberated from built-in subsidies and subordinated to the open play of the market, and the various benefit schemes of social security were either terminated, or revised to follow the principle of "pay according to contributions," instead of the "pay-as-you-go" system of the postwar decades. All these changes greatly affected the situation of the poor. Consequently, research on poverty in the 1990s has made the follow-up of the shifts in the socio-demographic composition and the living conditions of the poor its first priority. As a result, several approaches are being tried in contemporary studies of the phenomenon. In addition, the ongoing reforms have invoked studies to assess the general socio-economic impact of changes in the administration of welfare services, and, in particular, to measure their effects on the situation of the poor. Such policy-oriented research is contributing to the better understanding of the nature of contemporary poverty and to a richer characterization of the different groups within the ever broadening classes of the poor.

Let me summarize briefly the most important results that were produced by the numerous investigations during the past few years. In response to the question "who are the poor?" one can see the recurrent emphasis given to the material aspects of poverty in contemporary research. Three different approaches are most frequently followed to measure poverty and to differentiate between the poor and the nonpoor: (1) poverty as a manifestation of income inequalities; (2) poverty as the manifestation of inadequacies in consumption (measured by consumption-based subsistence minima); and (3) poverty as the manifestation of dropping below the minimally acceptable level of living (measured by income-based poverty lines).

In the first approach, poverty is defined in *relative* terms: the poor are those who occupy the first (and, according to some broader definitions, the second) decile(s) within the income distribution of the population. Great emphasis is given here to the inequalities of income and the absolute distance between the living standards of those in poverty and the rest of society. "Income" is not an individual category: it is understood as the share of the individual from those resources which are regularly at the disposal of his or her household. The strength of this approach is its focus on the structural character of poverty: the poor are seen in their relation to the nonpoor; they are those who possess fewer resources for everyday life. This approach directs attention to policies influencing the entire distribution of income and invokes the application of measures of a macroeconomic character (attention is drawn to necessary changes in the systems of taxation and social security in the first place). The shortcomings of this approach are partly conceptual, partly practical. Since emphasis is given to those inequalities which appear between the haves and the have-nots, the approach hides the internal differences among those who belong to the latter category. Thus, it is difficult to differentiate between the very diverse problems and needs of one-parent families, elderly pensioners receiving small pensions, the unemployed, or families with several children. They all might belong to the undifferentiated "first decile" of the income scale, though the nature of their poverty is obviously very different.

With regard to the political implications, this approach calls for universal programs and diverts attention from provisions which should fulfill specific needs of one or another group within the same income bracket. Equally important are, however, some technical limitations of the method. First, given that "households" are the central unit of measurement, these investigations do not provide any information about people not belonging to any household. Thus, the poor living in institutions, homeless people, and many of the sick poor are left out. Second, the approach applies the concept of "regular" income. However, one of the decisive characteristics of the living conditions of the poor is a high degree of irregularity in the flow of income. Their income might even exceed the upper borderline of the first decile from time to time, still they remain poor because of the strong oscillation in the magnitude of their resources from one week/month to the other. Third, the results of studies applying the relative concept of poverty are greatly determined by the availability, for interrogation, of households with different levels of income and by their willingness to respond. Since participation in these investigations is voluntary, there is no way to get information about those who refuse to cooperate in the research. Refusal rates have been very high in recent years (some 30-35 percent). As analyses of the data on typical groups that do not respond show, the refusal rates are exceptionally high both in the highest income brackets and among the very poor; in large cities; and among the younger members of households (CSO 1996d).

As a result, the samples that measure the entire income distribution are very skewed. Consequently, the results on the level and composition of poverty have to be viewed with great caution. The situation is further complicated by the exceptionally high proportion of unreported income: as calculations based on macroeconomic figures and various income survey data show, some 20-37 percent of interviewees' income remains unreported. This missing portion relates to those irregular elements of the household income that are derived from casual work, ad hoc contracts or day labor in the informal economy. It may also be in the form of labor for which no payment is made. Despite these limitations, research on people's income status tell us a great deal about the worsening financial situation of the lower middle class. But they are conceptually and methodologically inadequate for the investigation of the lives of the really poor.

By attempting to define a normative term for the measurement of poverty, the second approach tries to avoid many of the limitations of the first one. Conceptually, it applies an absolute view of poverty. Investigations driven from this conceptual framework aim at responding to two sets of questions: (1) they try to arrive at a satisfactory single indicator of poverty; and (2) they attempt to define the magnitude of the population that, according to the chosen indicator, could be described as "poor." Obviously, both sets of questions are raised by practical necessities. The indicator (best measure) of poverty should be justifiable and thus, it should be accepted by the public for policy purposes; the size of the poor population (and its change over time) has to be known in order to allocate adequate resources for programs of poverty alleviation. Although both tasks are clear and easy to accept, their realization suffers insurmountable difficulties in contemporary Hungary.

Let me first address the problem of the "good" and most widely acceptable indicator of poverty. At present, there are a great number of such indicators, but there is no consensus about "the" best one among them. The lack of consensus follows partly from clashing traditions in the methodology of the computations, and partly from practical reasons. Any of the computed minima prove to be higher than the level of income applied by the authorities in charge of welfare assistance to define entitlements, amid the chronic shortage of resources for distribution. From a conceptual point of view, two clusters of computations can be differentiated. The first set takes the actual consumption of the poor as the point of departure, and argues for the legitimacy of certain items being characteristic of the culture of poverty. The second defines the minimum in terms of some "universal" health norms and applies the "average" composition of consumption with some arbitrary reductions in its income equivalents. Apart from these differences in their underlying philosophy, all consumption-based calculations combine certain normative elements and some empirical findings about the actual patterns of consumption.

Concerning the methodological principle that should be applied to orient practical work in welfare assistance, serious attempts have been made in the past three to four years to compromise the various traditions of computation and to arrive at an agreement enjoining the support of the broadest possible circle of experts, statisticians, and politicians. The most important part in the recently published variant of the recommended computation (CSO 1996e) is the compilation of a food basket meeting some basic health requirements. After taking the money equivalent of this basket using average market prices, other components of the subsistence minima are computed from empirical survey data provided by the regular Household Budget Surveys on those households which, in their actual food consumption, are nearest the normatively defined basket. In this way, strong normative prescriptions are combined with specific features of consumption in poor households, and the computed minima reflect the actual needs of the various household formations more or less correctly.

Although these computations provide scientifically acceptable indicators, there are a number of unresolved difficulties with them. The first problem relates to the insensitivity of the minima: these computations have a rather static view of poverty, and are unable to follow the highly fluctuating character of the composition and level of consumption in poor households. One can easily identify a great number of households which frequently cross the borderline both downward and upward. Policies based on fixed minima are unable to follow these frequent changes. Further, the subsistence minima are also insensitive to variations in the composition of households and the type of settlement where a certain poor household lives. Given the great differences in patterns of consumption, in the share of expenditure, and also in market prices of the commodities in different parts of the country, it is important that the computation take note of these. True, calculations for scientific purposes can be (and are) refined according to the actual differences in household formations and types of settlement, but with increased refinement, the derived minima lose their policy relevance. Authorities and public services are unable to handle ten to twelve different standards in their actual programs of daily assistance.

Two further elements of the critique of the subsistence minima as the point of departure in measuring poverty will be briefly mentioned here.

The first is the problem of dwelling: the prices of houses are still so high that people with ordinary incomes cannot afford from. As in-depth studies on housing have demonstrated (Vajda and Farkas 1992), the greatest proportion of houses are still built in the form of work exchange within the family, kin, and the neighborhood. This is the only possible way to minimize expenditure and to substitute money spending with labor and/or the offer of different favors. However, such a strategy requires considerable sacrifice over quite a long period of time. The level of daily consumption has to be reduced substantially, and, in addition, extra-long working hours are expected from all members of the household, regardless of their sex and age. However, none of these components of the daily living of a rather large section of society is taken into account in the computations. The concept of the subsistence minimum, reflecting only the current standard and way of life, cannot handle this problem. Thus, all the computations take it for granted that all the households already *have* housing, and calculate only the costs of the maintenance of houses and not of their purchase (or any consumption equivalent of the latter). The needs of those *not* possessing any dwelling, or of those who are in the process of acquiring one, are mostly ignored in such calculations.

The second problem follows from the peculiarities of the level of consumption in Hungary. As empirical findings in the Household Budget Surveys show, people generally spend more than their registered income. The puzzle can partially be explained by the relatively high proportion of unreported sources of income in the monthly household revenue. More important is the above-indicated decisive role of production in the informal economy and the interhousehold transfers of commodities, services, and favors (which all work as substitutes for cash expenditures in meeting a great variety of needs, housing being an outstanding item, though just one element among them). These components are strongly underreported in people's returns – not because of their forgetfulness, or their desire to evade reporting, but because of the very nature of these "sources," which are not seen as income. However, their utilization is shown in the accounts of consumption. Thus, surveys based on the costs of consumption items end up attributing higher income to the respondent households than what they really claim to possess. As a consequence, the minima derived from the "priced" elements of consumption are surprisingly close to the average per capita income of the entire population, and are, thus, unable to differentiate between the poor and the nonpoor.

Income-based computations of the poverty line try to overcome this problem. The poverty line is usually taken as a derivation of the mean or average income – either 70 or 50 percent of the average monthly per capita value is most frequently the point of departure, and the poor are those whose income falls below this level. Studies based on this approach usually attempt to characterize those groups which they define as "definitely poor," and also describe the situation of those who are "endangered," i.e., who live in the neighborhood of the poverty line. Using this method, we have a relatively good idea of the size and composition of poor households, their sources of income, the number of economically active and dependent members, the rate of unemployment etc. In scientific discourses about the further refinement of this approach, the simplistic computation of per capita values has been heavily criticized recently. Since not only the number of household members, but also their age and economic status influences the level of spending (and consumption) in a certain household, it is strongly recommended that computations of the poverty line be standardized accordingly. In response, an equivalence scale is applied with increased frequency to calculate 70 (or 50) percent of the average income per consumption unit. In these computations, the various household members get different scores: when defining the aggregate "size" of the household, the head is usually counted by a weight of 1.0, other adult members by 0.7, and children by 0.5.

A great advantage of the poverty line based method of measuring poverty is its attempt to combine both relative and absolute poverty. Since the poverty line is bound to the average level of per capita (consumption unit) income, it avoids the above-mentioned inflexibility of the consumption-based computations. However, it defines a certain level of income as a strong measure for action. The shortcomings of the method follow from those limitations of the income surveys which were outlined above. These surveys do not provide data about those social groups which do not live in households; the rate of refusal is too high to take the results as valid and representative ones; the proportion of unreported income is extremely high in contemporary Hungary, and – perhaps more important – both its standard and internal variation differ a great deal among the various social groups. These computations take into account only the regular elements of the household budgets. They are, thus, highly insensitive to those irregular changes in income which have such a great impact on the composition of consumption among the poor.

With all its limitations, it is still this third approach which provides, however, the best possible estimation about the number of the poor and the internal structure of poverty in Hungary today. In addition, the yearly adjustment of the poverty line makes it possible to see people's transitions in and out of poverty and to sort out the chronic and transitory elements of the living conditions of the poor. Therefore, before turning to a detailed analysis of the causes, let me briefly show some basic data about the extent and recent changes of poverty. Tables below are derived from the database of the yearly repeated Household Panel Surveys run by the collective of TÁRKI and the Budapest University of Economics. The survey is based on the follow-up of a countrywide representative sample of 2,000 households.

Table 1.1   Changes in the proportion of the poor 1992-1996 (in percentages)

Year	Ratio of persons living in households with a per capita monthly income below 50 percent of the average
1992	10.1
1993	10.3
1994	11.6
1995	12.4
1996	14.0

Source: Sík and Tóth 1997

Table 1.2   The proportion of the poor, according to age, level of schooling, type of settlement, and ethnic group membership, 1996 (percentage of persons living in households with a monthly income per unit below 50 percent of the average)

Age	%	Level of schooling	%	Settlement	%	Ethnic group	%
0-5	26.4	0-7 grades	22.4	Village	20.1	Gypsy	66.7
6-14	21.6	8 grades	19.2	Small town	13.3	Non-Gypsy	9.2
15-19	19.1	Primary and vocational training	10.8	City	11.6		
20-29	13.2	Secondary school	5.4	Budapest	4.5		
30-39	13.6	Higher education	0.8				
40-49	15.5						
50-59	7.3						
60-69	4.3						
70 and over	8.9						

Source: Sík and Tóth 1997

Table 1.3   How many times were individuals belonging to different quintiles of the 1996 income distribution below the poverty line between 1992 and 1996 (poverty line: less than 50 percent of the per capita monthly income in the given year)

How many times poor, 1992-96	Quintiles of Income Distribution, 1996					
	Lowest 1	2	3	4	Highest 5	Together
never	9.4	21.1	21.9	23.8	23.8	100.0
once	42.0	20.5	17.6	9.1	10.8	100.0
twice	62.7	8.9	23.5	1.2	3.7	100.0
three times	75.4	24.6	–	–	–	100.0
four times	100.0	–	–	–	–	100.0

Source: Sík and Tóth 1997

As the data indicate clearly, the proportion of the poor within the population has shown a steady increase during the 1990s. The chosen poverty line (50 percent of the average per capita monthly income) provides a sharp division: those who drop below this limit live in truly deep poverty. (Comparative calculations based on the above-described subsistence minima result in a higher proportion of the poor for 1992. The Central Statistical Office estimated their ratio to be around 15 percent, and adjusted calculations for the subsequent years also indicated a steady increase, reaching 18-19 percent by 1996). As indicated in Table 1.2, the risk of poverty is highest among the very young: contemporary poverty hits children and their families in the first place. The high occurrence of child poverty has proved to be a constant feature in past decades. Studies in the 1980s already called attention to the ever more marked shift in the internal composition of poverty from rural to urban, and from elderly to younger groups (for a detailed discussion, see Szalai 1993). These tendencies also seem to prevail today: little schooling, loss of employment, several small children in the family, and the lack of rural agricultural backing to compensate for the decline in cash income result in the frequent occurrence of poverty among young urban families. Although these families might escape this situation from time to time, poverty is rarely a transitory phenomenon in their life. Taking the period between 1992 and 1996, the proportion of those who were below the yearly poverty line for more than twelve months is 26 percent on the national average, but proves to be as high as 37 percent in the case of school children, and 29 percent for young adults (below the age of thirty).

With the chronic economic crisis of the past eight to ten years, a similar increase can also be seen in the case of rural poverty. As more detailed analyses of the data reveal, the rise is due to a jump in the number of the poor in some pockets of the country. Villages previously providing the majority of commuting unskilled and semiskilled laborers to heavy industry (concentrated once in the North and Northeast of the country) suffer extra high rates of chronic unemployment these days. Similarly, the situation has become markedly worse in the traditional agricultural regions of the East and the South: people cannot find industrial employment anymore, and work in agriculture does not provide enough income to attain a decent standard of living. Due to these factors, the depth and the duration of poverty has been significantly increasing in these regions. As survey data show, these are the very parts of the country where the proportion of those permanently entrenched in poverty has grown with the greatest speed during the 1990s.

II. The Economic Dimension of Poverty

Hungary has experienced a continuous increase in poverty during the 1990s. Looked upon from a macroeconomic perspective, three sets of issues have directly contributed to the shaping of this trend: (1) the uneven socio-economic impact of the lasting economic crisis, which has impacted certain groups more than others; (2) the negative consequences of the systemic changes on employment stability and on access to various kinds of gainful work which has led to unequal risks of unemployment and marginalization; and (3) the socially uneven repercussions that the rapid changes in the prevailing property relations and state finances have had on household economies of the various social groups.

1. Consequences of the lasting economic crisis

Measured by the internationally accepted indicators of economic growth and productivity, the performance of the Hungarian economy has shown clear signs of an unstoppable decline since the beginning of the 1980s. The yearly GDP ceased to increase around 1982 and, from 1985 onward, statistics signalled an absolute decrease year after year. After a decade of steady decline, 1994 was the first year with a modest rise, though the improvement was only enough to regain the per capita value of the GDP in 1980. The decreasing yearly performance of the economy has generated further tensions which have put strong constraints on innovative economic policies in the 1990s. On the one hand, decreases have led to detrimental shifts in the structure of production, especially in exports and imports; and on the other, the attempts to countervail the losses through financial injections via international loans have made the country highly indebted.

Hungary's worsening position in the foreign markets is clearly indicated by the unfavorable trend in trade. Its index in 1995 reached only 89 percent of the corresponding measure of 1980, while the ratio of international trade in the yearly GDP has grown from 19 to 31 percent. Attempts to correct this situation have led to an export-oriented economic policy. Despite the growing internal and external indebtedness of the state budget, central subsidies to the exports occupy an increasing proportion in budgetary spending. The high priority given to the financing of exports has induced fierce competition among firms, contributing to a large extent to the rapid bankruptcy of enterprises in heavy industry, chemical production, textiles, vehicle production, electric equipment, etc. As a consequence, wages began to fall (in real value) along with the downsizing of these industrial units.

As to the magnitude of foreign indebtedness, it would be enough to cite a few telling figures. The already high U.S.$1,536 per capita value of foreign debt in 1990 increased a further 7 percent by 1995 (to U.S.$1,647 per head), amounting to around 91 percent of the gross yearly per capita disposable income of the population. This heavy burden on the economy makes the scope of "free" decisions in spending very limited. What is perhaps even more important, it makes the country greatly dependent on the "benevolence" of the major agents of the international financial world. The IMF and the World Bank play a dominant role in shaping Hungary's economic and social policy. The government feels obliged to follow their rigid prescriptions. This strong contingency determines the often insensitive application of strict neo-liberal rules, especially in those areas where rapid withdrawal of the state is urged. Such neo-liberal principles were behind the drastic cuts in price subsidies which led to the acceleration of inflation in recent years. Similar considerations have guided reforms in welfare provisions, which ultimately concluded in the effective devaluation of such important benefit schemes as pensions and family allowances.

The acceleration in the rise of consumer prices has led to a sharp decline in real income and in the level of spending on daily consumption. In addition, it has caused a substantial drop in savings and investments among households. In this manner, the previously accumulated resources of the greater part of the population have slowly vanished, further contributing to the shrinking of economic production and to the increase of unbearable inequalities of income and wealth. As clearly shown in Table 1.5, the direct impact of inflation has been most dramatic for the poor. Since items with a relatively high proportion of earlier subsidies have greater weight in their consumption, cuts in subsidies contributed to group-specific inflation rates exceeding the national average. The annual reports on returns for utilities (rents, electricity, etc.)

show an ever increasing number of indebted households concentrated in the poorest parts of the cities and large towns. Police reports encounter the frequent forceful eviction of the most seriously indebted who, despite all earlier warnings, remained "reluctant" to settle their bills. One can see the rise of new ghettos around the cities inhabited by the victims of this new notion of law and order.

Means-tested welfare assistance (discussed later in the chapter) is inadequate to compensate for the losses that the poor suffer on the market. Their real income falls further and further behind the nonpoor. The internal shift in the composition of resources of the monthly budget of the poor points toward the increasing weight of such unstable and nonguaranteed elements as income from casual work or incidental assistance from local support programs. Thus, not only the level, but also the security of their daily living has been badly affected in recent years. As the data on the changing resources of households belonging to the lowest and the highest decile of the income distribution reveal, between 1993 and 1995, the weight of those components of the monthly household budget which preserved their real value changed from 12 to 20 percent within the revenue of the poor, while the corresponding proportion grew from 20 to 30 percent in rich households. This is a clear indication of unequal access to channels which, despite the unfavorable macroeconomic conditions, are capable of stabilizing the household economies.

What is even more telling, however, is a glimpse into some characteristics of those components of the monthly household budget which, by preserving their real value, served to slow the fall of the overall household income. In the case of the poor, all these types of resources were ad hoc and/or transitory: they were only able to attain casual daily labor, welfare assistance, and childcare grants. On the other hand, in rich households, the income components resisting the loss of real value were either driven by the most prosperous parts of the economy or were legally guaranteed: profit from business, pensions, and long-term state support given for house maintenance were those items of the revenue which proved to preserve (or even increase)in real value amid conditions of general decline. Thus, not only the standards of living, but also the ways of life seem to diverge from one another. Adaptation to the market and the restructuring of social security offer opportunities only for the better-off groups, while the poor are left with marginal access to work in the most unstable segments of the economy, and to increased dependence on the local welfare offices.

2. Changes in employment and their consequences on poverty

With the turn toward marketization, radical changes have been taking place in the structure of the labor market and also in the legal regulations

Table 1.4 Changes in consumer prices, real wages/salaries, and real income, 1990-1995 (previous year = 100.0)

Year	Consumer price index	Real wages/salaries per earner	Per capita real income
1990	128.9	96.3	98.2
1991	135.0	93.0	98.3
1992	123.0	98.6	96.5
1993	122.5	96.1	95.3
1994	118.8	107.2	102.7
1995	128.2	87.8	95.3
Total increase/decrease 1989-1995 (percent)	399.4	− 20.3	− 13.1

Source: CSO 1996b

Table 1.5 Consumer price indices by income groups, 1990-1995 (Previous year = 100.0)

Year / Group	1990	1991	1992	1993	1994	1995	Total increase 1989-1995 (in percentages)
households with low income	129.8	134.2	123.1	123.6	119.4	129.2	08.8
households with medium income	128.8	135.1	123.2	122.7	119.0	128.5	42.3
households with high income	127.8	135.1	122.3	121.6	118.1	127.5	386.7
All households	128.9	135.0	123.0	122.5	118.8	128.2	399.4

Source: CSO 1996b

of employment. The most important new development in the post-1989 period was the suspension of compulsory employment. Neither companies nor individuals were forced anymore to follow the principle of full employment once prescribed by the law. The new "employment policy" expects firms to deal with matters of employment only in the context of productivity and marketability. This has encouraged enterprises to adopt tough measures against their employees. In many cases, a drastic reduction of the workforce has proved to be the first and easiest step toward market adaptation. Thus, the abolition of compulsory rules on employment induced large waves of dismissals. These especially hit those who had held peripheral positions in production.

The threat of dismissals has induced a large set of reactions among the employees. Since neither the old, nor the newly organized trade unions regard it as their task to formulate alternative production policies with an emphasis on job protection, reactions remained mainly individual. One of the responses may be termed as a "run-ahead" tactic: those with better qualifications, good personal contacts, and adequate family support left their old workplace in due course and tried to find employment either in the newly emerging small firms in the private sector or in the state-owned larger ones that were still actively functioning. As survey data suggest, there was a high rate of turnover in the 1990s not only among the young, but also in the middle-aged groups; and not only among men, but also among female employees.

The second response to the changing job situation has been an intensive utilization of all those pathways to temporary (or final) nonemployment which provide fixed regular income through social security. Compared to unemployment compensations, these payments are relatively high, and, in addition, one does not have to worry about their future termination. The pathways are numerous: besides the expanding early retirement programs, one can enlist in job-protected childcare leave until one's child reaches the age of three, disability pension plans, and also those programs which provide some payment for those offering home care for the chronically sick. True, taking advantage of these plans means a substantial reduction in one's former monthly income, but the gain in the increased amount of free time is usually utilized for compensation. People with social security benefits are the main workforce of the informal economy, and one can increasingly find them also among the part-time entrepreneurs in a wide range of services.

As labor statistics show, enrollment rates have been rising in all these plans during the 1990s. Some 496,000 persons withdrew from employment through one or another program of social security in 1990 (representing 8.3 percent of the working age population), and their number grew to 637,000 by 1995 (amounting to 10.5 percent of the respective population)(see Laky 1996). The adoption of these pathways is, however, a risky enterprise. In principle, one can gain (by combining social security payments and income from business or the informal economy), but the general result is a substantial loss of income with clearly declining opportunities for compensation. This is due not only to the lasting economic crisis of the country, which has diminished the purchasing power even for products of the informal economy, but also because access to jobs in the informal economy requires wide contacts, which people on social security slowly lose. By leaving behind their old workplace and coworkers, they also leave behind the major mediators of the supply and demand of the informal economy.

A third strategy adopted more due to the constraints of the shrinking official labor market than to a conscious choice for a long-term change in career is for less qualified people to look for jobs in the expanding black market. Although the magnitude of this market is anyone's guess, its existence is known to everybody. A number of small-scale services, work in construction, simple office work, etc. takes place without registering with the government, liberating the employer from paying wage taxes and social security contributions, and offering livelihood – even if in a very uncertain and unprotected manner – to those who would otherwise find themselves on the dole.

These briefly outlined individual responses to the uncertainties and instabilities of employment usually do not appear in a clear form. People try to combine the financial/legal protection provided by social security with higher earnings made from work in the unregistered part of the economy. However, many of them are turned down in their attempts to adopt these forms of self-defense against economic hardships. Following a recent excessive increase in the number of recipients, control over enrollment in various social security benefits has been tightened, with a sharp rise in the number of refusals for disability pensions and early retirement, and with new regulations introducing means testing for access to childcare benefits. In addition, many remain excluded from these plans because they fail to meet the strict preconditions of entitlement. Further, such options for temporary (self-)protection are rarely available in cases of massive dismissals. When entire firms are closed down, the employees hardly have any other choice than to become "unemployed."

Closing down operations has been a frequent response to the challenges that the necessary structural changes of economic adjustment put forward. Whole industries, once so much a part of production under socialism, proved to be noncompetitive amid the conditions of an open market. Their closure meant firing hundreds of thousands of their workforce. This was the fate of the once prestigious working class – coal miners, steel workers, mechanics, electricians, etc. Between 1992 and 1995, 36 percent of mining workplaces were eliminated; 29 percent in manufacturing; 11 percent in electricity, gas, steam, and water supply; and 36 percent in large-scale agricultural production and forestry. Altogether, some 1.4 million workplaces have been downsized since 1990, affecting more than one quarter of the employees. True, downsizing in some industries has been accompanied by expansion in others. First of all, it is the service sector which has enlarged during the past years, both in terms of employment and in its contribution to the GDP. Within the tertiary sector, earlier nonexistent (or seriously underdeveloped) areas have been growing dynamically: banking, agency, retail trade, personal services, all kinds of social services, health care, education, and public administration have provided employment to thousands of those (especially female) workers who left as the industries were declining. The effect of this "mass movement" is clearly shown by the fact that, between 1980 and 1994, the share of the service sector in employment grew from 40 to 60 percent.

In spite of these dynamic changes, however, the new (or expanding) industries have been able to absorb only a part of those who lost employment in the old, declining ones. As a consequence, the numbers and yearly rates of unemployment were on a steady increase in the first half of the 1990s, with a first modest decline in 1995 when nearly 546,000 job seekers were registered in the labor offices, representing 11.4 percent of the economically active population. Risks of unemployment show a great variation according to sex, age, level of education, and region. Gender-specific unemployment rates indicate higher risks for men in all age groups. In 1994 the respective average ratios were 12.8 percent for men, and 8.7 percent for women. Unemployment becomes the experience of nearly one-third of those young school dropouts who do not continue their studies beyond the primary school. Besides massive youth unemployment, it is the male workforce in its twenties which has the fewest opportunities to find employment: in 1994 their unemployment rate was 20.6 percent. Great differences also appear according to the level of education. Those with no more than eight grades of primary education represent 41 percent of the unemployed (they comprise only 25 percent of the employed), while the share of those with a degree in higher education is as low as 3 percent among those on the dole (they comprise 15 percent of the employed).

Although these patterns prevail in all parts of the country, their impact is further accentuated by huge regional variations. In areas that once had high concentrations of heavy industry and large-scale agricultural production, every fourth former employee is on the dole in these days, while in large cities (including the capital) with a high diversity of employment opportunities the average rates of unemployment remain around 5-6 percent. Massive disparities in the risks of unemployment are increased with markedly unequal chances for re-employment. On the aggregate level, chronic unemployment has been on the rise: while the proportion of those seeking jobs for more than a year was 39 percent in 1993, their ratio grew to 50 percent by 1995. In 1995, the average length of unemployment was already eighty-three weeks, with a variation of ninety-five weeks among those with elementary schooling, fifty-seven weeks among those with a secondary school certificate, and with unconditional opportunities for immediate re-employment for those with a diploma.

The prevailing programs and benefit plans which partially compensate for unemployment are rather weak and dubious. With the Employment Act of 1991, two major funds (financed partly from wage-related contributions of firms, and partly from the state budget) were set up to cover the costs of unemployment benefits and various measures of an active labor market policy. However, the available funds could not keep up with the growing number of unemployed. The entitlement regulations have become more and more rigorous, leading to shorter durations of coverage and higher proportions of a priori exclusion. Those who have exhausted the maximum duration of entitlement but are still without work, are referred to the local governments for support from their means-tested unemployment compensation plans. At present, entitlement for such a compensation is defined in terms of the per capita income: if it remains below 80 percent of the minimum old age pension in the household where the unemployed lives, a regular monthly assistance is given exactly at this value for two more years. However, the pension minimum is about a third of the subsistence minimum, thus, unemployment compensation hardly "compensates" for anything. Amid the rise of lasting unemployment with sharply uneven risks, even this last thread is broken among those most in need. As survey data for the year 1995 show, the proportion of those receiving either benefits or compensation was as low as 21 percent among the unemployed with unfinished primary education, while in the case of those holding a degree, the respective ratio was 60 percent (Laky 1996). Active labor market programs (retraining and job creation plans) hardly help. They cover only a few thousands of the unemployed, and reach best those who become participants at a relatively early stage of unemployment.

Given these peculiarities of unemployment, it is not an exaggeration to state that the loss of employment has become the most important risk factor for poverty. Its effect is particularly dramatic in its contribution to the previously mentioned increase in child poverty. As survey data indicate, the occurrence of unemployment is highest in families with several dependant children (Laky 1996). Income statistics show the relationship between unemployment and poverty from another angle: in 1995, the unemployed made up 18 percent of the population of the lowest decile, while their ratio was only 2 percent in the highest one. And it is worth adding that 27 percent of all those unemployed were in the lowest tenth, while only 3 percent were in the highest income bracket (CSO 1996c). In the course of the yearly follow-up of the group-specific incidence of poverty and people's transitions in and out of this situation, the Household Panel Survey found in 1996 that while the risk of deep poverty (measured as less than 50 percent of the average per capita income in the household) was 14 percent of the entire population; it was more than double this (29 percent) among the unemployed. In addition, the unemployed have significantly higher risks of remaining in permanent poverty than people in general. The respective ratios of those living below the poverty line for more than one year clearly indicate this difference with a 24.6 percent occurrence on the average, while it is 42.6 percent among the unemployed.

3. Income inequalities and the changing resources of household economies

Despite all the difficulties discussed above in estimating the exact magnitude of poverty, it can certainly be said that in recent years, Hungarian society has experienced a sharp increase in the inequality of income and wealth. This clear trend of marked social differentiation can be related to a number of factors. Let me briefly mention the most decisive ones among them:

1. With the shifts in the socially disparate access to gainful employment and the simultaneous deregulation of former central control on the attainable wages/salaries, remarkable inequalities have emerged in the proportion of earnings. Taking the decile distribution of personal income, earnings from employment in 1995 represented only 30 percent of the per capita gross income among the bottom ten percent, while it was 62 percent among the top tenth of households, representing a 11.7 times higher level in absolute value (CSO 1996c).

2. With the ongoing changes in property relations, capital interest has become an increasingly important source of income in the better-off households, while the poor have only very uncertain and limited access to such income. In 1995, no more than 3 percent of the yearly income was derived from business in the first decile, while its proportion was already above 7 percent in the top tenth, providing a 13 times higher sum in absolute value for households in the latter group(CSO 1996c).

3. The importance of income from the market has been accompanied by a diminishing role of income derived from social security: pensions, sick pay and child-related benefits constitute a decreasing part of the budget of all social groups, but in the case of the poor, the losses are above average. A thorough comparison of the data of the two subsequent Household Budget Surveys of 1993 and 1995 reveals that in 1995, households in the lowest decile received sick pay at a real value of 45, pension at a real value of 71, and family allowance at a real value of 81 percent of the corresponding sums in 1993. For those in the highest income

bracket, the figures were 63, 141, and 44 percent, respectively. Thus, the withdrawal of the state from the sphere of income distribution has left relatively more support for those whom one also finds in better positions on the market. The restructuring of the various benefit plans has not led to increased compensation for the losses that the more disadvantaged groups have experienced due to the restructuring of economy. Instead, the recent changes in central income distribution point toward the intensification of the spontaneously generated inequalities in the level of living. The case of the poor is left to marginal and uncertain low paid segments of the labor market, or to the welfare offices of the local authorities and the rapidly emerging NGOs. However, neither the coverage, nor the level of payments through the numerous assistance schemes is adequate to compensate for the losses. Despite all efforts to raise efficiency and targeting, means-tested assistance can reach at best some 30-35 percent of those in need, and the average value of the aid remains around one-third of the theoretically computed subsistence minimum (See Horváth and Szalai 1994).

As for the distribution of wealth, it is rather difficult to give any estimations about the actual value of assets at the disposal of the families within the various social groups. However, certain data on business and some information on the changing housing conditions and the possession of valuable household supplies can provide some indication. As for the role of the rapidly proliferating private businesses, the poor seem to be seriously underrepresented among the new entrepreneurs: in 1995, only 2 percent of persons belonging to the first decile made their living mainly from entrepreneurship, while their proportion was 6 percent in the highest one (CSO 1996c). "Enterprises" for the poor usually mean small grocery stores, shoe repair or sewing services in dark and wet cellars round the corner, with a modest return to cover payments for taxes, rent, and utilities. However, businesses of the rich include Western-style modern factories with computerized systems, well-appointed reception desks, and properly attired managers meeting their clients and partners in lavishly decorated lobbies or offices. Regular payments and fringe benefits to the managerial staff follow Western patterns: people on the top do not lag behind their West European colleagues anymore.

These differences in the actual levels of return do not appear, however, in the income survey data, or, if they do, part of the business-related return of the rich is reported under the headings of other components of their household budget. Some of their extra income appears as a constituent of their regular monthly "salary," another as a "transfer to other households," "spending on charity," etc. However, some indirect indication of the magnitude of inequality in the business sphere is provided by a recent survey comparing the possession of productive assets in households with varying levels of income. As shown in Table 1.6, the differences are significant between the two extremes of the income scale. Counted for 1,000 households in the respective income brackets, the rich owned 28 times more machines for agricultural production, 31 times more vans, 15 times more shops, 6 time more retail stores, 173 times more offices, and 10 times more vacation homes than the poor (CSO 1997). These differences signal a sharp segmentation in the world of business. At the lower end of the scale, one finds the self-employed (some 400,000 persons) who run their businesses with the sole motivation of keeping pace with inflation, but they are neither willing nor able to expand their enterprises. At the other extreme, there is a rapidly emerging small class of nouveau riche in banking, agency, mass media, and other services whose businesses are dynamically growing, both in the number of employees and the amount of yearly profit. Though the exact magnitude of their earnings is unknown, statistics on the distribution of the yearly collected personal income tax indicate that they pay tax on several million forints of gross income per annum.

Table 1.6 The possession of productive assets in the poorest and the richest households, 1996

Item	Average number of items for 1,000 households with	
	20,000 forints[1] or less	150,000 forints or more
	total monthly income	
Machine for agricultural production	7	195
Van	9	278
Shop	3	46
Retail store	6	40
Office	0.4	69
Vacation home	20	201

Source: CSO 1997

1. To get a sense of the level of income presented here in Hungarian forints, it seems worth providing the equivalents in U.S. dollars. Taking the rate of exchange at the time of the survey, (U.S.$1 = HUF 150), households in the lowest income bracket received some U.S.$133 per month, while those in the best financial situation could count on an income of at least U.S.$1,000.

The highly unequal distribution of wealth is also reflected by data on the housing conditions and the possession of valuable durables. When interpreting the figures in Table 1.7, it has to be noted that the modernization of housing and the accumulation of durables were the major areas of investment during the 1980s, when restrictions on private property did not allow people to invest extra income in business. Thus, the table shows the outcome of rather long-term processes: the poor were always on the margins of the informal economy where the huge mass movement for modernization through work exchange took place. With the turn toward open marketization, the position of the poor has not improved either. As discussed above, large groups of them have lost their jobs (and with this, they have experienced a significant loss of personal contacts for future work exchange), and, in addition, their households have suffered the greatest loss in real income. Thus, the poor have been unable to catch up: they could neither increase their participation in the informal economy, nor could they accumulate and use saved resources to improve their housing conditions. As a result, the standards of their apartments are significantly below those of the better-off. They live in smaller and less equipped dwellings, frequently without running water and sewage. In addition, the poor have fewer and overused durables. A detailed survey (Horváth 1993) of the quality of equipment in households with different levels of income showed that, in a great number of cases, the poor bought their refrigerators, television sets, washing machines, etc. from second-hand shops several decades ago. Moreover, many of the tools they own for housekeeping or gardening are useless as they badly need repair. In contrast to this, most of the durables at the disposal of the rich are recent acquisitions, kept continuously in good care. In order to maintain high quality, payments for repair have become a noticeable item among the expenditures of those in the upper strata. As survey data on consumption show, the rich spend six times more on repair services than the poor do.

III. The Social Dimension of Poverty

As mentioned earlier in this chapter, "overspending" on social benefits and services is widely seen as one of the most questionable legacies of socialism. It is strongly criticized as hindering economic advancement by inducing extra taxation, and also by "interfering" with the healthy competition among economic actors in a free market situation. Therefore, drastic reduction in state expenditure on different programs of social policy is proposed not only by the government but also by various business organizations. In its two reports on Hungarian social policy (1991, 1995), the World Bank came up with a similar criticism: while social

Table 1.7   Indicators of housing conditions and the possession of valuable durables in the poorest and the richest households, 1995

Characteristics of the housing conditions and the possession of certain durables	In households in the 1st decile	In households in the 10th decile	On the average
	of the per capita income distribution		
Percentage of apartments			
with one room	21.3	8.0	12.7
three or more rooms	10.5	21.5	17.1
with bathroom and flush toilet	64.5	94.6	83.2
with drainpipe	37.3	69.2	47.5
with telephone	17.6	63.1	38.2
Number of certain durables per 100 households	·		
car	16	59	35
freezer	29	71	55
microwave	9	39	20
color television	62	107	83
hi-fi set	8	24	13
personal computer	3	13	6

Source: CSO 1996c

policy related expenditures have been on an increase in proportion to the yearly GDP, the efficiency of the services financed by them has not improved at all. The low degree of targeting is one of the major drawbacks – the programs cover too many people with too little assistance. Therefore, not only reductions in spending, but serious reforms in the provisions are required.

Although much of this criticism can be justified on the basis of data about the efficiency of various measures in reducing inequalities or, especially, in mitigating poverty, paradoxically, the roots of the problem can hardly be identified in "overspending." Neither can recent Hungarian governments be blamed for their reluctance to initiate reforms to change both the financing and the administration of the various benefit plans and services. Instead, low efficiency follows partly from the struggle of different social groups to ward off impoverishment by maintaining their old entitlements, and partly from the weakness of the government to come up with coherent guiding principles for welfare distribution and clearly defined entitlement regulations for assistance.

In the brief overview below, the major changes in the legal regulations of welfare distribution will first be outlined. This will be followed by the presentation of a few comprehensive data about the actual shifts from universal benefits toward means-tested assistance. Finally, the ambivalent relationship of the better-off groups toward the state's role in income distribution will be discussed in its effects on intensifying the competition for the scarce resources which, as a final result, lead to the low efficiency of the prevailing measures of social policy in mitigating poverty.

With the systemic turn in 1989-90, the principles as much as the mechanisms of the socialist way of central redistribution of income were seriously challenged. First, the very basis of entitlements for various social security provisions was questioned. With the suspension of compulsory employment, income security through employment-bound benefits could not be maintained anymore. Second, with the turn toward marketization and the open acknowledgment of the necessity of strong differentiation in earnings, new needs have arisen. As we saw, both absolute and relative poverty have been on the increase, and special programs had to be set up to handle the previously unknown problem of unemployment. Third, with the commitment to marketization, strong claims have emerged for the restructuring of state expenditures. The previous steady rise of spending on social security could not be financed anymore amid the massive need for central support to be given to privatization, foreign trade, international credits, and the restructuring of governance. Fourth, a definite decrease in the role of the central state was claimed both on economic and political grounds. Central administration was seen to be too expensive and ineffective to reach those in need, and, simultaneously, the right of the communities to control their lives was unanimously demanded by a number of civil and political organizations. In short, there were strong arguments supported by a range of powerful groups to introduce meaningful reforms in social policy. It was clear at the outset that the reforms should concurrently affect the system of social security and the financing of local programs for welfare assistance.

In line with the claims, new principles and regulations were introduced, and a number of the old ones were suspended. Concerning social security, the most important was the redefinition of the bases of entitlement. Replacing the old rules of "automatic" access to benefits on the basis of employment in the socialist sphere of production, the new notion of contribution-based plans was introduced to reduce "uncovered" provisions. The application of the new principle has not promoted too much change in the situation of those employed and their dependent family members. However, the new regulations provide access for the unemployed on entirely new grounds. Unless a person pays his or her contribution, he or she loses entitlements to free medical care, pension, sick pay, maternity benefits, and childcare provisions. In theory, local governments, labor exchange offices, and public services should intervene in all cases when serious poverty endangers the capability to pay. Knowing however that the number of those poor who were dropped from all public plans has been increasing (the unregistered unemployed or those who have exhausted entitlement for both unemployment benefits and income compensation for the long-term unemployed, homeless people, school dropouts in casual work, etc.), it is easy to see that the new regulations have altered not only the mechanisms of financing, but they have led to the reduction of access to the various benefits to the clear detriment of those in the most insecure life situations and deepest poverty.

The "cleaning up" of social security and the new restrictions to halt the wasteful "overuse" of its provisions was thought to be compensated by the expansion of welfare assistance, both in terms of the range of programs and the volume of finances spent by the state on them. The Social Welfare Act of 1993 made it the task of the local governments to set up yearly plans for welfare assistance and to outline the rules of entitlement. The Act laid down some guiding principles but did not define the scope of needs that should be met by assistance; nor did it declare any national minima to guide means testing for the selection of beneficiaries. Thus, the local regulations based on the new Act show substantial variations both in the types of and in the magnitude of the financial support that the municipality is ready to pay to the poor. In richer communities, one-time assistance for families with school children or for the widowed elderly with small pensions can be several times higher than in the poorer ones. Not only the magnitude of assistance, but the actual content of the local programs varies to a great extent, too. In some communities, local authorities contribute to certain needs which, in others, are paid for by the families themselves (subsidized school meals, school books, certain home maintenance costs, and meals on wheels for the elderly and the sick are probably the best examples of discretionary local intervention).

In a thorough analysis of the local regulations drafted in the sixty-three settlements of a county in Western Hungary, Ágota Horváth found no less than 10 times differences in the aggregate amount a family can draw from assistance. Moreover, local regulations defined income limits in a very diverse manner. For the very same type of assistance (e.g., educational aid for families with dependant children) in several localities, only those could apply whose per capita income remained below the yearly minimum of the old-age pension, while in others the upper limit of entitlement was defined at a per capita income reaching 250 percent of the pension minimum. Further, in some settlements receiving unemployment compensation was a cause for exclusion from any other assistance schemes, whereas in others extra attention was paid to the financial needs of the unemployed (Horváth 1995). Thus, it is not an exaggeration to state that with the introduction of the Social Welfare Act, *all*

universal regulations have been eroded in programs for income maintenance, and the situation of the poor has become dependent on the arbitrary judgments of the decision-making bodies of their respective
communities. For better or worse, this dependence might lead to utterly
different fates. It might bring about substantial support assisting social
(re)integration into the community, but it might equally lead to the
extreme marginalization of the most needy, followed by their gradual
exclusion from all forms and institutions of normal life.

Turning to the financial aspects of recent reforms, the picture is perhaps even more controversial. Although time spans really show a slow
increase in the proportion of spending on social security and on various
assistance plans within the GDP, a closer look at the trend reveals that
the impression of "growth" is simply an artefact produced by the somewhat more speedy decrease in the GDP than that in the welfare section
of the state budget. However, counted on real value, aggregate expenditures on social security and welfare have actually been *decreasing*:
between 1993 and 1995, the loss was 12 percent in the case of social
security, and 4.2 percent for the welfare programs administered by the
local governments. All this happened amidst a substantial *increase* in the
number of recipients. Compared to 1993, there were, in 1995, three
percent more retirees on old-age pensions, 8 percent more in the disability pension plan, 91 percent more in the local plan for unemployment compensation, 33 percent more received compensation for house
maintenance and utilities, 26 percent more recipients were in plans for
the physically handicapped, and, because of not having a solvent family
member at all, on 25 percent more occasions funerals were paid for by
the municipalities. The findings in the last column of Table 1.8 are
hardly surprising. With the exception of the aggregate sum drawn from
the various welfare assistance plans, the real per capita value of all other
benefits decreased even more dramatically than the macrolevel data
would suggest.

However, the losses were allocated very unevenly. It was again the
poor who bore more of the burden than the majority. Those items
which lost their value excessively during the two years under consideration (sick pay, pensions, family allowances, and unemployment benefits), represented 38.1 percent in their gross per capita cash income in
1995, while the respective ratio in the case of the rich was only 15.8 percent. At the same time, with the somewhat increased real value of childcare provisions and the locally provided various forms of welfare
assistance, the poor could "protect" only 15.5 percent of their income.
However, the very rich were equally able to capitalize more on the welfare programs in 1995 than two years before. Both the proportion of
this type of source and its real value also grew in the budget of the

households in the upper segment of the income scale. It is hardly a consolation that social transfer payments altogether are less important in the upper groups than in the lower ones: they made up 16 percent of the monthly budget of the better-off households in 1995, while the corresponding proportion was 54 percent in the case of the poor. These differences in the weights of the transfer payments mean that, without various benefits and financial aid, the per capita real income in 1995 in households of the first decile would have been just 39 percent of their gross income in 1993, while the loss in the rich households (in the tenth decile) would have been much more moderate. Without payments from social security and local welfare, they still would have collected a real income of 78 percent of its value in 1993.

Thus, the Hungarian "safety net" is quite a peculiar "net" of protection. It is true that without it, the situation of the poor would be dangerously precarious. However, it also substantially helps all other groups, including the rich. And what is more, certain types of payments effectively increase inequalities. Instead of mitigating relative poverty, they contribute to its steady expansion. This is the case with all earnings-related benefits (pensions in the first place, but also sick pay and provisions for maternity leave). But in the final outcome, a similar role is played by the childcare provisions (clearly increasing the inequalities between the poor and those in the middle of the income scale), family allowances, scholarships, and assistance for those caring for the chronically sick.

When seeking explanations for the low degree of efficiency in the programs for income redistribution and maintenance, an analysis should go beyond the scope of social policy. Amid the ongoing restructuring of Hungarian society, it is the peculiar competition of a great number of social groups for state financing which pushes the needs of the poor to a residual position and which maintains the above-outlined ambiguities in the rules and regulations relative to the access to various benefits and assistance. The roots of the current discord date back to the decades of socialism, and are closely linked to the ways in which people built up their daily life with a simultaneous footing in the formal and informal economies. In this regard, strange ambiguities came to light with the change of regime. It turned out that both pillars in the two-pillar way of life are still equally important.

The conflicts of the past five to eight years have revealed that while the bourgeois aspirations for autonomy embodied in the informal economy urge a reduction in the political power of the state and its capability to intervene, embittered struggles are being waged to preserve the state sources and institutional channels that provide economic backing for the private sphere. While the drive for decentralization in place of the

Table 1.8 The 1995 real value of transfer payments per recipient, as a percentage of their value in 1993

Type of payment	First decile	Tenth decile	All households
Pension/pensioner	90.0	94.4	93.8
Sick pay/employee	42.4	66.3	58.2
Childcare provision/recipient	116.0	49.6	97.4
Family allowance per 0-18 aged dependant	80.1	65.4	70.9
Unemployment benefit/unemployed	42.5	37.1	38.4
Welfare assistance per household member	204.7	135.6	147.6
Gross monthly income per capita	83.6	93.2	90.4

Source: Author's own calculations on the basis of the data of the Household Budget Surveys for 1993 and 1995.

Table 1.9 Characteristics of social security benefits and welfare assistance

Type of transfer payment	percent in gross yearly per capita income (1993)			percent in gross yearly per capita income (1995)		
	First decile	Tenth decile	All hhlds	First decile	Tenth decile	All hhlds
Pension	12.6	9.1	20.4	10.7	13.8	23.0
Sick pay	0.9	0.5	1.0	0.5	0.6	0.6
Childcare provisions	4.9	0.7	0.9	6.6	0.3	1.4
Family allowance	21.6	2.0	6.4	20.9	0.9	4.7
Unemployment benefits	11.8	0.5	2.8	6.0	0.2	1.1
Welfare assistance	3.6	0.1	0.8	8.9	0.2	1.3
All transfer income together	55.4	13.3	32.3	53.6	16.0	32.1

Source: Author's own calculations on the basis of the data of the Household Budget Surveys for 1993 and 1995.

former overcentralization is unstoppable, there has not been the slightest decline in competition for the state's centralized funds. An endless stream of lobbyists besiege the offices of the policymakers to wring "special" donations and support from the increasingly indebted central budget. Despite all the efforts for rationalization and the cautious reform steps, the battle for benefits provided under social security continues; this is especially so for central spending on pensions, which represents the single biggest item in the budget. Strikes and demonstrations signal the resistance shown against the closure and privatization of the big state firms. Each day brings new petitions emphasizing the obligation of the state to compensate various strata of the population for their losses caused by inflation. It would appear that Hungarian society, now in the process of systemic changes, wants the state to be weak politically, but stronger in its economic power than ever before. The developments quite clearly indicate that while the era of totalitarianism has come to an end, the era for denationalization is still far away.

Of course, the ambivalence toward the presence of the state can be explained by many factors. In the first place, the economic motives are obvious. Independent economic activity entirely separated from the state requires stable capital backing and a well-established market, but neither of these conditions could be created in the past decades. This is why there will be a need for strong state support in finances for a long time to come, even though it now openly facilitates the accumulation of private capital rather than strengthening the structural bases for the unlimited power of an omnipotent ruling party. At the same time, the need for a state economic presence is kept alive by the fact that the restructuring of production has also begun to erode market relations that had hitherto been regarded as more or less stable and "permanent." The privatization of state firms has disrupted a state order that was thought to be secure, while the collapse of the Council of Mutual Economic Aid (CMEA) and the Eastern markets has confused and endangered the established export relations. All this has greatly increased the risk of full independence and has intensified social demands that the state play a buffer role.

However, the causes of this ambivalent relationship include not only direct economic components, but also cultural and attitudinal factors. The boomerang effect that accompanies liberation from state political power is the first to be noted. Paradoxically, the decades of resistance to the state as oppressor are now quite clearly being reversed. A wide range of those various corporate bodies and interest alliances, which earlier clung to the state distribution policy merely out of fear and defenselessness, now make angry claims on it for "fair protection." Behind the opposing principles of privatization intended to "regulate" the plundering of public assets, intensely competitive demands for compensation can be detected. Widely varying groups consider that the time has come for the state to compensate them for their historical grievances and their decades of "lagging behind," to give them open assistance for the advancement they "deserve" but have never achieved; and they outbid each other in submitting various claims for compensation that are all "legitimate" when considered separately. Getting these claims to be accepted and embodied in legislation is a matter of brute political force.

In this way, privatization and the creation of a bourgeoisie is the direct result of the latent bargaining positions established over the past decades.

Other arenas of economic life throw an even clearer light on the ambivalence toward state and bureaucratic integration. The large number of civil organizations, associations, and foundations now being set up are model cases of the simultaneous demand for self-organization and bureaucratic recognition. In this, they are faithfully continuing the traditions of the informal economy – now within institutionalized frames – which demanded undisturbed autonomy in formulating needs, and support from above for their satisfaction. The situation is similar in the acquisition and regulation of income: business managers and trade union activists are unanimous in protesting against all forms of central restriction on wage bargaining (interpreting even the attempt to reach uniform agreements as a sign of central intervention). At the same time, and with the same momentum, they also rely heavily on the very same central state: they all use the old channels that have proved successful in obtaining individual treatment to win compensation for themselves from various bodies of the central budget in the face of the inflation they regard as some kind of unavoidable fatality. There is little sign of the bourgeois virtue of self-restraint. In the name of the traditional "they" and "we" dichotomy, the atomized actors of the economy enter the competition where the stakes as yet tend to be minimizing personal risks rather than making real gains. The desire to minimize risks in itself gives the actors a tendency to formulate advantages for themselves in face of others in various "exceptions" and "concessions" and in other forms of bureaucratic protection. The still excessive presence of the state in the economy, as well as the understandable open aspiration of the state bureaucracy to reinforce its own position of power, at best only help a broad strata of society recognize that the creation of a private market in the Western sense is a "foreign" prescription for the process of embourgeoisement in Hungary. The Hungarian path still leads through nationalized modernization.

The poor are the victims of this tacit new compromise that is gradually taking shape. In the first place, they have been eliminated from the competition being waged for the carving up of state property and are also being excluded from all the advantages which the slowly emerging propertied strata are enjoying. They do not profit from tax benefits linked to property, and they do not receive the credits requiring property as security either. In this way, the poor are unable to take part in the most efficient social procedures which now help the majority to preserve and slowly improve the standard of living. In short, they behave "differently" from the rest of society. As time passes, it is this obvious "otherness" that gradually distinguishes the poor from the majority of

Hungarian society rather than their distressed state in a material sense. In contrast with the more fortunate, these people rely solely on their income derived from "official" sources for daily livelihood, and this gives the appearance that they are being supported by the "public." The uniformity of their daily resources then creates the false impression that in reality it is they who "use up" the thin trickle of already dwindling state sources. The majority are, therefore, in agreement on reducing state expenditures for support of the poor: all initiatives for cuts in this area with the aim of reducing "squandering" are given the green light.

But it is not only their exclusion from the carving up of property that pushes the poor into a kind of segregated second order. The process is also assisted by the struggle being waged to maintain a strong state but at the same time to redefine the "meaning" of its strength. Attempts at redefinition serve to justify the expropriation of public sources, now with the aim of privatization, in the hope of rapidly creating a bourgeois stratum that will save the nation. A new principle of legitimization has triumphed in this large-scale process. Those who also contributed through their own efforts to the maintenance of public sources acquire the right to a share of them. This private contribution presumes either the existence of a surplus in income, or membership in the inner circle of institutions that are qualified overnight as "private" with state bureaucratic assistance. In this way, all those – the poor – whose poverty is precisely due to their loose and ever weaker links to management and administration, find themselves prematurely outside all forms of the institutional net and are being "legally" forced to the sidelines. The largest of these groups – the steadily growing army of the long-term unemployed – has already been discussed. The ranks of the excluded are also being swollen by the residents of the small villages that have now become social backwaters – the elderly former agricultural cooperative workers who have been left without any livelihood as a result of the privatization of agriculture, the former long-distance commuters who have been left without a roof over their heads now that the workers' hostels have been closed, and, above all, the Gypsies.

As we saw, the official formulation of their classification in the second order is being left to the discretion of the local authorities. It has been defined as solely their task to rapidly create a policy on poverty which, as was discussed above, casts out all former elements of universalism, and provides assistance on an individual "behavioral" basis instead of with prescribed legal guarantees. The law of the second order is the acknowledgment of this system of direct patriarchal dependency, or more precisely, the renunciation of the right to autonomy in the interest of a meager livelihood. In other words, the poor are being deprived of key personal and political rights they have only just gained

— and all this happens without public recognition, though clearly in the interest of the nonpoor majority. The process seems to be supported not only by the bureaucrats who distribute this patronage and are thus daily reinforced in their power and indispensability, but also by all those social groups that are united in their strong wish to restrict the competition for state resources.

IV. The Political Dimension of Poverty

As a logical consequence of the social struggles outlined above, the case of the poor is rather vaguely represented on the political agenda in contemporary Hungary. On the macrolevel of politics, it can be stated with certainty that the issue enjoys very low priority. This follows partly from the unquestioned superiority assigned to privatization and economic restructuring (backed with the consent of the strongest and most vocal interest groups), and partly from the experiences of those broad layers which have suffered impoverishment during the past years and regard the real poor as their rivals in the competition for compensation. A further factor explaining the low interest in poverty is the lack of organized political forces acting on behalf of the poor. The poor neither have much influence on party politics, nor do their interests appear on the agenda of the various trade unions.

At present, the decisive divide lies between liberals and nationalists on the Hungarian political scene. Out of the six parties represented in the parliament, the two governing ones committed themselves to marked steps in market reforms and drastic measures in decomposing the legacies of the once omnipotent socialist state. The four parties currently in opposition emphasize "national" interests and give priority to the protection of certain conservative values. The issue of the poor simply does not fit into this divide. As for the liberals, their case appears as a "failure" in adaptation, thus, unworthy for support; and as for the nationalist-conservative forces, the social strata labelled "poor" are too heterogeneous to symbolize any "national" values (and let me add: since the Gypsies are overrepresented among those in deep poverty, they cannot even aspire to such a powerful role due to the strong prejudices against the Romany minority).

Outside the parliament, in theory, the trade unions could give voice to the interests of the poor. However, this is not the case. First, the union movement is in a lasting crisis: as representatives of the hard-liners under communism (who have blocked economic reforms several times and have initiated sanctions against the most successful workers of the informal economy, blaming them for "anti-socialist" attitudes and behavior), the old trade unions have become discredited. They have lost some 1.5 million of their members, and they have not been able to maintain influence in negotiations on the shop floor. Second, the new trade unions – mushrooming around 1989-90 – were marginalized shortly after their formation, because they were too weak and too divided to come up with alternative programs for the necessary restructuring in industry. Third, the largest groups suffering from poverty have never been strongly unionized: mothers with small children, retired workers with low pensions, unskilled Gypsy workers, and long-distance commuters now unemployed have never occupied strong positions in the unions.

In contrast to its weak representation in national politics, poverty occupies a rather decisive place at the local level. In a survey looking at the formation of local social policies in seventy-five communities,[2] we found clear commitments to develop antipoverty programs. True, there were great variations in the definition of poverty and in priorities given to one or another group among the poor, still, *some* efforts were made everywhere. There was a tendency to opt for one of the two major alternatives: either to prevent the increasingly impoverished lower middle class from dropping into deep poverty, or to focus attention and spending on the most needy. (The two policies are rarely combined.) The first option was more characteristic of the urban authorities, while the second was more characteristic of the rural authorities, and this tendency points to an unintended ghettoization of poverty in itself. Nonetheless, interviews with the local mayors and key public administrators revealed that "holes" in the local safety net had to be less attributed to disinterest toward or ignorance of the most burning needs of the poor than to the lack of adequate resources in the local budget. Besides the complaints about financial uncertainty, policymakers and field experts unanimously requested clearer regulations and revisions in the Social Welfare Act. They also articulated the necessity of normative provisions adjusted to the specific needs of certain groups (the homeless, children in foster care, families with small children, elderly people in need for permanent care, etc.).

Although the poor rarely have organizations to represent their interests in an institutionalized way, many of the mushrooming civil initiatives prove to be very sensitive to their needs. As the regular surveys of the Central Statistical Office on the nonprofit sector show, in 1994, more than 15 percent of the 40,000 foundations and associations were established to fulfill certain welfare needs. True, financial assistance for

---

2. The survey (based on a representative sample of the local authorities) was done by the research collective of the Institute of Sociology of the Hungarian Academy of Sciences in 1993-94. For the summary of the main results, see Szalai 1995.

the poor is just one of their goals, still, they play an increasingly important role in complementing the activities of the local governments – providing shelter, daytime warming rooms, play houses, family counseling, medical advice and various other forms of support. The complementary role of these organizations is especially important in larger towns and cities where the nonprofit organizations are the crystallizing agents of a wide range of voluntary donations and support (see CSO 1996a). Besides the material help offered by them, the most effective associations and foundations also function as important pressure groups. Recent legislation on certain entitlements for the disabled or the new law on child protection would hardly have been created without their lobbying on behalf of those in special need of support and guardianship.

The local developments outlined here indicate that a certain degree of solidarity rooted in the common experiences of coworkers, neighbors, and other communities still prevails in a Hungarian society otherwise divided by conflicts, competition, and rapidly growing social distances. However, expressions of solidarity hardly go beyond the boundaries of visible communities. Suspicion toward the state, the general feeling of uncertainty, and the low level of trust in the newly developed democratic institutions all work in the same direction. The integration of diverse groups is very difficult, and thus, protection remains very weak. Thus, in the foreseeable future, it would be unrealistic to expect a surge in representation of the interests of the poor in the national fora of policymaking. Their case remains the responsibility of small communities. If they happen to recognize it, then the poor have a chance to escape their current situation, but if not, the endless social reproduction of poverty can be anticipated.

V. Conclusion

Long-term socio-economic trends show a continuous expansion of poverty in Hungary since the late 1970s, which has hit the urban segment of society in particular. However, the trends of a steady increase in the number of those living below the subsistence level have rapidly accelerated during the past few years as the former state-socialist order has been systematically transformed. The causes behind the unfavorable recent development are often identified in the working of the market. The findings of the studies reported here raise strong doubts about such a direct correlation between marketization and the evolution of apparent castelike social differentiation. They indicate that, instead being due to any "fatalistic" determinants, the recent expansion of poverty is partly bound to the prevailing dogmatic neo-liberal interpretation of the necessary economic transformation, and partly due to those legacies of the state-socialist past which have not yet been terminated.

Analyses of the long-term data sets on trends in living standards and conditions during the past decades brought to the light the historical antecedents of the current state of affairs. The discussion stemming from these analyses resulted in the conclusion that the gradual increase of poverty was due to the malfunctioning of socialist redistribution amid the emergence of a dual socio-economic order, which was based on the coexistence of the state-controlled formal and the market-regulated informal economy. The analysis confirmed that the poor were increasingly left without formal support in those years, when the majority staved off poverty through an expanded participation in the informal spheres of production. Thus, the market in itself cannot be made responsible for the growth of poverty. Rather, the genuine causes should be identified in currents of effective disintegration. This chapter has argued that the new trends toward the rapid creation of a class of "secondary citizenry" are rooted in a long-maintained neglect of those who were once the base and main workforce of the socialist economy, but who were never elevated from their continuously reproduced poverty.

In identifying the groups at highest risk, the increasing occurrence of severe symptoms of child poverty has to be emphasized first. However, surveys on the nature of poverty revealed less visible, though equally disturbing, symptoms of serious deprivation among the elderly, and in families of the long-term unemployed. Attention has to be drawn also to the hopeless situation of large groups of young school dropouts whose perspective proliferates the broad layer of those facing an irreversible fall into destitution.

As to the recent institutional initiatives to mitigate poverty on the local level, the incapability of local programs to reduce these serious tensions has to be underlined. At present, social workers and welfare officers can offer only temporary solutions. Poor resources for financial assistance and a serious shortage of available social services set severe limitations on any generous actions and restrict practical aid to a kind of day-to-day fire fighting. Besides the chronic shortage in finances, the efficiency of actions for combating poverty is further decreased by deep controversies in shaping antipoverty policies and by continuously reproduced inconsistencies in the concrete decisions about welfare programs. Beyond these controversies and inconsistencies, one finds a disturbing confusion about the prevailing interpretations of the genuine causes of poverty, and the most promising "remedies."

The most common explanations identify the continuous decline in economic growth as the major cause. It is argued that the recent expansion of poverty follows directly from the chronic stagnation of economic performance over the past decade and a half. Any rise in the standard of living would presuppose a positive turn of the trend, i.e., a substantial improvement in productivity and a stable increase in the yearly GDP. Although such reasoning might have a justifiable logic from a purely macroeconomic perspective, one would seriously doubt any automatic and direct benefit for the "even" growth of all households. A thorough revision of the facts does not confirm a linear relationship. Such a one-to-one relationship can hardly be justified when looking at data on the distribution of personal income and consumption during the recent period of definite decline. Disaggregated statistical data show that several social groups have effectively gained in the meantime, even in comparison to their previous standards. In other words, one faces two simultaneous phenomena in Hungary today: a speedy and significant rise in the standard of living and a substantial accumulation of wealth in the upper segments of society, accompanied by a definite deterioration of the living conditions and an increase in absolute poverty toward the lower edge of the income scale. Thus, neither the current unstoppable expansion, nor the much hoped for future decrease in poverty can be bound simply to macrolevel indicators of the state of the economy. It is most probable that further cuts in social spending in favor of production would simply intensify the prevailing inequalities, without any promise of reducing them.

Another reasoning presents current poverty as the necessary price for a successful transition from state-socialism to a market-regulated economy. It describes the phenomenon as the unavoidable accompanying feature of the current changes, suggesting that it will automatically disappear after the full accomplishment of economic restructuring and marketization. There are, however, disturbing problems with this theory. First, the steady growth of poverty started well under socialism; thus, it hardly can be related to those systemic changes which began with the collapse of the old regime in 1989. Second, such arguments suggest that poverty is a "fated" phenomenon, a price which should be paid by some people for the advancement of society as a whole. However, the legitimizing principles of the uneven share of the burdens remain unclear. Third, faith in "automatic" improvement disregards the internal logic of poverty. It is forgotten that the lack of adequate income is just one (although usually the most decisive) of its features, which is in close correlation (and in a self-sustaining interrelation) with other aspects of life (e.g., all-round defenselessness, poor health, low education, lack of utilizable skills and qualifications, frailty of personal relationships, etc.). It is rather difficult to believe that all these aspects of poverty will be suddenly and spontaneously eradicated by a simple rise in personal income. This complex solution seems to require a wide range of well-targeted additional interventions, too.

Similar to the above-cited neo-liberal approach (which expects automatic improvement from rapid marketization), the third strand of thought (a kind of socialist conservatism) also starts with the historical demarcation line of 1989-90. However, its explanation for the recent expansion of poverty goes the other way round: it identifies the major cause as the "too" rapid withdrawal of the central state. It argues that the hurried deconstruction of the "old" state has left behind a vacuum in social policy, impacting first and foremost those vulnerable groups whose daily livelihood was the most dependent on central redistribution. Thus, the denationalization of social services in the name of privatization and the decentralization of certain benefit plans are the most responsible factors for the recent increase.

Although these arguments seem rather convincing from a synchronic perspective, there is a serious "catch-22" built into them. It cannot be denied that drastic cuts in central payments cause an immediate deterioration in the situation of those households whose financial resources were mainly dependent on transfer payments before. However, a diachronic approach indicates a somewhat different picture. A closer look at longitudinal changes in income distribution shows that the very same groups have always belonged to the poorest segments of Hungarian society; thus, central redistribution was never able to make substantial corrections in their financial situation. Instead, the relative alleviation of poverty was a product of the gradual "liberalization" of the oversight of the central state, which created a limited scope for autonomous economic activities for the larger part of society. Those who were able to maintain their livelihood with two pillars (i.e., keep one foot in the state-controlled, and another in the informal economy) achieved substantial improvements over the last two decades (that is, well before the collapse of socialism). Whereas those who were reliant only on the state have lost everything, in absolute and in relative terms.

Looked at from an historical perspective, it is justifiable to say that from the 1970s onwards, gradual marketization has meant effective protection against poverty, while centralized redistribution on its own has acted for the maintenance and reproduction of it. It also follows that the current institutional withdrawal of the state is in fact the completion of a process which was started decades ago. The gradual erosion of the omnipotent rule of the party-state over society has in a way "prepared" it even under the seemingly unbroken endurance of the old regime.

As demonstrated by a number of data collections on income distribution and welfare, the state of the old communist rule never helped those who could not help themselves. Therefore, its withdrawal can hardly be interpreted as a phenomenon of unprecedented and "new" neglect. Instead, the institutional decomposition of the socialist legacy is perhaps the most important precondition for a genuine change in the prevailing inequalities and in the self-sustaining inequities of central redistribution. On the grounds of a number of investigations (both, qualitative and quantitative), one is strongly inclined to take a fourth position. I equally doubt the "transitory" character of poverty in contemporary Hungary and those simplistic interpretations, which, while striving to alleviate it, believe in the aptitude of mere economic measures.

Some concrete recommendations for policymaking and for short- and medium-term actions follow from these conclusions. In order to prevent the ultimate splitting of Hungarian society, it is most urgent that the legal guarantees for universal social rights be laid down in a categorical manner. The establishment of the painfully missing institutional framework for their realization similarly cannot be postponed for long. Clear regulations to provide unconditional access to basic health care, childcare, and social services to the individuals and families in greatest need should be the top priority for legislative actions. The introduction of guarantees requires centrally allocated and well-targeted funds, and further, a clearly defined division between both the responsibilities and the resources of the central state and the local governments. Such a badly needed program would necessitate important amendments to the current Social Welfare Act and the Act on Local Governments, as well as modifications to the regulations on "contribution-based" access to health care or entitlements for welfare assistance. Amending legislation on social policy is on the agenda for the systemic transformation in Hungary. Therefore, one can only hope that the current painful gaps in access to social security and other statutory benefits will shortly be closed – at least on the level of adjusting the rules to the much changed conditions of people's life.

Some recommendations for research

Finally, let me address some of those issues that relate to poverty which should be explored in more depth by further research. The first set of questions relates to the definition of poverty. As discussed earlier, income- or consumption-based definitions lead to a substantial reduction of the concept, and restrict statistical data collections to the problems of the "consolidated" poor. Thus, it is not incidental that relatively little is known about those most marginalized poor who do not live in households, or whose household formations are extremely in flux. Since actual policy measures draw to a great extent on the available statistics, ignorance about the most needy groups contributes to the failure to provide for them.

In addition to research focusing on marginalized groups, more has to be revealed about the educational and occupational aspects of poverty. It seems that the importance of education substantially grows amid the ongoing restructuring of the labor market: those without the necessary levels of education and training have clearly decreasing opportunities to find decent employment. However, at present, knowledge about the interrelations between education and job opportunities is very limited – research in this area would be of utmost value. Without explaining in detail the causes of poor performance at school and failures in finishing (or continuing) education, little help can be given to the poor, and little can be expected from retraining programs for the unemployed, which are now up in the air.

Third, mechanisms of the microlevel transmittal of poverty should be put under closer investigation. Scattered research evidence shows that, amid certain conditions and in certain subgroups of the poor, poverty is "inherited" from one generation to the other, and the "culture of poverty" becomes a strong factor in itself in blocking actions for poverty alleviation. However, little is known about those patterns of socialization, access to and use of educational and labor market institutions, forms of interpersonal relations, attitudes to the prevailing majority norms, work habits and use of time, etc. which are "responsible" for the continuous reproduction of poverty. Qualitative research based on a close study of the decisive family life cycles of childhood and young adulthood in subsequent generations of various subgroups of the poor is highly needed.

Fourth, the various institutions created for poverty alleviation should be investigated in their efficiency. Not only should their internal rules of service delivery, their selection of people to assist, and their methods of "economizing" the available resources be studied, but staff-client relations and the positioning of the various organizations amid a range of similar service-providing agencies for the nonpoor should also be researched.

All the above-listed sets of questions are highly relevant in Hungary amid ongoing reforms in the fields of social security and welfare. Since to the best of my knowledge, similar reforms are either planned or are actually being realized in all the post-socialist countries, international comparative studies on poverty and antipoverty actions would likely meet with great interest and a high degree of commitment on the part of social scientists in these societies.

Bibliography

Andorka, Rudolf, and Zsolt Spéder. 1994. "Szegénység a 90-es évek elején" (Poverty at the Beginning of the 1990s). *Társadalmi riport, 1994* (Social report, 1994), ed. Rudolf Andorka, Tamás Kolosi, and György Vukovich. Budapest: TÁRKI.

Bocz, János. 1996. *Szociális nonprofit szervezetek* (Nonprofit organizations in the welfare sphere). Manuscript. Budapest.

Central Statistical Office (CSO). 1994. *Statisztikai Évkönyv, 1993* (Statistical Yearbook, 1993). Budapest: CSO.

_____. 1995. *Családi költségvetés, 1993* (Household Budget Survey, 1993). Budapest: CSO.

_____. 1996a. *Nonprofit szervezetek Magyarországon, 1994* (Nonprofit organizations in Hungary, 1994). Budapest: CSO.

_____. 1996b. *Statisztikai Évkönyv, 1995* (Statistical Yearbook, 1995). Budapest: CSO.

_____. 1996c. *Családi költségvetés, 1995* (Household Budget Survey, 1995). Budapest: CSO.

_____. 1996d. *Az 1996-os jövedelmi felvételre nem válaszoló háztartások* (Nonresponding households in the income survey of 1996). Budapest: CSO.

_____. 1996e. *Módszertani ajánlás a létminimum meghatározására* (Methodological recommendations for defining the subsistence minimum). Budapest: CSO.

_____. 1997. *A háztartások felszereltsége, vagyoni helyzetének egyes jellemzői* (The possession of durables and some features of wealth in households). Budapest: CSO.

Csontos, László, János Kornai, and István György Tóth. 1996. "Adótudatosság és fiskális illúziók" (Taxpayers' consciousness and fiscal illusions). In *Társadalmi riport, 1996* (Social report, 1996), ed. Rudolf Andorka, Tamás Kolosi, and György Vukovich. Budapest: Századvég-TÁRKI.

Ferge, Zsuzsa. 1996. "A rendszerváltás nyertesei és vesztesei" (Winners and losers of the systemic change). In *Társadalmi riport, 1996* (Social report, 1996), ed. Rudolf Andorka, Tamás Kolosi, and György Vukovich. Budapest: Századvég-TÁRKI.

Galasi, Péter. 1995. *Income Inequality and Dynamics in Hungary: 1987, 1992-1994.* Budapest: The World Economy Research Institute, HAS.

Horváth, Ágota. 1995. "Törvény és Anarchia avagy törvényes anarchia: a Szociális Törvényről és az önkormányzati szociális rendeletekről" (Law and anarchy or lawful anarchy: on the Social Welfare Act and the welfare regulations of the local governments).

In *Az államtalanítás dilemmái: szociálpolitikai kényszerek és választások* (Dilemmas of denationalization: constraints and choices in social policy), ed. Edit Landau et al. Budapest: Active Society Foundation.

Horváth, Ágota, and Julia Szalai. 1994. *A helyi önkormányzatok segélyezési gyakorlatáról* (Some characteristics of welfare assistance on the local level). Manuscript. Budapest.

Horváth, Zsuzsa. 1993. *Városi szegénység és szociálpolitika* (Urban poverty and social policy). Manuscript. Budapest.

Laky, Teréz. 1996. *A munkaerőpiac keresletét és kínálatát alakító folyamatok* (Major trends in labor supply and demand). Budapest: Labour Research Institute.

Mészáros, Geyza, and István Sebestyén. 1996. *Az önkormányzatok és a nonprofit szervezetek kapcsolata* (Relations between the local governments and the nonprofit organizations). Manuscript. Budapest.

Milanovic, Branko. 1995. *Poverty, Inequality, and Social Policy in Transition Economies.* Transition Economics Division, Research Paper Series No.9. Washington, D.C.: The World Bank.

Sík, Endre, and István György Tóth, eds. 1997. *Az ajtók záródnak?!* (Do the Doors Close?!) Budapest: TÁRKI, Department of Sociology, Budapest University of Economics.

Szalai, Julia. 1990. "Some Thoughts on Poverty and the Subsistence Minimum." In *Social Report, 1990*, ed. Rudolf Andorka, Tamás Kolosi, and György Vukovich. Budapest: TÁRKI.

———. 1993. *Social Policy and Child Poverty: Hungary since 1945.* Innocenti Occasional Papers. Florence: UNICEF.

———. 1995. "A helyi önkormányzatok szociálpolitikájáról" (Social policy of the local governments). In *Az államtalanítás dilemmái: szociálpolitikai kényszerek és választások* (Dilemmas of denationalization: constraints and choices in social policy), ed. Edit Landau et al. Budapest: Active Society Foundation.

Tóth, György István. 1994. "A jóléti programok szerepe a szegénység enyhítésében" (The role of welfare programs in mitigating poverty). In *Társadalmi riport, 1994* (Social report, 1994), ed. Rudolf Andorka, Tamás Kolosi, and György Vukovich. Budapest: TÁRKI.

Vajda, Ágnes and János E. Farkas. 1992. "Housing." In *Társadalmi riport, 1992* (Social Report, 1992), ed. Rudolf Andorka, Tamás Kolosi, and Györy Vukovich. Budapest: TÁRKI.

The World Bank. 1992. *Hungary: Reform of Social Policy and Expenditures.* Washington, D.C.: The World Bank.

———. 1996. *Magyarország: Szegénység és szociális támogatások* (Hungary: poverty and welfare assistance). Washington, D.C. and Budapest: The World Bank.

Chapter Two

EMERGING POVERTY IN BULGARIA

Sasha Todorova

Institute of Sociology, Bulgarian Academy of Sciences

Introduction

It was only after the political changes of 1989 that the phenomenon of "poverty" began to be discussed in Bulgaria. In the totalitarian society of the pre-1989 era, poverty was not part of the formal ideological paradigm and was, therefore, not a point of reference for the social policy of the government. Rather than talking of the poor, the phrase used then was "populations with low incomes." In the first years of the transition period, this phrase was replaced by an undifferentiated and, therefore, an almost immeasurable notion of "the needy." That is why in the research writings of that period there is a conspicuous absence of any reference to poverty as a social phenomenon; the only exceptions being some socioeconomic analyses of the 1970s and 1980s which attempted to estimate the living and social minima, and the number of people who lived under such conditions.

Another reason for the absence of any reference to poverty in the earlier period was the fact that social security was placed high in the hierarchy of the overall policy of the state. The basic necessities of life were guaranteed to each and everyone by the state, though at a minimum level, by the monthly wage which had no direct linkage with a person's work – that is, contribution to the economy. Moreover, public health and education were the responsibility of the state. The state also guaranteed maternity privileges to all women. Despite the unsatisfactory housing conditions, especially in the large cities, no Bulgarians were homeless. Drawing a comparison between themselves and the rest of the population, every member of society could see that there was no significant difference in meeting the material needs in labor, recreation, and physiological reproduction during the socialist period. It was almost impossible for a Bulgarian to imagine living below the poverty line. Marginal groups, primarily Gypsies, comprised a small portion of society, but they were looked after by the Ministry of Welfare.

Now after seven years of transition from a centrally planned economy to a market economy, and from a totalitarian regime to a democratic polity, Bulgaria is in deep economic crisis. Poverty has begun to surface and there is a crucial need to study and measure the "poverty" phenomenon. Unlike the countries of other regions of the world, a formal definition of this phenomenon has been absent in Bulgaria. Its limits and scope have not yet been formally recognized (Republic of Bulgaria 1996, 16) and there is no systematic mapping of poverty profiles (although envisaged in the government program in the future). The understanding of poverty in Bulgaria is based on secondary sources such as data collected for other research – statistical data regarding household budgets, sociological research on living standards, the structure of privatization and individual adjustment, economic analyses of the incomes and expenditures of different social groups. The differentiated data concerning sources of income, consumption models, economic activities, and the living conditions of the poor are gathered only sporadically and are not published officially (Minev and Zhelyazkova 1996).

The definition of the phenomenon of "poverty," prevailing in the scientific literature, stresses the "privation of things necessary for a normal existence and an acceptable quality of life" (Fotev 1996), and the "lack of material values necessary for creating and sustaining *basic* living conditions" (Yossifov and Naoumov 1996). The researchers share the opinion that what is necessary for the effective study of the phenomenon of poverty is its correlation with wealth.

The fact that Bulgarians define poverty in different ways deserves further investigation. Of course, there is no such thing as an absolute definition of poverty. It changes in response to the changes in the criteria employed by the society to determine "the limit" of the necessary needs for reproduction of the individual – the minimum of "entitlement" or *Anrecht*. The more a society departs from the idea that physiological needs are necessary for an individual's reproduction, the more it connects the notion of poverty with the possibility of meeting, not only these demands, but also a number of social needs. In other words, the idea of poverty is first of all defined on the basis of the living standards reigning in society rather than by the personal living standards.

The following is a range of indicators which express Bulgarians' various ideas about poverty:

when one has to economize on food	I
when one has to beg for food	II
when one has food to eat but nothing else	III
when one finds it difficult to maintain the living standards one is accustomed to	IV
when one is unable to pay one's rent, electricity, or gas	V
when one has no savings	VI
when one requests assistance from social services	VI
when, one cannot always afford heating in winter	VI
when one has to ask relatives and friends for help	VII
when one cannot afford to repair a leaking roof or a broken floor	VIII
when more than two persons have to share a room	VIII
when one cannot afford housing	IX
when one cannot afford to invite guests	IX
when one cannot travel on vacation	IX
when one cannot afford a television set	X
when one cannot afford a car	X

The range of indicators expressing the subjective definition of poverty shows that it is strongly connected with the individual's ability to meet elementary physiological needs. On the basis of the logically possible combinations of poverty indicators, a new artificial scale was created according to the criterion of whether a certain need is met or not. A total of four groups of poverty representation were thus established. (The survey, "Sociological Problems of Poverty," was carried out by a team headed by Professor Georgy Kostov at the Institute of Sociology of the Bulgarian Academy of Sciences (BAS)in 1992 and repeated in 1993. One thousand heads of families were interviewed [Kostov et al. 1993].)

1. *a primitive idea of poverty*, describing poverty as the impossibility of meeting one's physiological needs (indicated by the belief that "one should save on food") – 14.1 percent of those interviewed have such an idea of poverty;
2. *a daily-life idea of poverty*, relating poverty to the impossibility of meeting one's daily needs (indicated by the belief that "one cannot maintain the usual living standards") – 23.3 percent;
3. *a socializing idea of poverty*, indirectly related to the impossibility of meeting physiological and daily needs and directly related to the way in which they are met (indicated by the question "how and to what extent does the individual make use of social services,

or, if not, how does he or she manage without any assistance whatsoever?") – 40.1 percent;
4. *a civil idea of poverty*, relating poverty to the impossibility of meeting the needs of higher living standards, including a number of social needs (indicated by "when the individual has to restrict his or her social activities and communications" – 20.6 percent) (Rakadjiiska 1994).

The fact that the most widely shared idea of poverty is the third one stems from the fact that prior to the collapse of communism, a majority of Bulgarian households were able to maintain conventional living standards without any assistance from the state. Those who had to depend on social services were generally regarded as being below the living standard. This is now the public's definition of poverty.

The Bulgarian sociologists A. Yossifov and I. Naumov (1996) have mapped out four major "cultural models" of poverty combining specific values, adjustments, behavioral patterns, and a well-defined system of symbols.

Normal poverty: In most research, poverty is regarded as a characteristic feature of those people who have a low income and those who live below the average living standards for the society. It is generally accompanied by an inferiority complex and passive behavior. Such people do not rely on their own effort and cherish no hope for changing their status quo. The social subgroup in this model consists of outcasts, the neglected and/or the socially underprivileged. Included in this subgroup are a big proportion of the elderly, prisoners released from jails, people with strongly devalued professions, and members of some ethnic groups.

Ideological poverty: This is poverty by choice; it is raised to the level of a virtue, a morality norm. The behavior of such people is passive, nonaggressive, and expressive of a disregard for human vanity. Versions of this include "wanderers," "hippies," "nonconformists," and other groups who reject the social standards that have alienated them from society. Such poverty can be found mainly among the youth and also among the most elderly people.

Fatal poverty: This is the poverty of those who, either due to their being unfit, or because they make bad decisions, can neither adapt to their social environment nor join the norm of the material social standards. This is the poverty of the unlucky ones who, partly due to their individual characteristics, sway between depression and aggression. Anomie is characteristic of their state of mind. They accept poverty as fate, as something only too natural and beyond them to overcome. They look upon themselves as poor but find nothing bad in their poverty, and they do not envy others who are better off. They do not have any motivation to work or to change their situation. As such, they are fatalists. Such poverty is found among mendicants, particularly among members of the Gypsy ethnic group in Bulgaria, who lead a frugal life and bestow all their wealth on their newly married couples. In addition, such fatalistic poor are also found among the disabled, the homeless, and the sick.

Pseudo poverty. This is the phenomenon of relative poverty. Irrespective of their possessions, which may be sufficient for a life above average standards, some regard themselves as poor compared to others who possess more. This is in accordance with their cultural level and system of values. In Bulgaria, this feeling of relative poverty is widespread.

The Profile of Poverty:
The Definition, Measurement, and Distribution of Poverty

In compliance with the prevailing conception of poverty in Bulgarian scientific literature, the poverty line is defined according to an objective-subjective dichotomy with a special emphasis on the objective criterion of *the level of living*. Of course, some other techniques are also employed for its measurement.

The National Institute of Statistics (1996b) conducts a sample survey on family budgets (incomes and expenditures). It calculates the social and living minimum on the basis of the "consumer basket" which includes 497 kinds of goods and services in the first round and 476 in the second round. This survey of household budgets covers a sample of six thousand households. In this survey, a respondent is asked to conduct a self-analysis in a diary and is then interviewed to confirm the responses.

The information collected in the survey relates to the volume and structure of the total and the money incomes of the households from different sources, the volume and structure of each household's expenditure on different items, the quantities of necessary basic foods and commodities, and the average prices of the purchased quantities of basic food and commodities. Total income includes monetary income and the value of the foods and commodities the household has produced, received free of charge, or borrowed. It also includes the taxes, rents, etc., received by the household. Expenditures include monetary expenses and the cost of the food the household has used, has given as a gift, has lent, has used to feed animals or for seeds, etc.

This survey helps to draw a proper poverty profile in terms of: 1) poverty level; 2) the geographical distribution of the poor population; and 3) classification of the poor according to age, sex, ethnic group, and professional status. However, this approach does have limitations.

Because of Bulgaria's ineffective tax system, reported incomes cannot be compared with those actually received; in other words, there is great discrepancy between reported income and real income.

The Institute of Economics at the Bulgarian Academy of Sciences carries out an analysis of the structure of expenditures including the relative share of food expenditures. It also focuses on the social inequality of incomes defined by deciles and the Gini index.

The *consumer basket* model consists of two notions: the *social minimum* and the *living minimum*. The social minimum defines the upper line of poverty. This category includes those people who are not only able to buy things that are necessary for keeping the body and soul together, but also those goods and services which help develop their physical, cultural, and social potential. The *living minimum* defines the lower line of poverty, when people can barely maintain their physical existence and cannot afford access to other economic, social, and cultural goods. There are various methods for measuring the consumer basket, but in Bulgaria the most commonly used method is that of the normatively (expertly) determined incomes, expenditures, and consumption according to which people are related to various categories of rich and poor.

When defining the social and living minima, the following factors are taken into account:

- the type and amount of property owned
- the type and amount of work done
- the typre and level of people's education and qualifications
- their state of health
- the structure and amount of their incomes
- the state of the workforce
- the state of the environment

Though cumbersome, and difficult to obtain, the information gained from this approach gives an idea of social differentiation in terms of the living standards of the individual groups. It also helps identify the absolutely poor.

In order to determine the consumer basket, a family of four is chosen as a structural unit. This is done for the following reasons:

1. The relative share of families of four in the total number of households is high (23.1 percent in 1990).
2. There is a greater number of people in families of four (29.8 percent in 1990).
3. Consumption patterns of families of this size are regarded as most economical (Kostov 1996).

The Institute of Sociology has made an attempt to combine objective and the subjective criteria. In its survey questionnaire, the following questions were asked:

"Do you consider yourself poor?"
"What income, in your opinion, would enable you to make two ends meet?"
"How long could your family exist without getting any income?"
"What must you refrain from buying or deprive yourself of?"

Analyzing poverty through the relative share of expenditure on food makes it possible to outline the different levels of poverty. Thus, in Bulgaria, after the sharp rise of this share in 1991 – the first year of "shock therapy" reform – it gained stability at a level of 40-45 percent of expenditure, a level typical of poor countries. This share surpasses 50 percent among people with low incomes (Shopov 1995).

The Center for Studying Democracy uses statistical information on income stratification and the findings from a sociological survey of the social services to outline the parameters of the "risk groups." The analysis of the social services (the labor offices and the social care centers) traces out different factors contributing to poverty and accordingly develops strategies for poverty alleviation. But there are difficulties; the social office in Bulgaria mainly include members of ethnic groups who simultaneously represent the members of the parallel economic structures. To get financial assistance one is only supposed to sign a declaration of one's income, which is accepted by the social officers without any verification. For example, according to such declarations only 6.7 percent of the respondents have a car, while the survey results show that 23.6 percent of the respondents are car owners.

The risk groups in Bulgaria are as follows:

- Unemployed for more than nine months, comprising 47.7 percent of the total group, relying mainly on state support for their survival
- Unemployed youths, comprising 15.9 percent of the group, who are taking a more active role in their adjustment and demonstrate a readiness to join "requalification" courses, volunteer activities, or private business
- Invalids and the chronically ill, comprising 11.5 percent of the group (however, only 7.1 percent have been officially registered as disabled persons)
- Retirees, comprising 8.4 percent of the group
- Differentiated ethnic groups (among the Gypsies we witness the closest correlation between ethnic descent and poverty), comprising 19.1 percent of the group but only 3.8 percent of the entire population. The Gypsies inhabiting the rural areas are compara-

tively worse: 43.9 percent of the clients of social protection agencies with Gypsy descent live in the villages. They are poorly educated (57.8 percent of them have not even finished primary school), and half of them have no house of their own.

- Large families, comprising 8.6 percent of the group, the greater part of whom are ethnic Turks or people of Gypsy descent
- Single-parent families, comprising 16.7 percent of the group (6.3 percent of these are single mothers; 10.4 percent are widowed or divorced parents with children)
- Differentiation by gender: men comprising 24 percent and women 76 percent; 39 percent of them are under twenty-two years of age
- Individuals demonstrating asocial behavior, comprising 1.6 percent
- Children; 4 percent of this age group have limited social contact

According to research carried out in 1992 by the Center for Social Insurance and Social Assistance at the Ministry of Labor and Social Welfare, some 1,189,350 families were entitled to social assistance. They were distributed as follows:

family of one	7.2%
married couple without minors	36.5%
married couple with one minor	12.5%
married couple with three minors	1.5%
single parent with one minor	1.6%
single parent with two minors	0.6%
single parent with one major child	0.28%
single parent with one unmarried major	4.4%
single parent with two unmarried majors	8 0%
single parent with three unmarried majors	0.1%
an unmarried major living with both parents	16.1%
relatives or nonrelatives sharing lodging	2.3%

For defining the poverty line, this model is helpful. The information on family budgets is fairly reliable. It also tells us about the structure of privation in fairly objective terms.

Bulgarian poverty researchers share the view that the number of poor in Bulgaria is rising. Some groups are affected by the current crisis more than others. These are: farmers, Gypsies, the intelligentsia, employees in the budget organizations, and ethnic Turks (A. Yossifov and I. Naoumov 1996). There is greater poverty in some of the border regions. The unemployed are also in an extremely difficult situation, and their number is expected to further rise due to the introduction of the "currency board." It is necessary, however, to make differentiated poverty profiles for each group because they are not homogeneous entities. For instance, some of the farmers can meet their consumer needs through their agricultural production, while others do not have such an opportunity. Some of the retirees (who have very small pensions) have savings and income from rented property, while others share their households with their major children. Further, a significant portion of the ethnic Turks in Bulgaria participate in the parallel economy, though information on this source of income is not available.

In the changed scenario only those people who managed to participate in the redistribution of the state property were able to improve their status. Such people include the following:

- Representatives of the former and present economic nomenklatura (high-ranking state employees)
- Representatives of the former and present party nomenklatura (high-ranking party officials)
- Those participating in the parallel economy
- Those whose capital was restituted
- Some of those engaged in their own business or in commerce

However, these people represent only 6 percent of the Bulgarian population. This means that only a very small minority has benefited from the changed situation, and the vast majority (94 percent) find themselves in a "regime of survival," paying a high price for the new political and economic processes under way.

The Economic Dimension of Poverty

The delay in making economic reforms further deepened and expanded the economic crisis which began in the mid-1980s. The basic economic indices dropped abruptly, and this speeded up the process of impoverishment. The major factors for mass impoverishment in the post-communist era are listed below:

- Delays in structural economic reforms due to the back door privatization of the nation's wealth
- Foreign debt servicing has adversely affected the incomes of state employees and has limited the amount of the social policy in the national budget
- A high inflation rate has devalued the real income and savings of the people
- An ineffective tax policy

- The lack of a manifest political consensus and the presence of a behind-the-scenes collusion

Poverty in Bulgaria stems from the economic crisis. The scholars attribute impoverishment first and foremost to the harsh fall of the GDP, to galloping inflation, and to the rising level of unemployment. These major economic indices testify to the deepening of the economic crisis, particularly in recent years. Scholars have outlined a macroeconomic framework for the policies of poverty alleviation and reduction. During 1990-95, the GDP of the country decreased a significant 13.4 percent; in 1995, it stood at U.S.$1,543 per capita. In 1996 inflation reached 3,059 percent of the 1990 figure. Annual inflation in 1995 was a record 300 percent. Rising inflation accelerated the process of impoverishment by devaluing income and savings.

Similarly, the high rate of unemployment also intensified the process of impoverishment. The extreme growth of unemployment in the first two years of the transition period and the continued high rate of unemployment in the following years have turned many an unemployed poor. Long lines outside labor office are indicative of growing unemployment, and attendant poverty. Secondly, the economic reforms initiated by the government as part of its new economic policy have also significantly contributed to the impoverishment of the people. The political decision as to the nature of the so-called economic reforms, and the processes of their realization have proved to be ineffective, aggravating the economic crisis and accentuating poverty. So far, the economic reforms have failed to restructure property relations and stabilize the economy. With the delay in privatization and the continuation of the state monopoly, there have been streaks of back door denationalization, which have deepened the crisis and raised the social cost of the expected changes.

The reforms, being carried out through loans and credits, have encouraged neither production nor small business – both essential for limiting the crisis and eliminating inequality and poverty. For example, agrarian reforms have made it difficult to restore the ownership of land and have created conditions for the plundering of the accumulated operative wealth. Rather than opening new jobs in farming they have engendered unemployment and poverty.

Foreign debt is another significant cause of poverty because of the enormous amounts involved in debt servicing which, even in favorable conditions of economic growth, would be a heavy burden. The clauses of the debt agreement stipulate that upon attaining more than 25 percent of economic growth compared to 1993, Bulgaria will have to increase its rate of repayment; this implies that the fruits of a favorable economic growth will continue to be denied to the poor.

Lastly, the redistribution of the nation's wealth is being carried out to the benefit of the former *nomenklatura*[1] and the representatives of the corporate interests. This has resulted in a concentration of wealth in the hands of the economic elite.

Economic policy in Bulgaria has, however, given importance to the creation of employment with the hope of attacking the root causes of impoverishment. The following priorities characterize the strategy currently being implemented:

1. Employing social workers, to help the unemployed to look for jobs – fostering self-motivation and providing guidance.
2. Improving the orientation process by examining, adapting, and implementing the experience of countries with similar situations, and elaborating new projects.
3. Encouraging independent activity – building a system of services for orientation, motivation, education, and consultation; providing financial aid for initiating independent economic activity; conducting sociological surveys and marketing investigation to find potential new economic activities; setting up regional agencies for economic development; creating an information system for business services; and designing and implementing projects to encourage entrepreneurship.
4. Creating new jobs, introducing flexible forms of employment and maintaining already existing jobs. It should be noted that employers need consistent encouragement to pursue this agenda.
5. Promoting fairness in the labor market, including working with groups at a disadvantage in the labor market and developing social employment programs.
6. Introducing active measures to counteract the consequences of the restructuring, liquidation, and privatization of enterprises. This would necessitate designing and implementing regional projects for restructuring and employment, providing adequate pensions for workers due to their low education and qualifications, creating new jobs, and training employers in personnel management.
7. Improving the quality of the workforce by studying the demand for new professions and specialties, training and retraining, encouraging the little-educated and unskilled unemployed to obtain train-

1. The concept of the *nomenklatura* was widely known in the USSR and was used in all the countries of the Communist bloc. The nomenklatura were and are the power elite – the former and present high-ranking party and state officials – who take advantage of their position to derive benefits (monetary and material). Salarywise, there were no distinctions between a minister and his chauffeur, but it was the other privileges and perks that allowed the former to enjoy a much higher standard of living.

ing or retraining, widening the range of persons who are entitled to free training and retraining, and improving the education system to meet the changing requirements of the labor market.

8. Developing employment services through the improvement of office equipment for employment officers (e.g. computerization), raising the qualifications of those employed in the employment offices, further improving the services offered by the employment offices, and introducing a licensing process for nonstate organizations involved in employment counseling, as well as for the import and export of the workforce.

9. Protecting the national labor market through the introduction of licenses for issuing working visas to foreign citizens and for signing intergovernmental and other kinds of agreements on the export of the workforce.

Table 2.1 Structure of Expenditure on Active Measures (in percentages)

S. No.		1992	1993	1994	1995
1.	Employment Services	71.9	66.4	65.0	56.2
2.	Qualification	14.4	8.1	6.6	5.9
3.	Measures for the Youth	1.4	1.5	1.1	0.3
4.	Subsidized Employment	12.2	24.0	27.3	37.6
5.	Measures for Invalids	0.1	0.0	0.0	0.02
	Total	100.0	100.0	100.0	100.0

The policy in the field of employment does not fully correspond to the quality of the workforce in Bulgaria. What must be noted in this regard is the fact that, according to the National Institute of Statistics (1996a), a major part of the workforce (72.7 percent) is concentrated in the cities. Also there are are gender differences in it: men constitute 52.9 percent and women 47.1 percent of the total workforce. The age structure of the workforce is not favorable either: 29.9 percent belong to the age group 35-44 years, followed by 27.1 percent in the 45-54 years age bracket; the group of young people, between 15 and 24 years of age, constitutes only 11.8 percent. Educationally, the workforce is distributed as follows: higher education – 13.5 percent; college education – 5.6 percent; vocational school – 21.7 percent; secondary school – 30.0 percent; and elementary or less education – 29.2 percent. The average monthly wage for 1996 stood at U.S.$75.46 (13,280 leva); for those employed by the state it was lower than this figure (U.S.$51.16 or 9004 leva).[2]

2.   Bulgarian currency is called leva. In August 1997, U.S.$1 equalled 1800 leva; but in 1996, when this chapter was written, U.S.$1 only equalled about 176 leva. Compare

The functioning of the labor market can be evaluated according to several criteria. One of them is the labor offices' effectiveness in serving unemployed 'clients.' In 1993, 11 percent of the persons registered with labor offices were provided with jobs. In 1994 this percentage increased to 16 percent, and in 1995 to 29 percent. The effectiveness of the labor offices can also be assessed in terms of the preference given to those registered with them. The share of unemployed who prefer to look for a job through the labor agencies is approximately the same as that of persons who seek work through friends and relatives. This correlation is based on a survey carried out by the National Institute of Statistics (1996a). The effectiveness of the labor offices is also dependent to a great extent on the employers' attitude toward recruitment. More jobs were available in the second half of 1994. In December 1994, their number marked a 48.5 percent increase compared to December 1993; the highest increase was for the jobs for unskilled persons.

The number of persons who have successfully finished courses is considered an indication of the effectiveness of training activities to improve professional qualifications. During 1992-93, the number of such persons increased by 46.2 percent; while in 1994, it fell by 10.2 percent. In 1995, it decreased by 13.7 percent as compared to the 1994 figures. The weak economic positions of most of the employers and the low priority given to changing the structure of recruitment limited training activities.

The informal economy provides an alternative means of income for the poor. It includes not only in the sphere of material production, but also the field of services. The poor benefit from this informal economy by rendering their physical services. Those who enjoy high positions of power or who have the capital to invest also benefit.

People work in the informal economy without signing a labor contract; the employer pays his employee in cash with a verbal agreement. The labor relations in the informal economy remain hidden from the public, i.e., both the employer and the employee do not expose their relationship in order to avoid paying taxes. There are cases when social insurance is not paid at all, or is paid on the basis of the minimum wage while the employee is paid a much higher wage.

The number of those employed in the informal economy can only be estimated through sociological surveys. The latest survey (Hristoskov et al. 1996) shows that 13 percent of the officially 'unemployed' participate in the informal economy. They are most often employed without a

---

these figures with July 1990 figures when a U.S. dollar could be bought with just 2.97 leva! Thus between 1990 and 1997, inflation has increased 606 times. Therefore, a salary received in leva will be fewer dollars than the 1996 figure mentioned here: 13,280 leva today are as good as U.S.$7.30 and 9004 leva are worth only U.S.$5.00. This is a significant loss in income. *Editor*

signed agreement, and for shorter periods. The so-called self-employed working on their own farms or in the firms of their families, and do not paying social insurance account for 2 percent. The survey findings show that 23 percent of those who previously participated in the informal economy have turned to farming. Another 3.3 percent said that they produce goods both for themselves and for the market. This confirms the role of farming, and particularly of home farming, as a survival strategy for the poor. The survey showed that the self-employed participate in the informal economy as well. Nearly 80 percent of them have not reported their activities and their income to the government. According to some experts, the informal economy contributes 25-30 percent to the GDP.

The informal economy contributes, on the one hand, to the alleviation and reduction of poverty and, on the other, it helps the rich and the powerful to accumulate resources and concentrate capital. Therefore, it is generally believed that policy measures should be taken to reduce the informal economy, especially to put a check on those factors that engender criminal behavior, such as currency speculation, resale, smuggling, blackmail, prostitution, drug trafficking, gambling, and so on. This could be done by correcting the loopholes in labor legislation and by eliminating the disparity in the social and economic environment, processes, and relationships. What is particularly important is that economic policy be properly implemented. It is necessary to formulate ideas to liberalize employment policy, create favorable conditions for the development of private business, balance fiscal and tax policy to reduce the scale of the redistribution processes, and revive production while opening new jobs.

The large-scale redistribution of the nation's wealth deepens inequality further. The researchers of this problem quote data showing that "the share of the incomes of the richest 10 percent of the population has doubled (from 12 percent of the total income of the population in 1991, to 24 percent in 1993). The poorest 10 percent received 5 percent of the total in 1991, and only 3.2 percent of the 1993 total. The richest 20 percent of the population received 24 percent of the total income in 1991 and 39 percent in 1993. As opposed to this, the lowest 20 percent received only 10 percent of the total income in 1991 and 8 percent in 1993 (Shopov 1995).

As a result of this redistribution of income, large masses of people have become impoverished. In the transition period, the relative share of the population with incomes under the subsistence minimum has grown. In 1989, such people constituted 41 percent of the population; this figure rose to 62 percent in 1995. Those receiving incomes below the living wage were 24 percent of the population in 1989 and 47 percent in 1995. The degree of the income differentiation measured by the

Gini index for 1989 was 21.7 percent; it grew to 37.8 percent in 1995 (Stoyanova et al. 1996).

The economic policy that transfers losses to the public plays a definite role in this state of affairs, directly contributing to its impoverishment. This happens when subsidies for certain goods produced by a state monopoly are suspended, and no measures are taken to increase productivity; when bad debts are transferred into a state debt and their monetizing into inflation;[3] when greater tax and price pressure is exerted on the population; when sufficient anti-inflation protection is overlooked; when savings are devalued by a negative interest rate; and when income and social expenditures are limited within the framework of the budget policy.

Along with the impoverishment of the masses through the distribution and redistribution processes, a process of primitive accumulation is under way in Bulgaria now. According to Minev (1996), this process commenced as early as the beginning of the 1980s, but since the changes of 1989 it has accelerated. The delay in privatization, the inadequacy of legislation, and the abuse of the existing laws created conditions for capital transfusion. It is evident that the fair distribution of wealth will be possible only when the above-mentioned inefficiencies are eliminated. Adequate mechanisms for redistribution should be created to ensure that growth does not lead to further impoverishment of the masses, and that human capital is fully utilized. Only then will the country be able to enhance its rating on the human development index (HDI), constructed by the UNDP. In 1995 Bulgaria ranked forty-eighth in the world on this index.

The Social Dimension of Poverty

Bulgaria's transition to a market economy turned out to be the most difficult, the slowest, and the least successful of all the ex-socialist countries. The following are the major social problems that the country experienced immediately after the transition:

1. *A drastic increase in unemployment.* Although unemployment existed prior to 1989, it was officially unacknowledged. Moreover, it was certainly not as high as it is now. From a mere 1.7 percent in 1991, unemployment mounted to 16.4 percent in 1993. However, after that, until the middle of 1996, it started to decline. But again, as of September 1996, it began rising and

---

3. The state debt for 1996 reached 1,053 billion leva (U.S.$5,987,431).

stood at 12.52 percent by December 1996, with the number of the unemployed registered at the labor offices reaching 478,770. In 1997, this increase is expected to continue due to the restructuring of the economy, the closure of state enterprises that are incurring losses, and the dismissals of salaried workers in the government bureaus. The level of unemployment on 31 March 1997 had reached 14.5 percent with predictions of further increases in the months to come. The relative share of unemployment is expected to surpass 20 percent.

Fifty-five percent of the unemployed are women, 39.6 percent of whom are young, below the age of thirty. Only 16 percent of unemployed women are from the villages, thus suggesting a high concentration of unemployed women in the urban areas.

2. *Progressive impoverishment of large groups of the population.* The rate of impoverishment has been significantly growing in the last two to three years, and especially in 1996. Impoverishment is accompanied by a continued trend in the decrease of people's real income, lagging far behind the rate of inflation. The high rate of inflation and tensions between certain social groups and strata in Bulgaria have given rise to risk groups, the physical survival of whose members seems to be almost impossible without strong government intervention. All this has made the restructuring of social security and social protection systems only too imperative. Imperative also is the sporadic assistance provided to specific groups and individuals who have health and family problems. This assistance forms an all-round protection system without any restrictions whatsoever of a political, religious, or ethnic nature. Social protection will have to be based on the criteria and indicators of poverty that can be objectively assessed.

The first program – the purpose of which was to respond to the changing social and economic conditions – was associated with the labor market that came into being in 1989. The main measures taken under this program were (1) compensation payments, and (2) encouragement to the employers, through preferential treatment and various other stimuli, to create jobs. These measures, however, were targeted at the consequences of unemployment (the loss of labor incomes) but did not address to the need to stem unemployment. These measures aimed to assist the currently unemployed in finding work. Decree number 57 of the Council of Ministers, for the reorientation and effective use of the workforce, has been corrected and supplemented many times over during the 1991-1996 period. At present, the Decree envisages monetary compensation for (1) employees who have worked under a labor agreement for at least six months and who have been dismissed by their employers without any cause; and (2) individuals whose term of labor contract has not been renewed. The monetary compensation for those persons who had full-time jobs comprises 60 percent of the average monthly gross wage. For this purpose a special fund has been created for "professional training and unemployment." This compensation ranges between 90 and 140 percent of the minimum wage. Monetary compensation is decided on the basis of the length of service or the age of the unemployed. The period of compensation payment varies from six to twelve months. To receive this benefit, the unemployed person must be registered at the labor office in his or her residential area. In addition to monetary compensation, family allowances are also paid.

Compensation is paid to a person after he or she provides a written declaration that he or she is looking for a job, is at the disposal of the labor office, and will be available any time a suitable job is offered. Individuals must confirm their readiness to work every month. Young specialists who are not able to find a job within one month after they complete their studies and who are registered at the labor office are entitled to 80 percent of the minimum wage, but only for a period of six months. Young qualified workers receive the same amount in social assistance but only for three months. Young specialists and workers, just discharged from the army, are also entitled to social assistance. Those unemployed who have been registered at the labor office for more than twelve months get assistance equal to 60 percent of the minimum wage for six months. However, they must satisfy the conditions for social support and provide a written declaration that they are looking for a job and will accept any job offered by the labor office.

No compensation is paid to a person working under a labor agreement or receiving a pension. Similarly, farmers, service-class people, and businessmen are not qualified for such compensation. The payments are also suspended when a person joins an educational institution for further education. Those who refuse to accept an offer for a job, refuse to join a retraining course, or drop out of a course also forfeit the right to compensation.

As of 1994 the labor offices, jointly with the local government, state and private firms and organizations, have been implementing a National Temporary Employment Program. They have created jobs in socially useful activities. For this purpose, the labor offices remit the employer amounts which are equal to the minimum monthly wage plus the respective allowances to be paid to the persons employed under the program. This program guarantees employment to persons without any specialty or with primary or lower education. There is a similar national program for youngsters and invalids. However, high interest rates, inadequate markets, an unfavorable tax policy, and a deteriorating economic situation strongly decrease the chances for the unemployed to start their own business.

To be sure, the implementation of the Program for the Reorientation and Use of the Workforce initially helped to keep the prevailing chaos in the labor market under control. This program tried to locate the most unprepared and disadvantaged groups and to create special programs for them. The financial assistance provided to such groups under this program, however, is not enough. Despite the fact that women have constituted a larger part of the unemployed since 1994, there has been no program tailored to their needs. At this stage, the program is not an effective means for combating the black labor market. It cannot keep control over those who continue to receive compensation even after finding employment. Although the state gives some preferential treatment to those employers who hire partly disabled persons, many employers are unwilling to respond to these incentives. As a result, many invalids remain unemployed or work in very unfavorable conditions.

The weakness of this program stems from the fact that it is a *normative Act*.[4] But whatever effectiveness the program has is due, to a great extent, to the fact that the criteria to determine the range of persons it protects cover almost all the cases. There are two exceptions, however; this kind of financial assistance is not given to: (1) persons who have left work at their own will, or have been dismissed, or have been working under a labor contract for less than six months; and (2) persons who have been registered as residents of a given town or village for less than six months. There is currently a proposal to amend the program to guarantee the right to unemployment compensation to all persons for whom social insurance has been paid, irrespective of the reason for the person's unemployment or the duration of the labor contract.

This program operates through the National Employment Office, which is a branch of the Ministry of Labor and Social Welfare. It has opened 123 labor offices throughout the country. The budgets of these branch offices are independent of the budgets of the local bodies (the municipalities). The labor offices receive their funds regularly and directly from the National Employment Office. For this reason, there is no delay in the payment of compensations. The labor offices are independent corporate bodies and can sign contracts and agreements with the municipalities and the state or private employers. However, one of the major problems related to the implementation of the program is that

---

4. There are two kinds of documents in Bulgarian legislation. The first includes bills, which are passed by the National Assembly to become acts. The other type are worked out and adopted by the respective ministries. These hold less authority than acts; they remain independent documents and are called "normative Acts."

the size of the compensation and assistance package is tied to the minimum wage, and this does not cover even the most elementary needs. There is a delay in adjusting wages to rising inflation rates. Real wages over the 1990-1996 period have gone up by more than 60 percent. But this is not reflected in the amount of compensation paid to the unemployed. Therefore, whatever financial assistance they receive from the state is not enough to meet the basic minimal needs of their families.

The harsh decline in the living standards of the people and the explosive growth of poverty have necessitated social policy reform during the transition period. This reform has been carried out against the background of the ever deepening social, economic, and political crises, accompanied by the unprecedented process of the back-door redistribution of the nation's wealth. In fact, social policy has been playing the role of a "screen" or a "breath of air" for those who are sinking in the swamp of poverty. The limited possibilities for reintegration of the poor in the country's economic life, the deeply embedded idea of the role of the state in this process, and the lack of a tradition for the participation of nongovernmental organizations (NGOs) have all contributed to the present situation.

The major programs under which social assistance and social protection are provided are the following:

a) *Program for keeping incomes at the same level.* This is based on the so-called *base minimum income* (BMI). Through a system of coefficients, reading the number and age of the members of the household, its amount is corrected to form the *differentiated minimum income* (DMI). The amount of the monthly social assistance is added to the household income to form the DMI. Beneficiaries are subject to a check-up in order to establish the real state of their income and property. The plan for keeping incomes based on the DMI applies to all the poor households, irrespective of the reasons for their present state; and it is not time bound. It is built on the principle of solidarity and is financed by the consolidated state budget. Beneficiaries are encouraged to actively participate in the labor market. The program envisages the possibility of providing higher one-time or periodical financial assistance (up to six times a year), according to the decision of the social officers, to meet reasonable demands (clothing, textbooks, medicine, spa treatment, transport, etc.). Further, special provision is made for social assistance to invalids – for their protection, rehabilitation, and social integration. Similarly, there are provisions for one-parent families and orphans who cannot be accommodated in state orphanages. Monthly social assistance is granted in kind in case senior household members are not in a position to manage the household budget or do not look after their minors.

b) *Program for in-kind assistance and services.* This uses house calls to clients (providing them with foodstuffs, medical check-ups, cleaning); institutional care (homes for the aged, for invalids, for mentally deficient children, and old people); out-patient care (day homes for the aged, invalids, and mentally deficient persons); catering in canteens and vouchers for goods to be bought from specific shops at lower prices; free or discounted transportation for certain groups of people (invalids, retirees, mothers of many children); and spa treatment, etc.

At present, this program is more effectively carried out in the big cities, although even there it is not possible to provide free or reduced-price medicine. Because of the insufficiency of capital and financial means, the situation in the cities is also far from satisfactory. The services offered to clients are generally of low quality and the fees charged are extremely high, beyond the means of low-income households. There is also corruption in the provision of free and reduced-price medicine, since private pharmacies refuse to participate as they are not compensated on time by the municipal budget.

c) *Program for social protection.* This entitles to assistance every such household whose average monthly income has been lower over the last six months than the sum total of the DMI plus the value of the normative for minimum monthly needs on fixed prices for electricity, central heating, fuel, and running water. The protected norms are 44 square meters for a household of one to three persons and 74 square meters for a household of four, irrespective of the size of the house they inhabit. Assistance is received in the form of vouchers, which are provided by the regional social centers.

d) *Program for assisting mothers-to-be and all mothers who support their children.* This was initiated in 1968 and is now antiquated. It responds neither to the changed demographic situation and trends nor to the social protection needs of children and families in the midst of a cruel economic crisis. The program is universal and is mainly pronatal, encouraging the birth of a third child. However, around 52 percent of the families in Bulgaria have only one child, and 43 percent have two children. Some 70 percent of all the children in Bulgaria live with families whose incomes are below the family living wage. The amount of support money provided under this program is absurdly low and is the same for every family, irrespective of their income; it is measured by a percentage of the minimum wage. Moreover, the duration of the maternity leave depends on whether it is first, second, or third child. A maternity leave for up to two years is paid at minimum wage. Those availing themselves of the leave for the third year are allowed to retain their jobs but are paid no support money.

e) *Program for Pensions.* This is built on the principle of insurance. Pension installments are fixed by the state, but paid by the employer. Pension insurance is compulsory, all encompassing, permanent, and equal for all classes and groups. To receive a pension, a person must satisfy some conditions – have provided a specific length of service and be of a specific age (sixty years for men, and fifty-five for women). The amount of each pension depends on the wage the retiree received during the three years before his or her retirement and on the length of the service. However, the burden of pensions paid is extremely heavy for the state budget. Pension legislation is antiquated and ineffective, and the sums of pensions are not regularly adjusted to the fluctuating inflation rates. The real increase of the average pension for the 1990-1996 period is minus 40 percent. Currently a new pension act is being prepared, and as a first step, a National Insurance Institute was set up in 1996. However, in 1997 the pension superannuation funds were made independent of the state budget. Persons over seventy who have no income whatsoever are entitled to social pensions. The amount of the social pension constitutes a fixed percentage of the minimum wage; this is utterly insufficient and is far below the social minimum.

f) *Program for the protection, rehabilitation, and social integration of invalids.* Although still in its infancy, this program envisages a system of additional social assistance and alleviation (1996) for those not covered by the above-mentioned programs.

All the social programs (except for those referring to retirees) are of a universal character and have been built on a system of criteria which embraces all of the needy. However, these programs do not meet even the elementary needs of the beneficiary. In this sense, one can categorically state that the means provided are quite insufficient, although the social assistance programs envisage the possibility of granting additional assistance to some risk groups (invalids, nonworking and noninsured mothers whose children are under two years of age), as well as to persons in special conditions (orphans, refugees, released prisoners). The coefficients used to fix the DMI place families with children on unequal levels because of the extremely low coefficient assigned to minors (a child under sixteen years = 0.4; two adults without children = 1.8).

All activities for the execution of social assistance is carried out by the regional centers for social care and their branches. They are methodically subordinated to the Ministry of Labor and Social Care. Since the social centers have no independent budget, the municipalities provide the staff and financing for the programs. The reason that they face considerable difficulties in doing their work effectively and efficiently is that the municipal budgets are limited, and the necessary means are not regularly remitted. Along with this, the envisaged control of the financial and property status of those applying for social assistance is extremely difficult to maintain, and the shortage of funds in a number of cases is compensated by not paying some kinds of assistance.

Despite the mounting impoverishment of the masses, we still cannot speak about social conflicts on the basis of economic stratification. This does not mean that there are no social conflicts, on the contrary. At present, the social situation is very complex and even explosive, but the social energy created by these conditions has been transformed into political protests directed more toward the consequences of poverty than to its causes. What the demonstrators demand is political change and the ousting of the present rulers. However, they rarely think beyond the limited "bipolar" choices of the dominant two-party system[5] to find a broad social consensus on the social and economic stabilization of this country.

At the moment, the poor and the rich in Bulgaria coexist in two parallel worlds. The poor are deeply involved in the problems of their physical survival, and the rich do not seem to notice that the poor really exist. According to sociological opinion surveys, 64 percent of the respondents believe that it is the responsibility of the state and the municipalities to take care of the poor; 22 percent hold the rich responsible for the increasing poverty; 19 percent want charity organizations to assist the poor; and 12 percent feel that the poor should take care of themselves (Minev 1993).

In general, social attitudes toward the poor, mirrored in government policy during the transition period, are characterized by an ad hoc approach and lack of cooperation between the various sectors. The social policy of the government during the transition period has been paternalistic (Shopov 1995). Over the 1990-1996 period, the Bulgarian parliament sporadically changed governments six times, and yet none could solve the problem of growing impoverishment. The marginalization of the poor creates the real danger of a permanently fragmented society

5. Apart from the minor political parties which are of little significance, the Union of Democratic Forces (UDF) and the Bulgarian Socialist Party (BSP) reign over the political arena with opposing and often contradictory ideas of how society should develop in the future. Since their views stand at two opposite poles, this pattern of political formation may be called "bipolar."

(Fotev 1996). Further, the radical difference between the structure of the social and political formations also creates great difficulty in conducting a policy to reduce poverty (Minev and Zhelyazkova 1996).

Let us also make a reference to the European Union's B7-500 Program for emergency social assistance for the Republic of Bulgaria. Hyperinflation and political destabilization in the beginning of 1997 caused European Union to urgently intercede on the country's behalf. It allocated 20 million ecus worth of emergency social assistance to be used for households covered by the system of in-kind social protection and for social homes to purchase food and medicine (up to 10 percent of the assistance), heating, electricity, fuel, water, clothing, and linen (up to 10 percent of the assistance). This program has aided over 553,000 households, 48 percent of which are retirees. By virtue of the program regulations, a family of one (retiree) is entitled to 2.4 ecus monthly for February, March, and April 1997; a family of two (retirees) to 3.6 ecus; a family of three (two parents and a child up to ten years of age) to 5.2 ecus; and a family of five (two parents and three children over ten years of age) to 8.4 ecus per month.

The Political Dimension of Poverty

Over the last few years, the number of the civil associations and the NGOs has been growing. According to unofficial estimates, there are over one thousand NGOs in Bulgaria whose activities are oriented toward the problems of the poor. According to a 1994 survey, 46.6 percent of the NGOs are national, 23.8 percent are local offices of national organizations, and 9.6 percent are purely regional. However, a great number of NGOs and associations still have few activities. Five decades of state support have conditioned the minds of the people so that they still feel, even in the changed political regime, that the state should guarantee everybody the necessary income and jobs. A great number of people think that civil organizations are not in a position to solve problems by themselves but can only play a role in the process of their solution, i.e. by exerting pressure on the state machinery. According to a survey carried out by the Center for Studying Democracy, only 13.7 percent of the respondents think that civil organizations can significantly influence the solution of social problems, 36.2 percent believe that they rarely have such an influence, while 25 percent do not believe in the power of the NGOs at all.

In addition to its social and economic dimensions, the crisis in Bulgaria also lies in a growing lack of confidence in institutions. People are deeply disappointed with the incompetence and complete ineffectiveness of the powers-that-be, and in the last six years, there has hardly been any noticeable improvement. This has logically led to the people's rising dissatisfaction, often leading to their protests in defence of their own interests. All this will probably significantly strengthen the positions of the hitherto powerless civil organizations. It is only natural that these organizations should enjoy support from the state for their activities. However, the already existing organizations must work on behalf of the poor with greater enthusiasm.

In Bulgaria, the period from January to April 1997, was characterized by political destabilization, hyperinflation, and a very high rate of devaluation in the national currency. This brought about mass protests and early parliamentary election. The interim government managed to curb inflation and the devaluation of the Bulgarian lev and to pacify the mass protestors. But the expected rise in unemployment, along with the process of continuing impoverishment, limitations in free medical aid due to the extremely high price of medicine, heating, electricity, and so on might, yet once again, aggravate social tension. We hope that with the introduction of the currency board, the situation in Bulgaria will become more stable.

Bibliography

The Center for Studying Democracy. 1995. "Risk Groups and Their Challenge for Social Policy."Paper presented at a symposium, July 1995.

Chavdarova, T. 1996. "Methods of Determining the Poverty Line: Problems for Discussion." *Poverty and Fragmentation in Bulgarian Society: The Role NGOs Play in Encouraging Social Integration.* Sofia.

CISTI. 1995. *Sociological Problems of Poverty.* Sofia.

Fotev, G. 1996. "Poverty and Fragmentation in Bulgarian Society." *Poverty and Fragmentation in Bulgarian Society: The Role NGOs Play in Encouraging Social Integration.* Sofia.

Hristoskov, Y., G. Shopov, and I. Beleva. 1996. *Noninstitutionalized Employment and Self-Employment.* Sofia: Institute of Market Economy.

Kostov, G. 1970. *Problems with the Minimum Wage.* Sofia:Works of the Institute of Labor.

_____. 1996. "Poverty: Theoretical-Methodological and Methodical Problems." In *Poverty and Fragmentation in Bulgarian Society: The Role NGOs Play in Encouraging Social Integration.* Sofia.

Kostov, G., S. Todorova, Z. Toneva, and T. Rakadjiiska. 1993. "Sociological Problems of Poverty." *Sociological Review* 18, no. 2.

Kraleva, R. 1994. *How Do We Live?* Sofia: The Institute of Trade Union Problems.

Minev, D. 1993. "Poverty and Inequality: The Conspiracy of Silence." *Sociological Review* 18, no. 2.

Minev, D., and M. Zhelyazkova. 1996. "Poverty: Its Dimensions, Causes and Policy for Its Reduction." *Poverty and Fragmentation in Bulgarian Society: The Role NGOs Play in Encouraging Social Integration.* Sofia.

MLSW. 1992. *The Policy, Practice, and Financing of Social Support in the Republic of Bulgaria.* Sofia: The Center for Social Insurance and Social Assistance.

National Institute of Statistics. 1996a. *Employment and Unemployment. 1993, 1994, 1995, 1996. Annual Book of Statistics.* Bulgaria.

_____. 1996b. *Household Incomes, Expenditures, and Consumption.* Sofia.

Rakadjiiska, T. 1994. "Social and Economic Identity in Bulgarian Households According to the Status "Rich/Poor." *Sociology in a Society in Transition*, ed. N. Genov. Sofia.

Republic of Bulgaria. 1996. *National Program for Social Development.* Sofia.

Shopov, G. 1995. "Economic Stratification and the Unification of the Population." *Bulgaria, 1995: Human Development*, ed. N. Genov. Sofia.

Stoyanova, K., G. Shopov, B. Bogdanov et al. 1996. *The Social Reform.* Siela Publishers.

Todorova, S. 1996. "The Informal Economy." *Economic Sociology.* Sofia: "Economy" Publishers.

Yossifov, A. and I. Naoumov. 1996. "Poverty: Cultural Models and Mass Adjustment in Bulgaria Today." In *Poverty and Fragmentation in Bulgarian Society: The Role NGOs Play in Encouraging Social Integration.* Sofia.

Chapter Three

POVERTY IN ROMANIA

Traian Rotariu / Livia Popescu
Center for Urban and Rural Sociology, National University

Introduction

This study was carried out during a period of power transfer from the party which had governed since 1990 to a party coalition which now embraces a very different political orientation. Due to this political transition and the resultant "natural" time lag between the legislative/political changes and the current economic and social realities, the present analysis is based on data reflecting a past state of affairs. This is true both in relation to the real poverty phenomenon and to the political attitude toward it. Following the general and legislative elections held in November 1996, the governing bodies changed their political composition and subsequently their programmatic directions. At this point, it is hard to evaluate the impact of the new policies. Therefore, any comment can only be based on programs and declarations of intentions.

Economic reform will be speeded up by both accelerating and extending privatization and by encouraging foreign investment. The industrial giants, inherited from the communist regime and not affected by the reform initiated under the previous governments, will be included in the privatization and marketization processes. Subsidies for both industries and agriculture are to be significantly reduced. The universal social protection consisting of subsidies on essential food products, energy, and transport have already been abandoned or reduced to a large extent. The present government is aware, and has publicly admitted, that economic restructuring will bring about an important decline in the living standards of the majority of the population. Even if it is expected to be limited in time, such a deterioration will more severely affect the groups which are already in poverty. Unemployment is expected to rise and some of the envisioned passive and active measures are meant to reduce its social cost.

The former governments, during the period 1990-1996, based their reform policies on agreements and support from transnational bodies like the International Monetary Fund (IMF) and the World Bank, but compliance with such agreements was very often reluctant if not occasionally suspended. The new government has stated that its program will closely follow the agreements negotiated with the IMF and the World Bank. Subsequently, both economic and social policy will have a more explicitly liberal orientation.

In the domain of social policy, several changes are expected to occur. Some new selective provisions will be introduced, but this will not alter the already existing universal provisions. On the contrary, as in the case of the child allowance, their scope will be enlarged and the level of the benefits will be raised. Steps are being taken to reform the pension and the medical care systems as well. The situation of vulnerable groups (street children, families with numerous children, homeless people) has been acknowledged and the development of specific services for them is given priority attention by the government. Still there is considerable uncertainty as to the concrete realization of such a program under the conditions of an austerity budget.

I. Measurements and Definitions of Poverty

In the aftermath of the 1989 revolution, Romania has had the challenging task of tackling some serious social problems produced by economic backwardness and poverty: abandoned children, very poor quality medical and social care, and low living standards. This plight which the country faces has given it a bad reputation. The demographic and social indicators for the year 1995 – such as infant mortality (21.2 percent), life expectancy (69.5 years), the incidence of HIV/AIDS among the children (which is the highest in the world), the number of institutionalized children (46,744), and the incidence of tuberculosis (92 per 100,000 inhabitants) – indicate that poverty has remained a serious issue in Romania during this period of transition (1990-1996).

Paradoxically enough, poverty has had little political visibility until 1994. The social costs of the so-called mild transition, as opposed to the "shock therapy" that was adopted in other countries-in-transition, were underestimated (Zamfir 1995a, 422-23). The government agreed with the industrial workers that social welfare should primarily focus on job preservation and the provision of better salaries. The ruling party and important sections of the industrial working class (mining, energy production, heavy industry) favored state protectionism to ensure proper income distribution and to preserve the privileges inherited from the previous system of nonmarket economy. The postponement of structural changes in the economy was, in effect, advantageous for the powerful and unionized sectors of the labor force. But it did not prevent any of the "evils" currently associated with "shock therapy": hyperinflation, unemployment, the increased vulnerability of weaker social groups, and the overall deterioration of living standards (Popescu 1995).

The government policy of poverty prevention or alleviation was initially limited to unemployment compensation. Changes in the legislation aimed at responding to the problem of long-term unemployment. Due to an upsurge in poverty, the government acknowledged the need to supplement the existing welfare system with other safety nets. The Social Aid Law, issued by the parliament in 1995, represents an attempt to provide last resort income to the poorest people. Putting the law into effect required both a definition of poverty and the choice of a method to measure the poverty level. The first official definition of "deep" poverty was implicitly provided through legal entitlement to social aid benefits. The Ministry of Labor and Social Protection estimated that the number of people eligible for this provision constituted 10 percent of the country's population. The income level which entitles a person to social aid benefits is considered to be significantly lower than the subsistence minimum as it was defined by the Research Institute for the Quality of Life (RIQL) (Zamfir 1995c).

The various governments that ruled the country during the 1990-1996 period followed different policies regarding poverty alleviation. It is relevant to mention in this respect that the 1996 Human Development Report – a document coordinated by the reform minister of the SDPR government and the director of the National Commission for Statistics – deals with the poverty issue in a paragraph titled: "Social Equity and Stability: Limiting Social Tensions." The authors of the report have only taken into consideration the "perception of living standards" on a 10-point scale ranging from poverty (1) to wealth (10). According to the survey conducted by the RIQL, the average score was 4.25; this indicates that the self-reported standards of living are below the middle condition, that is, closer to the poverty pole of the continuum. The authors of the report consider these findings to be biased "by the respondents' disposition to exaggerate the negative aspects of their own living standards" (UNDP 1996, 46).

Given the fact that the government tends to minimize the problem of poverty, it is not surprising that the academic community and the media took the initiative in promoting public debate on this issue. At present, there is no official definition of poverty, and, therefore, no reliable statistics exist to measure its incidence. Nevertheless, indirect measures can be used to estimate the size and the dynamics of the problem. The Family Budget Surveys (FBS), carried out by the National Commission for Statistics (NCS), are the main official source of data for both the structure and distribution of incomes and the pattern of consumption expenditures. Every household in the sample for the Family Budget Survey is required to maintain a diary for all twelve months of the year, recording details of income and expenditure. The data collected through these diaries provide detailed information on the income and consumption expenditure of households, but not about their assets. As a taxation system for global income has not been established yet, the survey is based on the self-declared incomes. These are generally underreported: it is common knowledge that respondents do not declare all of their nonofficial (nontaxed, nonregistered) income in order to avoid taxation.

Another possible source of distortion comes from the altered representativeness of the sample. The way the sample is drawn, the groups placed at the extremes of income distribution (the poorest households and the most wealthy ones) somehow get eliminated from the sample. Therefore, these groups are underrepresented, and people in the middle reaches of income distribution are overrepresented. Despite this methodological limitation, the FBS provides a relatively dependable picture of the general features of income distribution and consumption expenditure (Plesca and Rata 1996). Since 1995, the methodology of the FBS has been changed in order to enhance the representativeness of the sample. The number of households included in the sample increased from an average of 9,000 (1992, 1993) to 36,000 (1995). The old permanent sample was retained as a separate set, to serve as a control group. The data are presented according to five categories of households: employees, employers, peasants, unemployed persons, and pensioners. The self-declared occupational status of the household head is used to classify the type of the household (NCS 1996).

The most recent figures published by the NCS relate to income distribution for the period July 1995-June 1996. The average total nominal income (486,000 lei; that is, U.S.$86.63)[1] consists of monetary income (70.5 percent) and the equivalent of gratuities or of food produced for consumption from the household's own resources (29.5 percent). The main sources of monetary income are wages or equivalent payments (60.7 percent), pensions (18.1 percent), cash for food products (6.6 percent), income from self-employed activities (5.7 percent),

---

1. One U.S. dollar equals 5610 lei.

and unemployment benefits (1.2 percent). The differences in income and consumption patterns between the household types are important. While the households of employers get 2.7 times the average income, the unemployed ones reach only 71.1 percent of this average (NCS 1996, 4). For the other three categories, the balance is almost nil, monetary income and monetary expenditure being very close to each other (NCS 1996, 10).

Consumption expenditure is often considered a better approximation of a household's living standard than is current income, since expenditure is based to a large extent on the expected life-cycle income. Thus, the extent of poverty can be assessed on the basis of the average *food shares* computed as a percentage of the expenses for food in the total consumption expenditure. The data indicate that, during 1990-1996, expenditure on food as a proportion of the total consumption expenditure has increased significantly. Figure 3.1 shows the evolution of this indicator for three groups of families: employees, peasants, and pensioners.

Figure 3.1 The evolution of food expenditure for three groups of families: employees, peasants, and pensioners. (as a proportion of the total consumption expenditure)

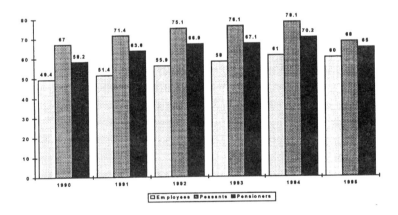

Source: NCS (1991-1996).

In Romania the fulfillment of food needs is not entirely market based. Recent surveys show that not only an important proportion of food for consumption is self-produced, but that this feature was reinforced during the 1992-1994 period and remained important afterwards (see Table 3.1). The high degree of self-produced consumption among peasant families indicates that private farming has not yet accomplished the transition from the traditional subsistence economy to the modern market economy.

Table 3.1   Percentage of self-produced consumption in the total expenditure on food consumption, 1992-1995

Type of family	1992	1993	1994	1995
Employee	31.3	33.1	35.4	35.0
Peasant	80.9	80.7	88.3	70.0

Source: NCS 1995, 1996; Spineanu 1995.

The data are not presented by the NCS in terms of poverty levels, but secondary analysis has been used by research teams to estimate income inequalities and poverty dynamics. A common approach is to compare the real value of the post-communist yearly average incomes with the 1989 average income, in order to highlight the changes in living standards. Despite the lack of reliable information on the poverty issue during the communist period, 1989 data are considered to be the only point of reference in this respect. The UNICEF Regional Monitoring Report, which has based its estimations on OECD methodology, has used two alternative poverty lines: (1) 45 percent of the 1989 average wage; and (2) 50 percent of the 1989 average wage. In both the cases, the data show a decline in the incidence of poverty in 1990 and a steady increase afterwards. If the poverty line is considered to be 45 percent of the 1989 average wage, the percentage of the population living in poverty decreased from 27 percent in 1989 to 18 percent in 1990 and, following the process of economic reform, it began rising again, reaching 51.1 percent in 1992 (UNICEF 1993, 8). It is very likely that the trend has continued with the erosion of income. As pointed out by Zamfir (1995, 70), the real value (percent of the 1989 level) of the main types of incomes was significantly low in 1994, as shown below:

average wage	54.7%
minimum wage	28.4%
pension	43.6%
child allowance	21.2%

The publication *Welfare in Romania during Transition: Analysis of the FBS Data (1989, 1992, 1993) – Technical Report* attempts to capture the changes in the inequality and poverty patterns using the data provided by the Family Budget Survey (Plesca and Rata 1996). The authors used different computing methods (Theil T index, Theil N index, Gini index, and variance logarithms, head count index, and Foster-Greer-Thorbecke index for e=2) and assessed their respective strengths in accounting for either the social inequality or poverty. The concern for the comparability of the data is obvious as the study presents the results according to three equivalence scales developed by OECD, EUROSTAT, and the Commission for Statistics.

The poverty line is defined as a fraction of the median income or consumption expenditure. The poverty indices have been computed for several alternative fractions of the median variables: 50 percent, 60 percent, 66 percent, 70 percent, and 80 percent.

Table 3.2 The Foster index[2] for measuring poverty by an individual's equivalent income in 1989, 1992, and 1993 (Commission for Statistics' equivalence scale)

| Year | Fraction of the median | | | | |
	50%	60%	66%	70%	80%
1989	.018	.030	.026	.043	.059
1992	.030	.045	.057	.063	.083
1993	.025	.039	.049	.054	.071

Source: Plesca and Rata. 1996, 22

The indices show that poverty increased between 1989 and 1992, but it decreased between 1992 and 1993. This trend is revealed for both income and consumption variables, regardless of the definition and the equivalence scale used (Plesca and Rata 1996, 16-19). However, what is interesting is that despite the decline between 1992 and 1993, the 1993 figures are still higher than the 1989 figure, which means that had there been a comparison of only 1989 and 1993 figures, it would have suggested a rise in poverty and not a decline.

The inequality analysis provides complementary information to the understanding of the poverty issue. If all the categories of income are divided according to ten deciles (from the first one corresponding to the

2. Foster-Greer-Thorbecke index is given by :

$$F = \frac{1}{N} \sum_{poor} n_i \left(\frac{z - y_i}{z} \right)^2$$

In the formula N represents the number of individuals in the sample, n_i represents the number of members in the household, z represents the poverty line and y_i the income per capita.

lowest incomes, to the tenth one corresponding to the highest), one notices that the increase of income is very important when moving from the first decile to the second one, and from the ninth decile to the tenth one. Within the middle region, the increase is comparatively smaller. The ratio between the income of the poorest 10 percent and the income of the richest 10 percent – which was calculated for 1989, 1992, and 1993 – indicates an increased polarization of the society. In 1989, the average income of the richest 10 percent was 6.71 times the average income of the poorest 10 percent. In 1992, the ratio grew to 7.87 and continued to rise to 8.49 in 1993. This suggests that the poor segment of the population is becoming even poorer while the rich segment is growing even richer. This observation is valid irrespective of the definition of poverty used (Plesca and Rata 1996, 12).

Independent surveys on poverty issues were carried out by the Research Institute for Quality of Life in 1994. The stratified random sample of households used in these surveys is considered nationally representative, and it gives a more appropriate picture of the whole range of income distribution than the former FBS sample. Three methods are used to identify and measure poverty. These are (1) the normative method, (2) the OECD method, and (3) the subjective method. The estimation of poverty incidence and the differentiation of poverty levels are based on two poverty thresholds, corresponding respectively to absolute poverty (*Subsistence Minimum* [SM]) and relative poverty (*Decent Minimum of Life* [DM]). There is a third threshold as well: the so-called *Ministry of Labor and Social Protection Minimum* (MM). This last one is actually the entitlement level for social aid benefits, and it corresponds to the condition of very severe poverty or misery. The ratios between the three minimum levels have been calculated for the standard family (two adults and two children) from the normative perspective: SM = 59.9 percent of the DM; MM = 31.5 percent of the DM, and 52.6 percent of the SM (Zamfir 1995c, 16-19).

The normative method is based on the basket of goods and services for the two minimum levels (SM and DM). The incidence of poverty as estimated by the Research Institute for the Quality of Life (RIQL) is given in Table 3.3.

The OECD method is useful but not relevant for the Romanian situation. In view of the peculiarities of the poverty phenomenon during the transition period in Romania, C. Zamfir (1995c, 23) has advanced the following reasons for not employing the OECD method: (1) the average income in Romania is so low that it cannot be used as an indicator of leading a decent life (DM) – in fact, even those whose income corresponds to the average income for Romania lead a life of relative poverty; (2) similarly, those whose income is equivalent of 50 percent of

Table 3.3 The distribution of the population following different poverty lines (percentage of the total households included in the sample)

below MM	9.8
below SM	34.9
below DM	74.8
above DM	25.2

MM = Ministry of labor and social protection Minimum
SM = Subsistence Minimum
DM = Decent Minimum of life

Source: Zamfir 1995c, 21.

the average income are unable to provide the Subsistence Minimum (SM) to their families; and (3) given the low level of average income, there is a considerable imbalance in income distribution: the segment of the population which is below this level is a small one and represents *absolute* rather than *relative* poverty. Poverty incidence measured through the OECD method gives a very different profile from the one established through the normative method, as shown below (Zamfir 1995c, 23).

1. below 40% of AI (Average Income)   9.2% of households
2. below 50% of AI   15.9% of households
3. below 60% of AI   41.5% of households
4. above AI   33.6% of households

The overall deterioration of living standards also has an important subjective dimension. The categories which have been used in the opinion polls are not exactly the same as those used in the normative approach, but some comparisons can still be made.

Since 1995, when this type of survey was carried out on a regular (trimestrial) basis by independent teams, people's perception of living standards indicates a relative stability. The proportion of the better-off (whose income is sufficient to cover all necessities without effort) has been the most stable over the period: 1 percent in 9 surveys. The percentage of those placing themselves "above the DM, but with some effort" declined from 9 percent (March 1995) to 5 percent (March 1996), and then rose to 6 percent (March 1997). The segment situated at the DM level remained around 23 percent over the 1995-1997 period. The category of persons perceiving themselves as close to, or above, the SM constituted 36 percent of the sample in March 1995, 38 percent in March 1996, and 40 percent in March 1997; while those below the SM rose from 31 percent in 1995 to 34 percent in 1996, and declined to 29 percent in 1997. It is significant that by cumulating the individuals at the subsistence level and below it the percentage varied from 67 in March 1995 to 69 in March 1997, with a peak of 72 in July 1996 (CURS 1997).

The poverty risk of the household depends very much upon the occupational status, the educational level, and the number of children in the family. The most exposed categories are persons without occupation (and not eligible for unemployment benefits), unemployed people, housewives, peasants, and children (both preschool and school-going) from families headed by individuals belonging to the categories at risk. In terms of education, those with poor education are at higher risk, but at the same time it is striking that more than half of the individuals with a high education also live below the DM level. The poverty risk of the family increases significantly after the second child. The risk is even more serious in a single-parent family. The influence of the environment is also important. Findings show that the proportion of the rural population living in misery (below the MM) is higher than that of the urban population. However, in the urban milieu what is more important is the number of people living below the DM. Table 3.4 presents the poverty risk for different groups.

Table 3.4 The poverty risk for different groups of the population, 1994 (in percentages)

	below MM	between MM and SM	between SM and DM	total below DM
Total population	**11.8**	**27.5**	**38.9**	**78.2**
Employers	1.7	10.2	23.7	35.6
Pensioners	5.8	21.9	40.2	67.9
Employees	4.1	24.4	45.0	73.5
Peasants	20.9	21.3	39.7	81.9
Students	13.4	35.1	36.0	84.5
Preschool children	19.3	34.3	33.7	87.3
Housewives	20.3	35.9	31.4	87.6
Unemployed persons	21.0	39.1	30.5	90.6
People without occupation	40.1	31.0	21.9	93.0
Urban	6.3	31.0	43.3	80.6
Rural	13.1	18.3	35.1	66.5
General / vocational school	14.8	32.6	35.1	82.5
Secondary / postsecondary schools	6.4	27.1	41.7	75.2
High school / university	1.6	13.4	49.9	64.9
Couples without children	5.8	12.1	38.2	56.1
Couples with one child	7.6	22.8	47.2	77.6
Couples with two children	6.9	35.5	42.7	85.1
Couples with three or more children	30.2	39.5	22.5	92.2
Single families with one child	11.1	40.7	33.0	84.8
Single families with two children	40.0	36.0	16.0	90.0

Source:Zamfir 1995c, 57-61

The majority of the conditions inducing poverty seem to be concentrated in the ethnic Romany (Gypsy) population: lack or low level of education, unskilled in labor, irregularly employed, and having numerous children. Subsequently, the majority of the Romanian population lives in severe poverty. Here is the breakdown: families living below SM = 62.9 percent; and families living below DM = 80.9 percent (E. Zamfir and C. Zamfir 1993, 217).

II. The Economic Dimension of Poverty

Privatization and marketization

The profile of the Romanian economy can be drawn in terms of the structure of GDP in 1996: 36 percent industry, 35 percent services, 17 percent agriculture, and 12 percent building industry (NCS 1996). The evolution of the main branches between 1990 and 1996 shows slight changes in their relative weight as well as a trend toward an increased contribution from the services sector, and a slightly decreased contribution from both agriculture and industry.

Compared with other East European countries, marketization and privatization processes have been distinctly slow in Romania. After the first steps of price liberalization were taken and the main legal documents expressing the privatization policies were issued by the parliament in 1991, reform processes faltered or even came to a standstill. As a result, Romania privatized only 13 percent of its big industries and thus lagged far behind other former communist countries in this respect (Spineanu 1996).

Yet, in the context of the oscillatory dynamics of the GDP, beginning in 1990, the weight of the whole private sector has steadily increased, reaching 52 percent in 1996. Since the vast majority (approximately 99.0 percent) of the private-owned enterprises are small or middle sized, these categories are the main contributors to the economic performance of the sector.

The critical review of the economic policy points out that due to the strong economic involvement of the state, the market and the private sector have not been able to develop properly (Zamfir 1995a; Serbanescu 1994; and Spineanu 1996) and, therefore, there has been no significant move toward market economy in Romania (Vosganian 1994). This is due to a variety of features mostly related to continuities with the past, such as a profitless industrial sector and a low level of free economic competition. The outcome is considered a "lame hybrid between a command economy and a market economy," which tends to accumulate the wrongs of the two systems (Serbanescu 1995, 4).

The absence of a coherent macroeconomic adjustment encouraged spontaneous illegal marketization and privatization. As a result, the "underground" or "parallel" economy has flourished within both the state-owned sector and the private one. The estimated contribution of this unofficial economy to the GDP varies between 25 percent (National Commission for Statistics) and 35-45 percent (Romanian Information Service).

Different perspectives on the private sector refer to its fragility: the legal inferiority of private property as compared with state property in the current Romanian legislation (Vosganian 1994); the nonindustrial (predominantly agricultural and trade) profile of the private sector; and the incapacity of the private sector to produce significant changes in an economic environment which is predominantly state owned and state regulated (Serbanescu 1995). At the end of 1995, almost half (49.2 percent) of the total employment was in the private sector. This proportion indicates a seeming advance toward privatization, but the composition of the employees in the private sector shows the structural limits of the actual changes in the Romanian economy: 46.5 percent are self-employed, the majority of them being individual farmers; 26.1 percent represent unpaid family members; 22.6 percent employees; and 4.8 percent employers (NCS 1996, 56).

Income and wealth distribution

The state continues to be not only the most important employer but also the owner of the majority of the industries and services. By carrying out this double role through wage, employment, and fiscal policies, the state interferes with market processes by either blocking or distorting them. The government salary policy in the state-owned industrial sector is pursued despite the market rules and tends to discourage economic efficiency and to offer income privileges on political grounds. The analysis of wage differentials points out the very privileged situation in the extractive industry, in the production of electric and thermal energy, petrol and transport. At the bottom of the salary hierarchy are the people employed in education, health care, and social services (Table 3.5). Such policies have deepened the categorical cleavages within the state-owned sector to an extent that overshadows the private/public income disparities. As a matter of fact, the earning differentiation in Romania today extends and reinforces the pattern established during the communist regime. The so-called productive, mainly manual, activities are opposed to "nonproductive," mainly nonmanual, activities. In other words, for the most part the working class sector is more privileged than the "service" class sectors (Popescu 1995). Statistics show that within the Romanian state economy the vocational- and secondary-educated labor force is paid higher than the people with degrees in higher education (NCS 1994). The government has derived important political/electoral gains from its salary policy, but the long-term economic and social consequences have undoubtedly been negative.

Table 3.5 Average net monthly earnings by branches of the national economy *(the global average net monthly earnings =100)*

Branch	1995
Agriculture	81.0
Extraction industries	158.9
Electric and thermal energy	150.2
Processing industry	98.4
Transport	119.9
Post and communication	125.8
Financing and banking	188.6
Public administration and defense	106.9
Education	92.1
Health care and social assistance	76.3

Source: NCS 1996

The chronic inefficiency of the state industries is likely to bring about a further deterioration of the economy and aggravate social problems. The preservation of wage differentials based not on economic performance but on political entitlement – a system inherited from the old regime – could slow down the social cohesion of post-communist society. This will jeopardize the process of building a solid social security system.

Apart from salary policies, the government is also very influential in establishing individual and group access to other areas of wealth distribution. The privatization of industrial property as well as of land and home ownership, carried on under state control, has favored groups which constitute the political clientele of the post-communist regime. Free competition has been occasionally restricted and legal entitlement criteria have quite often been abused. It is difficult to measure the extent of such phenomena, but some examples may help demonstrate the kind of benefits obtained by individuals and groups belonging to the ruling party.

Key positions in the administration of the state-owned companies are held by people who are members of, or are close to, the Social Democracy Party (SDP) which has been in power, under different names, between 1990-1996. By influencing the appointment of both managers and members of the administrative councils in the state sector, the ruling party reached two important goals: to control the strategic areas of the economy and to give its clientele important advantages in economic competition. Several independent newspapers recently brought attention to the privileges associated with membership (usually available solely to SDP members of parliament [MPs] and their families) in the administrative councils or in the Shareholders General Assembly. Those participating in these two bodies have actually been recompensed with huge sums of money (up to thirty times the average wage) and with preferential treatment in the privatization process.

Land property was privatized according to a 1991 law which aimed at partial restoration of the pre-communist ownership. Actually, reprivatization was limited to formerly cooperative property, leaving aside lands which have been appropriated by state agricultural and industrial companies. Also, restrictions concerning the size of the restituted property were imposed (ten hectares per former owner) in order to ensure a seemingly egalitarian design of land distribution. The political reason for this decision was to prevent the emergence of a wealthy class having its economic and ideological roots in the pre-communist period, rather than preventing the aggravation of social differentiation. The land law, in fact, restricts the restitution of middle- and large-sized properties to the owners prior to nationalization, but allows the appropriation of new ownership up to one hundred hectares.

It should be mentioned here that while industrial and land ownership were abolished under communism, ownership of private housing was allowed. The state had its own housing sector, resulting from intensive building activities and abusive, massive-scale nationalization which was carried on since the beginning of the 1950s. After 1990, this sector – created by the state building industry – sold the houses it constructed to the tenants at the original construction cost; for this, the buyers were given loans with low interest rates. The purpose was to evenly transfer the existing state ownership to private owners and to make it affordable for the majority of the population. Although affordability was real, some privileged persons took frequent advantage of this. At the same time, present legislation conceals the accumulation of home properties and profit making by individuals with preferential access to the subsidized privatizable sector. The privatization of houses that were previously nationalized has recently been regulated by a new law. The actual tenants will be entitled to buy these houses at a favorable price. The former owners will be recompensed with a sum significantly below the market value of the property.

In Romania, the post-communist distributive policies had effects that contradicted the official pro-egalitarian discourse. Those who accumulated wealth, legally or illegally, during the communist and post-communist regimes were provided favorable conditions. In contrast, the pre-communist owners are still being prevented from regaining their lost wealth and prestige. At the same time, no positive measures have been taken to empower the disadvantaged groups – such as women, youngsters, disabled people, and the Gypsy minority (Popescu 1995).

Redistributive mechanisms and social transfers

Chronologically, the first and major measure of universal social protection consisted of compensations for price increases and subsidies on essential food products, energy, transport, and housing. For the majority of the population and especially for those negatively impacted by the market logic, protection provided by the state has proven to be inadequate. Quite often, the benefit was only an eyewash because the items on which subsidies were to be paid were in short supply and, hence, unavailable. Moreover, the subsidies provided for electricity and gasoline resulted in a regressive redistribution. The people who possess electric goods and equipment for domestic use are in the minority (approximately 20 percent of the population), so also are those who own cars (8 percent); subsidies related to these items, therefore, benefited a very small number of the rich. In the case of house rents, regressiveness is even more significant. While state rents were frozen at the 1989 level (which equalled the price of a pack of cigarettes in 1995), the rents for private houses are as high as the average monthly earnings. The allocation of state flats was, and still is, highly favorable for people in positions of power; they live in heavily subsidized houses while the common people have to pay high rent for their private accommodations because subsidized public houses are in short supply.

The government budget depends on the performance of the economy. For many years, the budget depended heavily on taxes on salaries, and taxes on profit made only a marginal contribution. After the introduction of the value-added tax (VAT) and the growth of the private sector, this pattern of financing has somewhat changed. But even in 1996, taxes from salaries and indirect taxes constituted a major portion of the budget; while the contribution of profit taxes ranked third in government revenue (MOR 1996).

Maintenance of costly and inefficient state industries is negatively impacting the social security budget. There are delays in receiving contributions from the state-owned industries and services to the Social Insurance Fund, the Unemployment Fund, and the Health Fund. The coal mining industry, steel industry, energy production and railway companies – where the wages are the highest – are also among the most important debtors to the social security budget. The total of such debts represented 34.1 percent of the social insurance revenues in 1996.

Social welfare does not seem to be the first priority of the Romanian government. Although the share of GDP allocated to social programs slightly increased during the 1990-1994 period compared with 1989 (Table 3.6), the financial support of the welfare sector tended to decrease in real value as a consequence of the GDP decline (Table 3.7).

Table 3.6 Public Social Expenditure (percent of GDP)		Table 3.7 Real Value of Social Expenditure (1989 = 100 percent)	
1989	14.1	1989	100
1990	16.6	1990	120.3
1991	16.4	1991	109.0
1992	16.2	1992	96.0
1993	15.5	1993	77.1
1994	16.5	–	–

Source : Zamfir 1995

The composition of the public budgets since 1990 clearly indicates the reduced importance assigned to the social sector by the post-communist governments.

Figure 3.2 Main components of public expenditure, 1996

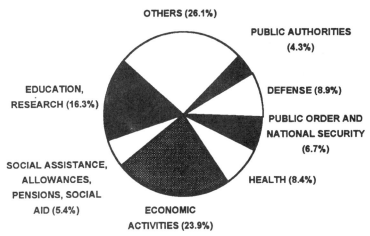

OTHERS (26.1%)

PUBLIC AUTHORITIES (4.3%)

EDUCATION, RESEARCH (16.3%)

DEFENSE (8.9%)

PUBLIC ORDER AND NATIONAL SECURITY (6.7%)

SOCIAL ASSISTANCE, ALLOWANCES, PENSIONS, SOCIAL AID (5.4%)

HEALTH (8.4%)

ECONOMIC ACTIVITIES (23.9%)

Source: MOR 1996

The share of public expenditure allocated to health, education, child-care, and other social services is constantly maintained at a low level. In contrast, the so-called economic activities, which mainly represent indirect subsidies for the inefficient state-owned companies, continue to share a major part of the government budget (Figure 3.2).

The overall underdevelopment of the Romanian economy is clearly reflected in its low profitability. For 1995, the GDP per capita was estimated by the NCS (1996) at U.S.$4,130 while independent sources used a considerably lower figure of U.S.$1,325.4 (Spineanu 1996). The consequent economic conditions are significantly impacting the living standards of the people. With the exception of some food items and energy, the price structure is increasingly market regulated. However, the average salary in Romania is among the lowest in Eastern Europe (U.S.$108.5 per month in August 1996). As opposed to this, the prices of some of the liberalized commodities are quite high in comparison with the prices of their European counterparts.

After a general increase in 1990, real wages have started to drop; they now represent 52.6 percent of the 1989 real wage (Zamfir 1995a, 422). Although, through the compulsory minimum wage, mandatory since 1993, the underpayment of specific jobs has been tentatively prevented, the continuous erosion of the overall minimum wage indicates an increasing inequality in earnings. The minimum wage dropped from 59.2 percent of the average wage in 1990 to only 30.5 percent in 1995 (UNDP 1996, 17; Zamfir 1995a, 422).

Unemployment compensation, which is provided either as unemployment benefit or as support allowance, depends on seniority in employment. Both its minimum and its maximum level are calculated in relation to the minimum wage. The minimum amount of compensation cannot go below 75 percent of the minimum wage, while the maximum amount cannot exceed the total of two minimum wages. In 1995, the average unemployment benefit represented 97.4 percent of the minimum wage, and the support allowance was only 60 percent of the minimum wage (NCS 1996).

In regard to the pensions, the situation is quite the opposite. Due to the indexation[3]/compensation policy, the difference between the minimum pension and the average pension decreased between 1990 and 1995; the ratio of the minimum to the average pension reached 88.5 percent in 1995, up from 53.5 percent in 1990. As a result of this policy, the majority of pensions (87 percent) are placed within a range of ± 10 percent of the average pension. Despite the increase in the real value of the supplementary pension, the level of the average pension remained lower than the average salary – 50.5 percent of the net average salary in 1995 (NCS 1996, 64). In the case of pensions provided by the Peasants Fund, the levels are even below those of the social aid benefits.

---

3. Adjusting the level of the wages and social benefits to the inflation rate.

III. The Social Dimension of Poverty

Generally speaking, the country's social security system has not changed radically since 1989. Although its basic components (public health fund, pension insurance, childcare allowance) have been maintained, and new ones (such as unemployment benefits, social aid benefits) have even been added, the actual social security provision is far from being adequate. The main deficiencies of the present system are the absence of coherence in the choice of principles for formulating policy and devising strategies, and the fragmented character of administration of social programs (Margineanu 1995; Zamfir 1995).

Social security in Romania depends on a combination of universal benefits (childcare allowance), insurance-based benefits (pensions, unemployment benefits, health care, maternity benefits), and a supplementary safety net provision (social aid). Childcare allowances became universal only in 1993 when full-time employment in the state-owned sector ceased to be the eligibility criterion. Accordingly, its coverage was extended to children from the families of individual farmers, the unemployed, self-employed, and privately employed persons; these were formerly excluded from benefits, both in the communist regime and in the first two years of the post-communist era. Still the eligibility for school-age children is tied to school attendance.

This increased coverage was, however, not able to produce any significant improvement as regards childcare since it occurred in a period of constant devaluation of the real allowance money. The share of GDP allocated for childcare allowances declined from 2.7 percent in 1990 to 0.9 percent in 1994; and further to 0.7 percent in 1995. Moreover, these allowances have not been adequately protected against inflation, which has led to a dramatic decrease in their real value (UNICEF 1993; Zamfir 1995a). In 1995, childcare allowances represented a meager 1.55 percent of a household's total net monetary income.

The Health Fund is the result of the employer contribution relative to the total wage bill (which stands at 2 percent) and serves to partially compensate for increases in the price of drugs and medicines. Individual eligibility is differentiated by the type of illness and the occupational status of the patient. Due to delays in the recovery of employer contributions and because of the Health Ministry's inefficient management of the fund there are difficulties in getting timely and appropriate compensation. Other components of health care are financed by the government budget. The entitlement to free medical services – which is presumed to be universal – is actually only available to those who are employed full-time or to students, pensioners, the unemployed, peasants, and the disabled. In addition, children are granted full gratuity.

The health care system in post-communist Romania has inherited an anomalous functioning from its predecessor, which the transition has rendered conspicuous. With a constantly low budget – 2 percent of GDP or 9 percent of public expenditure – medical services are constantly short on resources. This has resulted in poor facilities and equipment, and a lack of medicine and other items. In the absence of public financial support, medical institutions have had to rely on private donations (mainly international) and ask the patient's family to supply food, hygiene items, and medicine.

Following a policy rooted in the communist period, people in the medical profession continue to be distinctively underpaid. Their wages are considered to be below "efficiency" level, and medical practitioners are led, for survival reasons, to disregard contractual obligations and professional ethics (UNICEF 1993, 42). We are witnessing, in fact, a process of insinuative marketization and privatization in the public health care system. Medical personnel are getting paid directly by the client ("gifts" or "gratitude money"), and occasionally local markets are being formed for medical practice. Consequently, the quality of medical services depends upon the capability of the client to pay – the poor, who are unable to pay big fees to the doctors, get poor service; and the rich are able to buy better service with their money. Thus, the medical practice is becoming commercialized.

The insurance system which has been in place since the 1970s has two major constituents: State Social Insurance (SSI) and Farmers Social Insurance (FSI). Until recently they had separate administrations and different constitutive principles. As part of the envisioned unification, since 1992 the FSI is now administered by the SSI but still maintains its distinctive features. The SSI is based on a compulsory employer contribution which is differentiated by "work category." The proportion of the wage bill, paid by the employers, increases progressively with the degree of risk exposure, as it was defined in the communist system: 20 percent (category III); 25 percent (category II); 30 percent (category I). The work category system is based on the differentiation criteria existing in the wage policy and even introduces new ones, such as an uneven replacement ratio and different eligibility age for pensions (Labor and Social Protection Ministry 1993; Margineanu 1995). The pension plan also includes a compulsory contribution from the employees (3 percent of the gross wage) to the Supplementary Pension Fund.

Among the kinds of provision which are offered through State Social Insurance (SSI), pensions represent the most important part (90 percent in 1995). In addition to pensions, SSI also covers a number of situations, such as a temporary incapacity to work (accidents, illness, childbirth); infant care; cure, and rest. Over three million people benefit from a whole range of pensions "for work accomplished up to the age limit," sickness, disability, successor allowance, and war injuries. The pension provision is tied to the employee status and reproduces, if not reinforces, the inequality pattern generated by the salary structure. The eligibility criteria and the method of calculating pensions have remained unchanged even after the end of the communist regime. During 1990-1994, the decline in real pensions was sharper than the real average wage. In 1994, real pensions represented 45.8 percent of the 1989 level while the real average wage was 52.2 percent of its 1989 level (Zamfir 1995b, 157).

The Farmers Social Insurance (FSI) provisions cover the same range as SSI, but the cash benefits are substantially different. FSI is funded through small compulsory contributions paid by agriculture-related employers and voluntary contributions from the insured persons (which are 7 percent of the declared monthly income of the insurant). The FSI fund constantly suffers from a lack of resources and relies on transfers from SSI to cover its deficits. Consequently, the farmers receive much lower pensions and other benefits. The average pension of a farmer in 1995 was 18.6 percent of the average state insurance pension (NCS 1996).

Compensation for unemployment is paid through the Unemployment Fund which is part of the insurance system. This fund is made up from contributions by employers, who are required to contribute a sum equivalent to 5 percent of their total wage bill. Unemployment compensation is initially provided for a period of 270 days. Following this period, if a person is still unemployed he or she is eligible for the support allowance for another eighteen months. Both unemployment benefits and support allowances have preserved strong work incentive. These entitlements can be denied to an unemployed person in two situations which are considered to indicate the existence of alternative self-sufficient income sources: (1) if he or she has individual or family ownership of a farming area which exceeds 20,000 square meters in the plane or hill regions or 40,000 square meters in the mountain regions; or (2) if he or she is deriving from licensed activities an income representing at least half of the gross minimum wage after taxation. The means testing is even more restrictive in the case of support allowances. The ownership of a farming area is, as in the case of unemployment benefits, an excluding criterion. This entitlement is also denied if the unemployed person or his or her family members get at least 40 percent of the gross minimum wage from other sources. For both the provisions, the entitlement can be suspended if the insured person refuses an employment offer which matches his or her level of training and the place of work is situated within 50 kilometers of his or her home.

Income maintenance is achieved at different levels by two unemployment provisions using dissimilar formulas. The unemployment benefit is earnings related; it is different for different categories of people classified in terms of their seniority: (1) for up to three years of seniority, the benefit represents 50 percent of the net average earnings in the previous three months; (2) for those who have given five to fifteen years of service the benefit is 55 percent; and (3) for those who have served for more than fifteen years, the benefit is 60 percent. The law stipulates both minimum and maximum limits. In none of the cases can the unemployment benefit exceed twice the sum of the minimum wage. Similarly, the monthly sum cannot be lower than 75 percent of the minimum wage for the first category of the unemployed; for the second and the third categories of seniority, the lower limit is fixed at 80 percent and 85 percent respectively. The support allowance is a flat-rate benefit which represents 60 percent of the minimum wage.

The Unemployment Fund also finances the professional integration allowance which is provided to noncontributors. The eligible groups for this provision are school dropouts (sixteen years of age and above) and graduates (eighteen years of age and above) who have no source of personal income, who are unable to get employment within sixty days after leaving school or after their graduation, or who do not get more than half of the average minimum wage. Similarly, this benefit is available to those young men who were not employed before being conscripted for military service and who were unable to find a job within thirty days after their completion of military service. Handicapped children leaving their school and remaining unemployed also benefit from this plan. The integration allowance amounts to 70 percent of the minimum wage in the case of college graduates, and 60 percent in the case of pre-university and vocational school dropouts (Romanian Official Bulletin 1994; UNDP 1996).

The unemployment rate has followed an ascending curve between 1991 and 1994 – from 3.0 percent in 1991 to 10.9 percent in 1994. After 1994, the unemployment figures began to decline somewhat and fell to 6.3 percent in 1996. This clearly reflects the gradual pace of the reform processes during the first four years and the stagnation of the last two years. The continuous decline of the official figures for unemployment during 1994-1996 cannot be interpreted as a sign of economic recovery. The low rate reflects rather the containment of the transition to a market economy which resulted in the preservation of jobs despite their inefficient returns.

On the other hand, the number of persons who are eligible for these two unemployment provisions decreased significantly as proportion of the total number of unemployed people. Given the eligibility criteria, such a trend indicates a rise in long-term unemployment. Between 1993 and 1996, the eligibility ratio declined from 91.5 percent to 72.0 percent of the registered unemployed persons (UNDP 1991, 15; Statistical Bulletin 1996). Chronic unemployment and lack of employment prospects for unemployed persons aged fifty years and above have led, in 1995, to the enactment of the Early Retirement Law. Those taking early retirement – retiring five years prior to the standard retirement age – have now also become eligible for unemployment benefits, provided they have completed a required minimum years of service.

Also beginning in 1995, the employees included in layoffs resulting from the restructuring of state-owned companies were offered some options: full wage without presence at work during the notice period and a support allowance equivalent to six monthly wages or exemption from paying taxes on profit for two years, if starting a new business (PAEM 1995, 4-5).

Despite the adoption of legislation promoting active measures (training or retraining programs, wage subsidies for recent graduates), the structure of expenditure from the Unemployment Fund indicates that expenses on these items have steadily decreased from 2.9 percent in 1991 to 0.85 percent in 1995 (PAEM 1995, 5; NCS 1996, 62). The programs financed by the Unemployment Fund have been mostly ineffective in preventing long-term unemployment.

The groups which are most impacted by unemployment are manual workers (80 percent in 1996), women (52.4 percent in 1996), and young people under twenty-five years old (44.1 percent in 1995). Regardless of changes in unemployment rates, the proportion of these groups vis-à-vis the total number of the unemployed has remained high. For example, women constantly represented more than half of the total unemployed during the 1991-1996 period, but the proportion showed a descending curve from 61.8 percent in 1991 to 52.2 percent in 1996 (UNDP 1996, 15; Statistical Bulletin 1996).

The social security system is highly centralized. The revenues and insurance contributions are both administered by the government. The formal separation of the two budgets has not prevented the government from borrowing from the social insurance budget to cover deficits in the state budget. For those benefits or services which are locally provided, financial resources are distributed to the local authorities according to their estimated needs. Decision making is, however, centrally regulated.

The "social safety nets," which were critical under the communist regime, became totally inadequate during the transition to the market economy. Growing unemployment, falling wages and pensions, and difficulties in coping with changes have caused a surge of poverty which none of the existing provisions was able to alleviate. The Social Aid Law, issued by the parliament in 1995, represents an attempt to provide a last resort income to the very poor. The benefit is essentially means tested, but it sparked public controversy long before it became operational. Criticism has mainly focused on two issues: (1) the inclusion of occasional incomes in the formula used for calculating eligibility, and (2) the low level of the benefit, which is half of the subsistence level (Zamfir 1994). As the eligibility criteria are very restrictive in terms of goods and real ownership, C. Zamfir (1994, 126) thinks that the law could also become a "poverty trap" for poor people who would be tempted to sell their property in order to receive the benefit.

The provision of this benefit is based, to a large extent, on the resources of local budgets. Due to the scarcity of financial resources, both the criteria and the technicalities (the means testing) were reviewed shortly after the enactment of the law. A redefinition of the eligibility criteria was attempted by many local authorities who were unable to fund all the originally eligible persons. Thus, the criteria have become more restrictive and the work-based component of the scheme has been enhanced. The modest share of social expenditure and the GDP (0.38 percent in 1996) allocated to social aid benefits resulted in a limited coverage of the persons in real need. The present government acknowledged disparities in coverage and, in the absence of an appropriate evaluation of the plan, decided to extend its scope with 11 percent of the existing coverage and to apply a full indexation to the benefit (R.L. 1997).

At present, the social aid provision, in its actual administration, represents a mere "survival income"; it does not aim at enabling the users to have an independent life. The range of social services providing assistance in kind is very limited. As a matter of fact, the only generalized services are the residential ones. Their profile and functioning were inherited from the communist regime, and both their quality and adequacy in terms of user needs have been severely criticized ever since 1990. The notorious "orphanages" (children's homes) are typical of these kind of services. The children-in-care were not, and are not, orphans; they are either abandoned children or are children placed in residential care by their own parents. In both the cases, the family's poverty – its incapacity to fulfill the child's basic needs – is the main reason why the child is not admitted to the orphanage. In the absence of alternative services, the residential solution has been maintained and even reinforced despite the lack of cost effectiveness and increasing criticism by professionals. In the last three years, some shelters for "street children" have been organized mainly by the nongovernmental sector. An experimental program targeting needy families with children has been in place since 1995, but its further development is limited by a lack of resources. The family support services are locally administered and have been financially assisted by national and international NGOs.

At present, no assistance is provided to the homeless. During the winter of 1996 an attempt was made to temporarily host them in hospitals. The solution, however, proved to be fairly unrealistic and benefited a very limited number of people.

The "social canteen" is a means-tested service administered by local authorities and aims at providing hot meals to people with an income level close to the one which entitles a person to the social aid benefit. The eligibility criteria for this are defined regionally. While there is no clear evidence, officials and journalists have commented that the coverage is insufficient and that the system is abused by some people.

In the absence of any research evidence, it is difficult to identify either a single coherent discourse or a multiplicity of group-based ones. Although there is no empirical basis, some assumptions on collective attitudes have already been made both in academic literature and in the media. One of the most articulate contributions in this field is that of C. Zamfir which was made prior to the enactment of the Law on Social Aid. Referring to the "moral and political acceptability of social aid benefits," the author believes that the "possible attitude" of people toward the provision of social aid is shaped by the following underlying beliefs: (1) that groups whose vulnerability/difficulties are essentially beyond their control (old age, chronic illness, handicap) have an unconditional right to social solidarity and support; (2) that groups whose difficulties could be dealt with by an increase in personal effort and responsibility do not necessarily have this right.

Two categories are mentioned here: families with many children and the unemployed. In the first case, the author thinks that having a large number of children, which is likely to exceed the family resources, tends to be perceived as irresponsible behavior. Therefore, a social benefit which is provided irrespective of the size of the family is likely to be negatively perceived by the public. It should be mentioned that a very high, if not the highest birth rate, in Romania is recorded among the Gipsies. With respect to unemployment, Zamfir assumes that the public opinion perceives that it is not totally inevitable and is consequently remediable, at least in the long run. According to the belief that "whoever wants to work will find a job," the state is expected to create jobs rather than provide social benefits. It is difficult to estimate if, and to what extent, such a perception is shared by the nonpoor population. What can be said without much doubt, however, is that the attitudes that Zamfir considers to be specific to the Romanian population are imbued with the old ideology of the deserving/undeserving poor.

Data which could support an analysis of the politics of poverty are extremely scarce. Due to the quasi-generalization of the poverty risk, all the trade unions think that they can deal with poverty through their salary claims – hence the emphasis in their negotiations on the minimum wage. The nongovernmental sector concentrates on poor children, trying to alleviate their poverty through support in cash or in kind. The advocacy activities meant to enhance the political rights of the poor have had no significant results so far. Of course, there is no countermovement or antagonism against the poor. If there is any, it is against those individuals or groups that are not "genuinely" poor and are suspected of abusing the social welfare system.

The findings made available by opinion polls give some indication of the relationship between political orientation and self-perceived living standard. It is noticeable that those saying that their income is "not sufficient for meeting the bare necessities" tend to be either politically indecisive (37.5 percent) or supportive of the left-oriented parties – like the party in power until 1996 – (32.9 percent), rather than voting for the rightist parties (the present governing coalition). Although less pronounced, this trend is also present among persons perceiving themselves as having an income which is "strictly sufficient for the bare necessities" (CURS 1995). A regional analysis of voting behavior confirms this political orientation. Electoral support for the former president (a candidate supported by left-oriented parties) was very pronounced in the districts ranking lowest on the Human Development Index (HDI).

Conclusion

Romania had a comparatively late start in the reform process and hesitantly pursued the decisive steps needed for privatization and marketization. The continuous postponement of structural changes has not prevented any of the alleged "evils" generally associated with "shock therapy": hyperinflation, unemployment, the increased vulnerability of weaker social groups, and an overall deterioration of living standards. The absence of coherent macroeconomic adjustments left room for illegal privatization and created a favorable context for the expansion of the informal economy. Despite the official position that the consequences of unreported economic activities are entirely negative and, therefore, need to be restricted, some public statements made by the authorities have suggested that the informal economy is an unwanted but real supplement to, or replacement of, unemployment benefits.

The deteriorating condition of the public services and the low level of benefits are generally associated with poor economic performance. There is no doubt that the modest value of the GDP in recent years, and the moderate prospects for economic growth, do not allow Romania to spend much on social provisions. The structure of public expenditure indicates that the role of the state in the social sectors has tended to be minimal in recent years. Many analysts believe that minimalist social policies have been recommended to, even imposed on, the Romanian government by agencies such as the IMF and the World Bank (UNICEF 1993; Zamfir 1995a; Margineanu 1995). Although the important impact of these agencies cannot be denied, the government's own electoral agenda must not be underestimated. The groups with a political voice have been the winners in the short term while those with no political voice have been the losers in the long term (Popescu 1995).

The reform of social policy must be based on decentralization. Transparency in bureaucratic procedure is essential to transform decision making into a democratic and efficient process. The intermediate institutions – professional associations, citizens/clients groups, voluntary organizations – must be accepted as legitimate partners and must be encouraged to express themselves in public debates.

Research on poverty had a late start in Romania. There is a need to refine existing methods and techniques and adapt others. The small size of the academic community in the social sciences, as well as a lack of financial resources, are major obstacles in the pursuit of scientific research on poverty. Furthermore, it will be desirable to develop a regional cross-cultural comparative project so that social scientists from different countries can jointly develop new methodologies that are relevant for the region, and can learn from each other's experiences. True, a regional project may not solve all the problems, but it will certainly help overcome some of them. Such an endeavor may lead to the development of a more adequate methodology for poverty analysis while addressing questions such as these: How do we differentiate between absolute and relative poverty? How do we capture all the dimensions of the poverty phenomenon? What theoretical approach should we adapt or develop? What is the impact of the government's political orientation and real policies on the dynamics of poverty? This project initiated by UNESCO is a first, and useful, step in that direction.

Bibliography

Center for Urban and Rural Sociology (CURS). 1997. *National Opinion Poll.* Bucuresti: Fundatia Soros pentru o Societate Deschisa.

Labor and Social Protection Ministry. 1993. *Cartea Alba a Reformei Asigurarilor Sociale si Pensiilor.* Bucuresti: Departamentul informatiilor publice.

Margineanu, I. 1995. "Asigurarile sociale." In *Politici Sociale. Romania in Context European,* ed. E. Zamfir and C. Zamfir. Bucuresti: Editura Alternative.

Monitorul Oficial al Romaniei (MOR). 1996. *Monitorul Oficial al Romaniei,* vol. VIII, no. 298. Bucuresti.

National Commission for Statistics (NCS). 1994. *Romanian Statistical Yearbook.* Bucharest.

_____. 1995. "Dimensiunea Sociala si coalitia guvernamentala." *Romania Libera,* 20 May.

_____. 1996a. "Veniturile, cheltuielile si consumul populatiei." *Informatii statistice operative,* Nos.1-2.

_____. 1996b. *Starea sociala si economica a Romaniei in anul 1995.* Bucuresti.

PAEM. 1995. *Local Initiatives for Employment in Romania.* Bucharest: Fiman.

Plesca M., and C. Rata. 1996. *Welfare in Romania during Transition: Analysis of FBS Data (1989, 1992, 1993).* Technical Report. Charles University: Center for Economic Research and Graduate Education.

Popescu, L. 1995. "State and Market in Romanian Social Policy." Paper presented at the international conference *Transition to What? The Implications of Privatization in Eastern Europe, the European Union, the Balkans, and Beyond,* Democratus University of Thrace, Komotini, Greece, 26 June-2 July 1995.

Serbanescu, I. 1994. *Jumatatile de Masura Dubleaza Costurile Sociale.* Bucuresti: Editura Staff.

_____. 1995. "De unde sa mai vina schimbarea?" "22" 22: 4-5.

Spineanu, U. 1996. Documentar RL. *Romania Libera.*

UNDP. 1991. *Romanian Human Development Report.* Bucharest.

_____. 1996. *Romanian Human Development Report.* Bucharest.

UNICEF. 1993. *Central and Eastern Europe in Transition: Public Policy and Social Conditions.* Regional Monitoring Report 1. Florence: ICDC.

Vosganian, V. 1994. *Jurnal de Front.* Bucuresti: Editura Staff.

Zamfir, E., and C. Zamfir, eds. 1993. *Tiganii intre ignorare si ingrijorare.* Bucuresti: Editura Alternative.

Zamfir, C. 1995a. "Politica sociala in Romania in tranzitie." In *Politici Sociale: Romania in Context European,* ed. E. Zamfir and C. Zamfir. Bucuresti: Editura Alternative.

_____. 1995b. "Politica de Protectie Sociala." *Cercetari Sociale* 1: 156-72.

Zamfir, C., ed. 1995c. *Dimensiuni ale saraciei.* Bucuresti: Editura Expert.

Chapter Four

TOWARD POVERTY ERADICATION IN GEORGIA

Avtandil Sulaberidze
Institute of Demography and Sociological Research

Introduction

Georgia lost its independence as a state when it was annexed to the Soviet Union as one of its provinces. During this long historical period Georgia's consciousness was devastated, and it grew excessively dependent upon the economy of the USSR. It was isolated from the West and remained backwards in many respects. The opportunity to regain state independence came with the collapse of the USSR. Georgia began nourishing the rather unrealizable ambition to recover its lost ground in a short span of time and regain its place in the world community.

Similar to other post-communist countries, Georgia did not hesitate to initiate a process of reforms. And, similar to other countries, Georgia is also experiencing a certain disillusionment with regard to a quick transition to a rapidly developing economy. In its desire to speedily transform into a non-communist economy, the country somehow overlooked the fact that developmental plans need to be adapted to the cultural specificities and developmental needs of each country. The old mentality of revolutionary development surfaced, and less attention was devoted to the strategy of evolutionary socio-economic development. This resulted in an excessively radical course of reforms. The "shock therapy" model, used blindly and spontaneously following the persistent demands of a great number of scientists and politicians, brought about adverse socio-economic consequences and plunged the country into civil war and a series of ethnic conflicts. From the very beginning, the transition process deviated from its original course and took a wrong turn. This was caused by existing internal and external political problems, and was aggravated by natural disasters. And then the civil war and ethnic conflicts contributed to a drastic increase in the number of internally displaced persons (IDPs), whose social protection in this transformation period turned out to be a task of inordinate complexity.

The transition from an administrative command economy to a market economy is taking place against the background of a severe socio-economic crisis. To a certain extent, this is predetermined by various internal and external, objective and subjective factors. In contrast to the post-communist countries of Eastern Europe, the former Soviet republics needed to construct an independent economic complex. This meant overcoming a number of economic problems, such as the excessive economic integration of the USSR, which resulted in narrow specializations; the country's excessive dependence on delivered power sources and raw materials; the unavailability of spare parts; and a lack of technical assistance. These problems impeded the full production cycle and created difficulties in developing an independent economic system.

The rapid realization of reforms, in its turn, meant the following: creation of new proprietary relations, liberalization of prices, liberalization of trade, macroeconomic stabilization, privatization, liberalization of the labor market, the decentralization of governance and reorganization of industry, in-depth reconsideration of external trade, a search for new markets and a revival of old economic links, large-scale and profound institutional changes, etc. However, given the extremely difficult and truly unprecedented background against which the reforms were to take place, a large number of difficulties were encountered. In this, a certain responsibility must be assigned to subjective factors, such as political and criminal instability, civil war, politico-economic confrontation with the Russian Federation, an influx of refugees, and a rise in the number of the unemployed.

The complexity of the process of socio-economic transformation resulted in a drastic fall in the standard of living of the people. Due to the frequent change of government and ad hoc economic decision making, the country failed to identify an appropriate socio-economic strategy in a timely fashion. This resulted in a number of negative social consequences. In the period from 1991 to 1996, the number of unemployed increased from 180,000 to approximately 800,000. The social situation was aggravated by the introduction, in 1993, of the interim currency coupon, and by the monetary credit emission. Frequent correction of salaries due to commodity deficits intensified inflation processes and undermined the real income of the population (in particular, in the course of this period the minimum salary was reviewed five times, and its nominal level underwent a 22.4-fold increase). In the period from 1993 to 1994, which was the most critical one, the portion of labor remuneration in the subsistence minimum fell dramatically from 25.2 percent to 0.07 percent (according to the combination of 134 appellations of goods and services for an active adult male).

Given its socio-economic development and living standard, Georgia was recognized by experts as a Third World developing country. According to the UNDP's 1991 Human Development Report, Georgia held the sixtieth place in the international hierarchy in terms of the human development index (HDI). While this placement is acceptable, a point must be made here. Historically, the developed countries have been characterized by social inequality, and even today, a large part of their population lives below the poverty line. In contrast, Georgia, like other post-communist countries, enjoyed a certain social well-being under the communist regime, and the manifest social differentiation in living standards used to be less visible. Of course, the quality of life was below the modern standards of developed countries; but whatever living standard was maintained, all people had the same standard. That is why, during the previous regime, under the conditions of guaranteed employment and with free state social services, the concepts of unemployment and poverty were unknown.

People's expectations about moving to a market economy are being frustrated. They have become skeptical about the promises made by the reformers and about the new course chosen for development, because rather than improving, their situation has deteriorated in the changed milieu. The monetary, credit, and tax policies – carried out under the strict requirements of the International Monetary Fund and the World Bank – and the improvement of the internal political and criminal situation have created certain conditions for socio-economic stabilization in the country, but the state budget continually runs in deficit and does not permit the implementation of an effective social policy. The population itself has created a certain social protection mechanism.

Georgia is a country with a rather developed informal economy and a social structure built on strong kinship ties. In the present moment of crisis, the population has drawn on these resources. These very factors also contribute to further strengthening of the shadow economy. There is a lack of appropriate propaganda activities in favor of the market economy; these should be implemented along with the process of reforms and should aim to replace the communist mentality of free social protection with a new one, adapted to the market economy.

I. Measurements and Definitions of Poverty

Up until recently social research in Georgia was guided by communist ideology. The methodology used was highly charged ideologically, and many of the terms now being used were nonexistent in the literature. It was only at the end of 1980s, that the approach toward the problem changed. Previously categories and terms such as "consumer basket" and "subsistence minimum" were hardly mentioned. "Poverty" is now seen as a new phenomenon and has become the subject of much research in Georgia. The majority of authors (L. Chikava, I. Meskhia, L. Papava, I. Gogidze, A. Tsakadze, I. Archvadze, A. Sulaberidze, K. Kakhniashvili, R. Khorbelia, G. Grigolashvili, etc.) working on this theme have an innovative approach, and there are very few methodological differences between them.

The living level is calculated by means of a system of quantitative and qualitative indices, which express the level and extent of consumption of the gross national product (GNP) per person at a given point in time. In spite of the fact that the gross national product includes income earned both in material and nonmaterial spheres, it represents a very capacious macroeconomic index and gives us an idea of the financial situation of the country. It does not, however, include the results of transactions taking place outside of the market (results of the informal economy of both a positive and negative nature, free time and its utilization, the expansion of production and its accompanying negative results, etc.).

Together with the above-mentioned, the following variables defining the living level of a population are used by the scholars: real wages, real income, the level and structure of consumption, level of education and culture, level of medical service, the provision of apartments (housing), and population indices such as life expectancy at birth. The scientists attach particular importance to the concept of *subsistence minimum* while defining poverty. What can serve as a basis for determining this minimum? The consumer basket of one active adult male or the family budget? Given the physiological norms, should it include, apart from necessary produce, the service tariffs? What are the most essential foodstuffs which are to be included in the consumer basket taking into consideration physiological norms, and so on? Here, we have to mention that in the former post-communist European states, to say nothing of Western Europe, for quite a long time the subsistence minimum has constituted approximately 35-40 percent of the medium wage of the country. As for Georgia, this is impossible since the medium wage constitutes 37 percent of the subsistence minimum! Thus, this problem should be solved quickly.

Therefore, our approach to the problem is as follows: since the poverty line is much above the minimum wage, we have to introduce additional indices and criteria to define the poverty level. This permits us to follow the mutability of the direction of poverty – from absolute poverty up to the limit of the official subsistence minimum. According to many scholars, the subsistence minimum should be considered as the absolute poverty limit. We fully share this view, but only in conditions of a better and higher standard of living. In the case of Georgia, the following socio-economic categories and indices must be introduced: poverty line (subsistence minimum), physiological poverty (quota determined below subsistence minimum), and absolute poverty (a person without income). This model can also be used to study the subsistence minimum of the family. It enables us to better determine the most socially unprotected populations, and makes social policy much more purposeful.

The compilation method of an emergency consumer basket, elaborated by the authors of the UNDP Human Development Report is quite interesting and useful. It allows the calculation of the *minimum income* required, in a given month by persons of different age and sex groups or by an average family, to survive the present period. The calculations here differ in several respects from other, similar calculations: only those items are included that are considered absolutely essential at the present time; in this sense the basket approaches the concept of a poverty line. The food content of the basket is 2470 calories for an active male adult and correspondingly less for other groups. One major omission is cigarettes which, according to the survey, were and still are commonly bought, but are excluded from the basket as nonessential. The reasoning behind the exclusion of most items of clothing is that most people are now forced to make do with what they have (using their old clothes, furnishings, and utensils), hoping to renew them when times improve. No allowance is made, therefore, as is normally done in consumer baskets, for the maintenance, renewal, or acquisition of new equipment. The exceptions are items such as winter shoes, likely to wear out quickly, or oil, wood, and electric heaters and stoves required because of the lack of central heating and, intermittently, gas. It would be unrealistic to assume an unchanged basket throughout the year when the purpose is to gauge the cost of living.

In calculating the minimum cost of living of a family of four persons (or any other family size), the savings effect of communal living is smaller than it normally is. On the assumption that each individual is consuming the minimum amount of food, by definition nothing can be saved in pooling food – moreover, food is a considerably larger constituent of the total basket in Georgia than is the case in Europe generally. Items that normally benefit from pooling, such as furnishings, a television, or household utensils, are virtually absent from the basket.

The only major saving is in fuel, since a light bulb or cooking stove serves a small family almost as well in Georgia as it does an individual. No allowance, even formally, is made for rent, which would be a major expense in Western Europe. Most people in Georgia live rent-free in their own accommodations (recently conferred on them by the state) or with relatives.

The cost of maintaining an adult in reasonable health in the current emergency situation, as of 1 January 1995, is calculated at $31 per month. Corresponding costs for other groups are given in Table 4.1.

Table 4.1 The subsistence minimum for various types of family members

Type of person	Weights (in relation to an adult male = 1)		Rubles	U.S. dollars
	food	nonfood		
Active adult male (20-59)	1.0	1.0	127,900	31.2
Active adult female (20-54)	0.8	1.0	113,200	27.6
Adolescent (15-19)	1.0	0.8	117,000	28.5
Child (average, 0-14)	0.7	0.7	89,500	21.8
male pensioner (60-)	0.7	0.8	95,000	23.2
female pensioner (55-)	0.6	0.8	87,700	21.4
Average*	0.86	0.88	111,800	27.0

*Weighted average for Georgia, using ratios as above and numbers of persons in the respective sex and age groups as weights.

Source: HDR, Georgia 1995

As an example, the cost of maintaining a family of four persons consisting of an adult male and female, a child under fifteen, and a female pensioner is U.S.$94. Note that the amount is less than the sum of the individual values. An allowance has been made for the cost of sharing items such as fuel, light, and related equipment.[1]

Various humanitarian organizations working in Georgia use their own definitions of poverty. In order to identify families in need of assistance, Larry Dershem *(Food, Nutrition, Health, and Nonfood Vulnerability in Georgia, 1996: A Household Assessment)* determined food and nutrition vulnerability by using the criterion of "a minimal level of food security" at the household level and the consumption of only a limited number of food items by the household. Causes that contribute to food insecurity and malnutrition are multiple. Food security is partly based

1. The methodology is close to that developed by I.K. Gogodze and A.D. Tsakadze in "Determining Indicators for the Subsistence Minimum and Minimum Wage."

both on the ability of the household to produce food and its access to land. On the other hand, a household's purchasing power enables it to procure the necessary food and contribute to household's food security. The inability of a household to produce, or procure, food will affect the overall food basket of all the household members. The availability of various coping strategies within a household can ensure better food security and help to avoid short-term malnutrition. The extent of coping strategies and the length of time these strategies are used will also determine food security at the household level.

Compared to other definitions, this definition is broad in that nutritional needs are not linked either to cultural habits or to preferences of individual members of the household. The reasoning behind this definition is that the current food assistance situation in Georgia is probably related more to specific cases and less to the overall food needs of certain vulnerable groups in the population. It must be emphasized that the definition of food or nutritional vulnerability should not depend on the status of any particular individual in a household. Rather, it should depend upon the food security of the whole household – its ability to avoid situations in which one person can qualify for food assistance based on certain criteria, while the rest of the household is able to have a high standard of living either through their own production or a high income. In spite of certain shortcomings, this approach is generally accepted for studying household budgets, since in Georgia several generations usually live together and share a common budget.

The law on the subsistence minimum, passed in 1996 by the Georgian state parliament, is officially used for defining poverty. According to this law, the subsistence minimum constitutes the monetary expression of the minimum consumer goods needed, in accordance with the socio-economic development of the country, to ensure the satisfaction of normal physiological and social needs of a citizen. The law stresses that calculation of the subsistence minimum should be made on the basis of current average (purchase) prices. Through this, the figures for a consumer basket are compiled, taking into consideration the minimum norms of consumption of foodstuffs. At the same time, using the same norms, expenses for non-food items and for other essential services are computed; these reflect the actual level of consumption. The food basket of one adult male serves as a basis for the identification of the subsistence minimum.

The law on the subsistence minimum is of great political importance since it provides a guiding line for social policy. Subsistence minimum and poverty line are synonymous, but in reality the minimum wage is far below the subsistence minimum. Unfortunately, due to this, the parliament, at the second reading of the above-mentioned law, excluded from it the paragraph saying that "subsistence minimum and poverty line are synonyms." Because of this anomaly, the law could be considered "stillborn." However, this law is particularly necessary today because it (1) serves as a basis for the formation of state policy in the social sphere; (2) provides a guideline for the elaboration of a mechanism of state regulation of real incomes; and (3) determines directions for reducing the gap between the subsistence minimum and minimum wage, and for their equalization.

The government of Georgia embarked on the calculation of the subsistence minimum in 1995, even before the adoption of this law. Thanks to the assistance provided by international organizations, its methodology has been constantly improving and it nearly reflects the present social situation. Following requests by various international humanitarian organizations, this method is universally applied to determine the minimum income for a person or a family. The contents of the food basket are defined by merging normative and statistical methods. The first method takes into consideration minimum norms of foodstuff consumption, while the second measures the real consumption level. The minimum food basket and its price are calculated for an active adult male; the price of the minimum food basket for other groups of consumers is calculated in proportion to the normative need for calories. Presently the food basket includes thirty-eight kinds of foodstuffs and gas.

The assessment of the joint consumption effect is based on statistical regularities coming from the household assessment. By means of the existing methodology, the following types of consumers are defined, in accordance with their age:

1. preschool-aged child (0-7)
2. adolescent (7-16)
3. active adult male (16-65)
4. active adult female (16-60)
5. male pensioner (65-)
6. female pensioner (60-)

Families are classified into six categories according to their size, as follows: one-member family, two-member family, three-member family, four-member family, five-member family, six-and-above-member family.

The Ministry of Health determines and, when necessary, reviews, contents of the food basket as well as the norms of basic calories and foodstuffs for various types of consumers. Such revision is made every five years (the last revision was done in 1994). The social standard is defined and reviewed annually by the Ministry of Social Security, Labor, and Employment in coordination with the trade unions. The reason for revision of this parameter can be either changes in the real structure of expenses subject to the data coming from the household assessment, or the corresponding change in the structure of value of the complete minimum basket. Changes in the structure of expenses are determined by the State Department of Socio-Economic Information.

In the period from 1994 to 1996, under the aegis of various international organizations, special "selective observations" were carried out on the employment level, income, and the distribution of social assistance. On the basis of these observations and our own studies, we present an analysis of the changes taking place in Georgia in regard to poverty during the last five years. Some tables are compiled on the basis of the official statistical information.

Table 4.2 Minimum tax-free wage, minimum normative wage, and subsistence minimum, 1992-1996 (calculated for one family in U.S. dollars)

Particulars	1992	1993	1994	1995	1996
Minimum tax-free wage	4.1	0.3	0.7	4.8	7.1
Minimum normative wage per one person employed in a four-member family	11.0	21.1	28.1	43.4	34.2
Subsistence minimum for a four-member family	34.1	62.5	84.5	132.7	150.6
Percentage of minimum tax-free wage - with minimum normative wage	37.3	1.4	2.5	11.1	21.0
- with subsistence minimum calculated for one member in a four-member family	48.1	1.9	3.3	14.5	18.9

Before analyzing Table 4.2, we consider it necessary to briefly explain the data it contains. The minimal tax-free wage is approved by the state. It is more or less stable over the course of the year and is not subject to taxation (9 lari ~ 7 U.S. dollars). Apart from this, there is also a minimum wage (12 lari ~ 9.4 U.S. dollars) which is taxable. Basically, the minimum tax-free wage is used to analyze the living level. It should be noted that both types of minimum wages are symbolic, since they do not even reflect the cost of foodstuffs necessary for survival, to say nothing of the subsistence minimum.

Since, in principle, the minimum wage should reflect (be equal to) the subsistence minimum of the individual, and the state is unable to ensure this, a law on minimum wage has not yet been discussed in parliament. This, in its turn, has resulted in the parliament's inability to pass a full-fledged law on the subsistence minimum.

As one indicator of the living level, the government has introduced a third calculated version of the minimum wage, which shows the amount of the minimum wage necessary, in addition to other incomes, for one member of an average (four-member) family to live at the level of the subsistence minimum. This calculated indicator represents, to a certain extent, the reference point of the subsistence minimum. It helps us analyze the living level, since the difference between it and the minimal tax-free wage shows us the "poverty gap" which is to be "filled" by the state.

As becomes clear from the above table, in 1992-1996 the rate of growth of the minimal tax-free wage fell behind the rate of growth of the level of minimal normative wage per one member of the family. It is true that in comparison with 1994-1995, the "poverty gap" underwent a decrease in 1996, but it is still rather high and amounts to U.S.$27.10. The ratio between the minimal tax-free wage and minimal normative wage in 1996 (21.0 percent) still falls far behind the similar index of 1992 (37.2 percent) and represents only 55.8 percent of the 1992 level, to say nothing of "the golden times" of the 1980s. The above data point at the extreme level of poverty in Georgia.

The acceleration of the equalization of the tax-free wage with minimal normative wage is rather desirable, but this is a difficult task to accomplish, given the difficulties faced by the country; it depends on many socio-economic factors. Therefore, we consider it important to briefly examine some of them. In the first place, we need to mention change in the price index. In December 1996, its change, in comparison with December 1995, accounted to 113.5 percent, and was equal to 1.05 percent per month. In comparison with previous years, this is very low; and the low inflation level of 1996 which was far below the expected 29.0 percent perplexed even optimists. In 1995 the liberalization of the price of bread took place, followed by 12.7 percent inflation, although this caused no significant modifications in overall price dynamics.

In October 1995, the introduction of the national currency lari resulted in a 23.4 percent increase in prices over the course of the month, but the situation stabilized in November. Table 4.3 below shows the price index according to commodity groups in December 1996 in comparison with December 1995.

It should be noted that the strengthening of the national currency, the lari, entailed stabilizing prices in the market, although they nearly reached the level of world standards. The reinforcement of the lari is basically the result of transfers from the World Bank and the International Monetary Fund, and not due to economic recovery; this endangers the future solidity of the lari as compared to the dollar (on 1 January 1997, the exchange rate was as follows: 1 U.S. dollar = 1.27-1.29 lari).

Since, against the background of high market prices the economy still does not function properly, salaries are low and the purchasing power of the lari decreased to a certain extent. This, together with other factors

Table 4.3 Fluctuation in the consumer price index according to certain commodity groups, 1995-1996

Commodity and service groups	Fluctuation in indexation price index, 1995-1996
Total	113.5
Foodstuffs, beverages, and tobacco	108.1
Clothes and footwear	112.2
Rent, water, heating, and electricity supplies	117.3
Household goods	117.3
Medical care	129.4
Transport and communication	204.9
Leisure, education, and culture	107.2
Consumer services and hygiene	140.0

Source: Georgian Department of Socio-Economic Information 1997, 18

(for instance, a high level of unemployment and economic difficulties caused by the energy crisis) resulted in a significant increase in the cost of living. Therefore, a large section of population is forced to purchase low-quality foreign foodstuffs (mainly produced by Turkey and Iran) whose purchase dates have expired, since they are far cheaper than local products (if such exist). This, apart from socio-economics, raises the problem of the eco-demographic development of the country – the reproduction of the population, since the birth rate has decreased drastically with the increases in disease, mortality (especially among children), and sterile marriages. An important part of the population has left Georgia to go abroad (to the Russian Federation or West European countries) in search of employment. There is an increase in crime, drug addiction, and prostitution, all of which have reached levels never known before in Georgia.

According to official statistics, at the end of 1996, about 45.0 percent of the total population was economically active, 79.0 percent of whom were employed (77.0 percent as employees, 23.0 percent self-employed). The year 1996 was notable in many organizations and enterprises for prolonged vacations without pay, for temporary unemployment, as well as for staff reduction in state organizations and institutions. Against this background, we believe that the official statistical data mentioned above is a bit exaggerated.

In 1996 the salaries of those employed in certain branches of the economy slightly increased. As a result, the average monthly salary of an employed person underwent a 2.3-fold increase in comparison with previous years and amounted to U.S.$27.30. Simultaneously, it underwent a 3.3-fold increase in budget organizations, amounting to U.S.$21.10, and a fourfold increase in nonbudget organizations, amounting to U.S.$35.20. The salaries of those employed in the private sector are two to three times higher than of those employed at state and budget organizations. The results of the research conducted in the city of Tbilisi showed that the production income of one producer from Tbilisi amounted to 351.60 U.S. dollars, which is three times higher than the incomes of those employed in the private sector and twelve to thirteen times more than the salaries of state-sector employees.

In 1996, the old age pension amounted to 6.64 U.S. dollars. According to the situation of 1 January 1997, 27 percent of the unemployed registered at the State Employment Service benefitted from support amounting to 6.16 U.S. dollars per person in December.

The official information which appears in Table 4.4 below, gives us an idea of the 1996 poverty level in Georgia.

Table 4.4 Subsistence minimum dynamics, July-December 1996 (in lari)

Month	Active adult male	Average consumer	Average statistical family	1	2	3	4	5	6 and more	Minimum normative wage
				— Number of family members						
July	106.8	93.7	187.4	93.7	150.0	168.7	187.4	210.9	292.4	42.3
August	106.6	93.5	187.0	93.5	149.6	166.3	187.0	210.4	291.7	42.5
September	107.2	94.1	186.5	91.1	150.6	169.3	188.1	211.6	293.5	42.6
October	107.0	93.9	187.8	93.9	150.2	169.0	187.8	211.8	292.9	42.7
November	107.8	94.6	189.2	94.6	151.3	170.3	189.2	212.8	295.1	49.2
December	104.4	91.6	183.2	91.6	146.6	164.9	183.2	206.1	285.8	41.5

On the basis of the minimum monthly food basket, it is assumed that over the course of a long period of time, the nourishment expenses constitute a fixed part of an overall amount of expenses. It should be noted that, according to research done in 1996, nourishment expenses decreased to 53.0 percent of the overall family budget (compared to 62.0 percent in 1995). In spite of certain increases in the minimum normative wage, the percentage of a minimum tax-free wage and of a subsistence minimum remains unfavorable, being, in October 1996, only 9.6 percent for the average consumer and 8.4 percent for an active adult male. It is true that in December both subsistence minimum indices underwent a decrease, but the ratio of the subsistence minimum and the minimum tax-free wage introduced no tangible changes.

Figure 4.1 Distribution of the average wage by education level, 1995 (in lari)

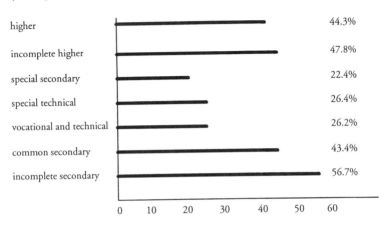

Theoretically, in the conditions of the liberalization of the labor market, better education should be a prerequisite for a certain advantage in wage. This was completely neglected during the Soviet period, when brainwork was not adequately reimbursed. As shown in Figure 4.1, this tendency still continues to exist in the transition period. The reason for this is that the labor market is still not able to create conditions which would stimulate the improvement of qualifications, while the sphere of business requires highly educated people. According to the findings of the joint research conducted in Tbilisi, the labor remuneration of an employed individual with a secondary education was one-third higher than that of an individual with higher education. The situation remains precarious in national research institutes, where many scientists are in search of alternative incomes. Under these circumstances, many of these institutes are likely to stop functioning. And should that happen, it will definitely result in an overcrowding of the labor market by unemployed intellectuals.

As for the structure of real income in the population, the official statistics take no account of a family's income from its own activities and from other sources, including the informal economy. According to the dynamics of combined household income given in Table 4.5, the most difficult year for Georgia was 1993, when incomes fell sharply and simultaneously increased the portion of food expenses in overall expenses. The point is that it was precisely in 1993 that the Interim Currency Coupon was introduced, which suffered a very quick devaluation and, in the conditions of hyperinflation which continued until October 1995, seriously affected family budgets. Table 4.5 confirms that incomes

Table 4.5   Dynamics of Combined Household Income, 1990-1995 (1995 consumer price index prices)

	unit of measurement	1990	1991	1992	1993	1994	1995
incomes, including those received in kind	million laris	3650	3430.8	1661.3	762.6	1223.5	1384.9
	in % 1990 = 100%	100.0	94.0	45.5	20.9	33.5	37.9
incomes, excluding those received in kind	million laris	3358.1	2927.0	1001.9	380.5	430.3	655.5
	in % 1990 = 100%	100.0	87.2	29.2	11.3	12.8	19.5
portion of food expenses in overall expenses	in %	45	53	66	74	61	62

received in kind play an important role in family incomes, and that their share has been increasing sharply beginning from 1990. Without incomes received in kind, many families would have died of malnutrition. For example, if in 1990 the difference between family incomes (including those received in kind) and family incomes (excluding those received in kind) was 292,000 lari, in 1993 (the peak of crisis) it increased to 322,100 lari, and in 1995 to 729,400 lari – after 1993 the incomes received in kind exceeded those received in cash. It is precisely here that the paradox is hidden which amazed foreign experts: people living below the poverty line are not suffering. Therefore, if not for undisclosed income, the social part of the state budget would have increased considerably.

We believe that in determining the poverty level, the amount of the wage is a rather unreliable parameter and does not speak fully about the family income. During the period of transformation, households are relying on a multiplicity of monetary (wages, remittances) and non-monetary income (food produced and consumed from a family farm, exchange of goods and services).

The study, *Vulnerability in Georgia, 1996* (team leader Dr. Larry D. Dershem) has identified thirteen sources of family income. The total sum of the individual incomes of 1205 families in the survey sample amounted to 345,166 lari, approximately 286.4 lari per family. We compared this study, conducted in eight regions of Georgia, with analogous studies carried out by the World Bank with 500 families (Tbilisi, June 1995 and 1996) and matched the results with the U.S. situation in Table 4.6 below.

According to Table 4.6, whereas the results of Dershem's study do not differ tangibly from the results of the 1995 World Bank study, this differ-

Table 4.6 Distribution of family incomes by quintiles in percentages

Quantum groups	Study by the World Bank, June 1995	Study by Dershem, February1996; percentage from the unified income	Study by the World Bank, June 1996	Family incomes in the U.S. in 1984
First quintile (the poorest)	1.5	1.0	2.7	5.0
Second quintile	4.3	4.6	6.7	11.0
Third quintile	9.0	9.8	12.4	17.0
Fourth quintile	18.0	19.1	20.3	24.0
Fifth quintile (the richest)	67.3	65.5	57.9	43.0

ence increases drastically as far as the 1996 World Bank study findings are concerned. Thus, in a four-to-five-month period following the Dershem study, the redistribution of incomes underwent certain modifications, which can be explained by seasonal factors. In particular, family incomes in February were smaller than during the summer period. With a view to examining this issue more precisely, let us again refer to the study carried out by Dershem in February 1996. The analysis of this study reveals that households rely primarily on three sources of income: (1) salary, wages, or personal business/income activities (86.0 percent); (2) state benefits (40.3 percent); and (3) loans from money lenders (23.9 percent). The primary nonmonetary income source reported was from food produced and consumed from the family plot (53.2 percent). There are differences between urban and rural households in regard to their reliance on various sources of income. A greater percentage of urban households rely on salary, wages, and personal business (91.5 percent) than rural households (80.3 percent). In contrast, a greater percentage of rural households rely on food from their plot (91.7 percent), on state benefits (43.1 percent), and on the use of previous savings (20.8 percent) than do urban households (26.2 percent, 38.4 percent, and 18.1 percent respectively).

In terms of rank, ordering the regions by the highest average monthly household income for February 1996, the region with the highest average is Kakheti (624 lari), followed by Guria (420 lari), Achara (401 lari), Samagrelo (397 lari), Kvemo Kartli (231 lari), Shida Kartli (224 lari), Tbilisi (214 lari), and Imereti (175 lari). The two regions in which salary, wages, and/or personal business represent a larger percentage of the monthly household income than in other regions are Tbilisi (47 percent) and Achara (43 percent). Compared to other regions, households in Shida Kartli and Imereti rely more on state benefits for their monthly household income (14 percent each). State benefits represent a greater proportion of the household income since the average monthly income is comparatively low in these two regions. In addition, these regions have a higher proportion of households containing disabled members. The nonmonetary value of food grown and consumed by the household represents a greater proportion of household monthly income in Guria (64 percent), Kakheti (49 percent), and Kvemo Kartli (45 percent) than in other regions. In the regions of Tbilisi (18 percent) and Imereti (17 percent), loans represent a greater proportion of monthly household income than in other regions.

An analysis of income by household type indicates that households with the lowest average monthly income for February 1996 were (1) one-parent households (84 lari); (2) divorced parents living with the family of one of their children (130 lari); (3) retired couples living alone (155 lari); and (4) "other" types of households (167 lari). The highest monthly income during this period was reported by households of (a) two or more couples (378 lari), (b) couples with or without children living with one parent (348 lari), and (c) couples with or without children (318 lari).

The poverty levels for separate districts of Georgia below, based on the same study, are given in Table 4.7.

Table 4.7 Households below the poverty line for February 1996, those perceiving their food situation as unbearable,* and those considering their household to be extremely poor** (in percentages)

	URBAN				RURAL			
	N	poverty	Food Unbearable	Extremely Poor	N	Poverty	Food Unbearable	Extremely Poor
Location (urban or rural)	709	71.5	23.5	14.0	496	42.7	16.7	6.9
Region								
Tbilisi	317	70.0	22.4	12.3	–	–	–	–
Shida Kartli	131	79.7	25.4	23.7	79	73.4	10.1	7.6
Kvemo Kartli	69	71.0	13.0	14.5	117	46.2	17.9	7.7
Kakheti	33	57.6	24.2	18.2	82	3.7	12.2	3.7
Imereti	130	76.2	30.8	18.5	86	72.1	25.6	10.5
Achara	47	61.7	12.8	8.5	43	32.6	2.3	2.3
Samegrelo	43	83.7	34.9	4.7	60	28.3	31.7	6.7
Guria	11	54.5	18.2	0.0	29	13.8	6.9	6.9

* Based on responses to the question, "Generally, over the last three months, how would you evaluate your household for having met the basic food needs of all household members? 1) bad and unbearable, 2) bad but bearable, 3) adequate, 4) good, or 5)good enough to provide assistance to relatives in need."

** Based on responses to the questions, "Compared to other households where you live, what is your household's standard of living? 1) extremely poor, 2) poor, 3) average, 4) above average, or 5) high."

Utilizing the criteria of the minimal level of household income for poverty by household size, evolved by the Georgian State Department of Socio-Economic Information, the above table shows the percentage of households falling below the minimum level of monthly income for February 1996, by rural and urban areas, and by region.

The table reveals that 71.5 percent of urban households and 42.7 percent of the rural households fall below the official minimal level of household income. Yet, when asked to self-evaluate their food situation over the last three months, only 23.5 percent of the urban and 16.7 percent of the rural households reported it as bad and unbearable. Even fewer urban and rural households evaluated the economic status of their household as extremely poor (14.0 percent and 6.9 percent respectively). A much smaller percentage of rural households compared to the urban households regarded their food situation over the last three months as bad and unbearable, and considered their household as extremely poor.

If we generalize the results and findings of these three studies, we shall see that, in comparison with previous years, in 1996 the real unified family income increased by more than 40.0 percent. The percentage of families with incomes below the subsistence minimum was 80 in June 1995, 71.5 percent in February 1996, and 65.5 percent in June 1996. In spite of this declining tendency, these indices are rather high.

Taking into account the data provided in Table 4.6, the following can be concluded: There is a gradual equilibration of unified incomes distribution among various income groups. In particular, incomes of the richest population category in 1995-1996 decreased from 67.3 percent to 57.9 percent, while the incomes of the most deprived 20 percent of population increased from 1 percent to 2.7 percent. The same is shown by the so-called Gini index, which reflects income inequality; it decreased from 0.58 in June 1995 to 0.5 in June 1996. It should be noted, that the group consisting of the richest 20 percent of population is itself sharply diverse. In 1995, the richest half of this group possessed incomes which were three times more than incomes of the other half, whereas in 1996 they were only two times more. In spite of this differentiation of incomes, a more positive tendency can be noticed when considering family incomes in decile groups.

Table 4.8 confirms the comparative equalization of income distribution that took place in different decile groups in 1996. The decrease in the portions of the last two richest groups entailed an increase in income levels in all the other, less rich groups. Bearing in mind that in July 1996 the average family subsistence minimum was 187.4 lari, only family incomes of the last three groups exceeded this figure. Therefore, about 60-70 percent of the households could be considered below the poverty line.

Table 4.8 Distribution of the population's income by deciles, 1995-1996 (in percentages and lari)

Year	1	2	3	4	5	6	7	8	9	10
July 1995, in %	0.5	1.0	1.6	2.7	3.8	5.2	7.4	10.6	19.0	48.3
July 1996, in %	0.72	1.75	3.19	4.63	5.79	7.49	9.42	12.04	17.13	37.81
July 1996, average laris	13.9	34.5	59.0	85.6	118	147.0	181.0	232.0	329.1	741.0

Table 4.9 Family Size and Poverty Level, 1996

	Family Size					
	1	2	3	4	5	6 or more
Number of families examined	51	68	111	120	75	75
Families below the poverty line (no.)	33	49	73	72	44	56
Families below the poverty line (%)	64.7	72.1	65.8	60.0	58.7	74.7

Table 4.9 confirms our calculations and is quite revealing. Families with more than six members or with three or less members represent a higher percentage of those who are below the poverty line. It is only the families with four or five members that show a relatively small percentage of poverty. However, this should not be overemphasized because the percentage of families living below the poverty line is high no matter what the size of the family, ranging between 58.7 and 74.7 percent. Size alone, thus, does not explain the poverty phenomenon.

We refrain from commenting on the poverty indices according to ethnic groups out of political sensitivity. We have also not separately talked about the 400,000 refugees living in Georgia, since they are included in the results of the study. It must be said, however, that the influx of refugees has contributed a great deal to the poverty situation in Georgia. The situation is likely to improve sharply upon their repatriation: the family budgets of their relatives and friends (where they are accommodated or receive support) as well as municipal and regional budgets (apart from Tbilisi, refugees from the Abkhazia and Tskinvali regions reside in sixty-one towns and districts of Georgia) shall be freed from the additional cost of the refugees. The finances thus released shall be spent on the improvement of the living standards of local residents, and on the development of small businesses.

II. The Economic Dimension of Poverty

An overwhelming majority of Georgian scientists (A. Sulaberidze, L. Chikava, V. Papava, G. Grigolashvili, I. Meskhia, I. Archvadze, N. Chitanava, T. Beridze, and so on) attribute the current crisis to the "shock therapy" method employed to effect the transition without properly adapting it to the local conditions. The appropriate supportive environment was not created prior to the liberalization of prices. That is why the transition dragged on for so long, causing the complete impoverishment of a socially unprotected population. Under these conditions, the transition toward a market economy turned out to be very painful and contrary to expectations. According to the World Bank, the rate of the socio-economic decline observed in Georgia in the last five years was much higher than in other countries, and amounted to approximately 27 percent annually. The gross domestic product underwent a five time decrease, and the cost of capital assets dramatically decreased (20 percent). Due to the sharp weakening of industry, the savings of the rich, rather than being invested in industry is being channelled into consumption. This process is called the "corrosion of national wealth" by some experts. In comparison with their actual cost, elements of capital assets are sold cheaply in order to use the cash receipts to meet basic demands, particularly for foodstuffs. This process takes place parallel to the formation of the state system, and to some extent, in the conditions of a juridical vacuum and in an environment of nihilism; this causes an exaggerated and utilitarian approach toward the production process. As far as business is concerned, it follows a simple path: "buy here, sell there".

An important part of the population is gradually losing hope of receiving assistance and support from state institutions and is trying to find ways to survive. The redistribution of national riches, which should be an objective and natural process, is obstructed by the decline of industry, political and military cataclysms, and a disregard for the supremacy of law. All these factors contribute to the spontaneity and unfairness of the process of redistribution of the country's wealth. As mentioned by a number of scientists (A. Sulaberidze, I. Archvadze, G. Grigolashvili, etc.), the redistribution of Georgia's national wealth is presently being accomplished not only by handing over records (redistribution acts), but also through new methods. One such peculiarity is that a large portion of GNP expenditure goes to people in power and their staff (Archvadze 1996, 109-22). According to the UNDP report published in 1995 on human resource development, the 1995 expenses for defense in Georgia amounted to U.S.$333 million, compared to U.S.$147 million in Armenia. The number of regular servicemen amounts correspondingly to 3000 and 50,000 (UNDP 1995, 206).

The redistribution of wealth is an objective process, but, given its social price, it is rather expensive in the conditions of a transition economy. In the course of two years, Georgia experienced four military conflicts and civil confrontations, and witnessed the criminalization of governing structures and economy. This adversely affected the size of its per capita GDP, the amount of foreign debt, and the scale of inflation and unemployment. Some separatist groups have practiced aggressive separatism through ethnic conflicts in order to annex wealth. This mode of redistributing wealth is certainly primitive, and in the modern context can only be described as a forceful appropriation of the country's wealth. In doing so these groups forget that a considerable part of their loot is wasted in engineering the conflict itself. The powers that support Abkhazian separatists have grabbed about 15 percent of Georgia's national wealth (U.S.$12 billion). By pillaging and looting the Georgians, the Abkhazians registered a fourfold increase in wealth; only in the capital of Abkhazia, Sukhumi, did the Georgians suffer a loss amounting to U.S.$1.4 billion. This clearly shows that the political objectives of Abkhazian separatists were inspired by economic considerations (Archvadze 1996, 120).

In general, from the analysis of processes and events which have been taking place in Georgia over the course of last years, the following aspects are revealed:

1. The redistribution of national wealth is a dynamic and large-scale project.
2. In comparison with current incomes, redistribution turned out to be a large-scale and serious event. As a result, the current differentiation of society with regard to the property rights of single items of great value is more important than the differentiation of society by income.
3. The social price of redistribution – the inflationary tax – was much higher for low- and middle-class families than for rich ones.
4. A utilitarian approach toward valuables dominates when the short-term interests overshadow long-term efficiency. Capital turnover has been "simplified" to the utmost and reduced to a minimum period of time.
5. There is a spontaneous tendency in the redistribution of wealth (i)from higher age groups to lower age groups; (ii)from village to city; and (iii)from traditional agricultural governing bodies (ministries, committees, etc.) to institutional structures corresponding to market structures.
6. In relation to the concentration of wealth, the proprietors demonstrated a lack of social responsibility.

7. There was an intensification of the redistribution of the nation's wealth between states and nations.

Against the background of the above-mentioned common aspects, we have to mention the major reasons why the country was hampered; in many respects they predetermined the impoverishment of the country and the wrong course of macroeconomic development.

In Georgia, as elsewhere in the former Soviet Union, the economic transition has not been planned properly, and therefore, it has not so far been successful. The government and the administration as a whole, trained on the autocratic model of the former centrally directed system of the Soviet Union, have great difficulties in dealing with present contingencies. Powers of decision are scattered and diffuse. In any case, they do not necessarily lie with the parliament or other organs of democratic governance. No rational decisions along humanitarian lines are taken. The legacy of the Soviet tradition of governance finds its expression in an authoritarian and vertical system of decision making, inefficient management, a lack of a sense of state or institutional responsibility, and an excessive state bureaucracy. Other remnants of the system include the lack of incentives for efficient work, inadequate salaries, a predisposition for involvement in parallel economic activities, corruption, and a lack of creative and innovative thinking.

The step-by-step policy of transition to the market economy, now being pursued, can be regarded as the second phase of the country's transition. This plan for a step-by-step transition was elaborated in 1991 by the Institute of Economy of the Georgian Academy of Sciences. The same year, the Institute of Demography and Sociological Research formulated a program of socio-demographic development. Unfortunately, the state took neither of these initiatives into consideration when it developed its program of socio-economic transformation. The official economic policy leaned heavily on the Georgian version of "shock therapy," having a great deal in common with the Polish and Russian "therapy" models. At that time, given its socio-economic situation, Georgia was not at all ready for "shock therapy treatment." The eyewash stage of economic reform led to suffering, causing major difficulties for the country's economy and society (Papava 1995).

The aims and objectives set out in the Presidential Program of Economic Reform, as well as in the above-mentioned programs served as a basis for the "1996-2000 Indicator Plan for the Socio-Economic Development of Georgia" approved by the Georgian government. Various research and scientific organizations, ministries, and institutions participated in the elaboration of the scheme of indicators, and full account was taken of the conclusions and recommendations of international financial organizations – the International Monetary Fund and the World Bank. This indicator plan represents the strategy of the government's economic policy and includes nearly all facets of the development of the country, such as a strategy for socio-economic development, a new phase of economic reforms, anti-inflation activities, fiscal and monetary policy, and the reform of the state enterprises. Here, however, we shall focus on the strategic directions of social policy.

With a view to implementing an active state social policy, the Indicator Plan proposes to strengthen the role played by the private sector in employment; to carry out an in-depth reorganization of the system of staff training, retraining, and improvement of professional skills; to improve organizational structures and the legislative base regulating employment and unemployment; to identify both the unemployed (particularly those seeking employment) and available jobs (vacancies) for each region; to conduct activities aimed at employing people in search of jobs; and to conduct activities, by means of labor exchange, aimed at the realization of a systematic state control over the employed and at providing social protection to the unemployed.

With a view to perfecting the organizational mechanism of the state's regulation of the labor market, the plan intends to design and implement common state and regional programs on the creation of working places and to encourage small and average businesses. In order to socially protect the unemployed, the system of assistance for the unemployed is to be strengthened, as well as the regulation of fund transfers from the labor remuneration fund into the joint state employment fund.

The scale of remuneration for the population's work should be based on the anti-inflationary principle of increasing salaries in relation to inflation. Minimum guarantees for social protection by the state should first be ensured for the poorest stratum of the population by means of adjusting minimum wages and minimum pensions to the subsistence minimum. The proposal suggests controlling the earned incomes of the population through guaranteeing the minimum wage, differentiating the wages of employees of budget organizations, as well as by means of taxation. The labor remuneration system should be regulated on the basis of labor agreements.

The state socio-economic policy includes a differentiation in the amounts of compensation given to various social groups, assigning priority to the poorest sections of society with a view to protecting low-income families and perfecting the family assistance system, and using of other methods of social protection. It attaches particular importance to pension reforms – the expansion of a system of financing social programs for pensioners, promoting private insurance organizations and companies, and so on.

The government's Economic Program, at the macroeconomic level, gives priority to the creation of one million jobs by the end of the twentieth century so as to substantially decrease unemployment and satisfactorily ensure the social protection of the unemployed. The policy implemented by the government in 1996 with a view to solving the problem of employment is rather passive: the state budget made provision of two million lari (approximately U.S.$1,560,000) to support the unemployed, but no provision was made for the creation of new jobs, the improvement of skills, and for training and retraining. The situation has somewhat improved in the 1997 budget, although the provisions made in this budget are also insufficient for the realization of an active employment policy.

Starting in 1997, the active policy of the government is to be based on the appropriate legislative base – a new version of the "employment law" (which will be adopted by the state parliament in 1997), new taxation legislation, and a state program on employment. According to the proposed employment law (in spite of certain shortcomings which apparently will be taken into consideration during its adoption), a state employment regulating mechanism is to be created which envisages a thorough revamping of the process of creating new jobs (organizationally and financially) in all branches of the national economy. In this context, particular attention is being given to the development of small businesses. The common State Employment Foundation, the activities of which have so far been restricted to the provision of assistance to the unemployed, now has the right to use a major part of its finances to create new jobs in small businesses.

The organizational structure of the Employment Service underwent serious changes: an Employment Department has been established, which acts as an executive organ for the active employment policy. This department is comprised of a section on labor market regulation (uniting the analysis and prognosis unit), a unit for coordinating the employment programs, a unit for organizing employment, as well as a unit for training and retraining. Its foreign relations section has already begun to liaise with various embassies and representatives of international organizations based in Georgia with a view to controlling the uncoordinated outflow of manpower. A wide mandate has been given to the Center for Professional Orientation and Training so that it can provide training and retraining according to the demands of the labor market. The employment law also provides for the creation of private employment bureaus and companies. The revival of the Department of Primary Vocational Education, which used to exist at the State Ministry of Education and was rather successful in Soviet Georgia, would definitely contribute to an active employment policy.

In our opinion, it would definitely contribute to the active employment policy if the law on employment could make a number of provisions – in particular, for an effective system of organization of temporary working places for seasonal jobs. In addition to this, provisions should also be made with regard to adapting higher, secondary, and primary vocational education to labor demands so that the problem of youth unemployment can be adequately addressed. At the moment the law does not pay any attention to the potential of vocational education.

For the assessment of the labor market, reliable information is available in the Report on Manpower Resources compiled annually by the State Department of Socio-Economic Information. It gives an idea of the actual situation with regard to both manpower supply and the existing demand. In particular, this report sheds light on the total structure of manpower resources (able-bodied people, adolescents up to age sixteen, and pensioners); the migrant labor force; the distribution of manpower resources according to employment and forms of ownership; the distribution of employees in different branches of the national economy; and the total number of the unemployed.

A national profile of professionally qualified manpower still remains difficult to compile. Only expert assessments exist on this subject. Information about the professional qualifications of the registered unemployed is, however, available and is reliable. However, the number of the registered unemployed is only 61,000 constituting 8-10 percent of the total number of the unemployed. Information on manpower migration is also not very reliable.

The informal economy has rather solid roots in Georgia. It existed even during the Soviet period, and was perhaps strongly entrenched here unlike in other Soviet Republics. The political and economic changes of the transition period facilitated its further expansion and strengthening. It plays an important role in generating the country's gross domestic product. Estimates suggest that the informal economy contributes 35 percent of the GDP, the formal economy contributes 55 percent, and foreign capital contributes the remaining 10 percent. These figures point to the negative role of the informal economy in budget receipts. In particular, as is generally known, people in the informal economy evade taxes.

The reasons for the growth of the informal economy are as follows:

1. Neglect of the supremacy of law and spontaneity and illegality in the redistribution of wealth during political and military cataclysms.
2. The asymmetrical nature of current incomes and of distribution of the accumulated property.

3. The superiority of the country's established institutions for self-preservation and survival over the programs for the "stabilization" and "system transformation" of the economy.

4. Instruments of an interstate redistribution of wealth: (i) utilization of foreign currency (the Russian ruble, the U.S. dollar, etc.) for payment within the country; (ii) the low level of domestic prices compared to the international market; and (iii) open economic borders (this caused an outflow of a large-scale material wealth from Georgia).

5. Taxation indulgence with regard to certain companies and organizations.

6. Patronage to households and unregistered companies by certain government officials leading to the concealment of revenue.

7. Nonregistration of income coming from lands.

8. A high level of latent privatization. According to experts, not less than 25 percent of the capital assets which used to be the property of the state were secretly privatized in the beginning of 1990.

9. The ineffectiveness of the taxation system and growing corruption in the government.

10. The use of humanitarian and scarce goods for mercenary ends (between 40 percent and 60 percent of humanitarian assistance is used for purposes other than those for which it is provided).

It should be said that, in order to get rich in so-called population employment activities (secondhand goods markets, bank machinations, etc.), separate clans employ impoverished parts of population and particularly internally displaced persons (IDPs), who play the role of distributors for minimal remuneration. In addition to this, a major part of this income is hidden by the clans from tax collection services.

The existence of a developed underground or unregistered economy served as an important cushioning mechanism during the catastrophic fall of production in the formal sector and the consequent decline in family incomes. Even today what baffles most people is the fact that while the formally registered income of many households is ten times less than the survival limit they are not only surviving but enjoying a reasonably good life. The discrepancy between stated income and lifestyle is indeed surprising. This paradox can be explained only when one acknowledges multiple sources of family income, both monetary and nonmonetary.

The informal economy in Georgia is not similar to the one that operates in some other regions of the world, where shadow economies tend to be essentially criminal and related to drug smuggling or arms trading. A significant proportion of the informal economy in Georgia is being gradually legitimized by introducing more comprehensive and sophisticated legislation, effective taxation and registration systems, along with a general improvement in living conditions and an economic revival. In this context, the informal economy has some positive aspects as it enables people to survive hard times, to accumulate capital, as well as to gain experience in small business and trading. It is also a potential resource for state revenues.

As to the appropriate means for the redistribution of wealth, these mechanisms are presently being created. So far, a strict fiscal regime has not been established in the country. It is necessary to improve the legislative base of customs and taxation systems. It is believed that the differentiated taxation system and the policy of protectionism will contribute to the legalization of wealth accumulated in the informal economy. In particular, by instituting low-rate tariffs, the number of taxpayers is expected to increase dramatically with a corresponding decline in the volume of hidden taxes. Ultimately, this will contribute to the national budget, and facilitate redistribution of wealth.

III. The Social Dimension of Poverty

It is because of poverty that a significant proportion of the population is excluded from full participation in development and nation building. Furthermore, the country is relatively vulnerable because of the many legacies of Soviet rule and economy that it has inherited. Vulnerability is a relative concept. At the present time, almost 99 percent of the population have incomes that are close to subsistence. The situation is such that anyone can come upon financial disaster if he or she suffers an accident or falls ill, or if a family loses its breadwinner. Singled out for description here are three categories of people who are possibly at greater risk than others, precisely because many of them lack family support. These are IDPs (internally displaced persons) from Abkhazia, and a much smaller number from the Tskhinvali region; elderly persons living by themselves; and orphans and other children in institutions. Individuals belonging to other categories may also be needy – for example, children under five, mothers of newborn children, or lone mothers; but their conditions, like those of the elderly in general, depend on the circumstances in which they live and their association with their family.

The elimination of poverty in Georgia is basically a political problem. A strong and sustained political commitment to empower the people is necessary. The elimination of poverty is primarily the responsibility of the government. It must create an enabling environment for the empowerment of people at all levels. Synergy between economic growth and poverty eradication must be fully exploited.

National strategies need to be developed which seek to strengthen economic and social safety nets for the vulnerable, expanding the coverage of social protection systems, protecting them from the erosion of benefits due to inflation, and strengthening traditional systems of social protection where appropriate. The most effective means for protecting vulnerable and disenfranchised people is to eliminate exclusion and to improve the status of the elderly, the disabled, children, and single parents in society, and to respect the cultural diversity and human rights of minorities, migrants, refugees, and IDPs. Social protection programs should create an environment in which everyone is given the opportunity to participate fully in all social, cultural, and political activities of the community.

Before examining the assistance provided by public service programs, we consider it necessary to analyze the activities carried out under the state social policy. In the first place, the state parliament needs to adopt a "subsistence minimum law." Particularly important is the 1996 Presidential Decree Number 162 on social assistance, which came into force on 1 January 1997. According to it, the following three types of families can benefit from assistance:

1. the family of an unemployed lone pensioner;
2. a family that has some disabled members; and
3. an urban family composed exclusively of unemployed members.

According to preliminary information received from the Ministry of Social Security, Labor, and Employment, such assistance is expected to be provided to some 100,000-120,000 families.

It is necessary to concentrate on households rather than on individuals when assessing the needs for food distribution, for it is the kin group that serves as a cushioning agent when an individual is vulnerable or suffers from poverty. It is also helpful to take into account variables such as the age structure of the family, the number of producers/earners and the number of dependents, access to land or productive employment, productive skills or educational level, and material assets. The aim of programs must be to reduce the dependence of the beneficiaries on humanitarian assistance and to build their self-reliance through innovative strategies for creating employment, to increase agricultural production, and to equip the workforce with the new skills necessary to rebuild the economy.

The government has formulated "basic directions for the improvement of labor remuneration for the period 1996-2000." It proposes to regulate salaries in the budget sphere by means of a common tariff scale, and in the nonbudget sphere by means of multilevel agreements. Proceeding from market relations, the agreements are concluded thus: at the state level – general agreement; at sectoral level – branch (tariff) agreement; and at territorial and enterprise levels – collective agreement.

Noteworthy are "the basic directions of social protection of the population for the years 1996-2000," which were prepared by the government and approved by the president. Naturally, these directions include a set of measures calling for the serious financial and economic recovery of the country. Therefore, parallel to economic advancement, the basic objective of state social policy is the stabilization of the population's quality of life and its further improvement. The following priority directions will be given utmost attention: the adjustment of the population's income – along with economic stabilization; the gradual adjustment of the minimum level of labor remuneration, pensions, stipends, and assistance up to the level of the subsistence minimum; the balancing of the economic and social interests of the three major population groups – the employers, employees, and the disabled; and the creation of a system of social guarantees with a view to supporting disabled people.

The increase in the poverty level and in vulnerability is caused, to a large extent, by ethnic conflicts in Tskinvali and Abkhazia which have rendered many people refugees or IDPs. With a view to protecting these people both legally and socially, the Committee on Refugee Settlement (which was subsequently transformed into a ministry) was established on 17 December 1992. Its basic objective was to receive and settle IDPs, and at the same time to elaborate the legislative base for the juridical and social protection of refugees, which would define the rights and duties of IDPs and the scale of assistance to them. In 1993, the recently established Committee on Refugee Settlement registered some 400,000 Georgian citizens (Georgians, Abkhazians, Russians, Ukrainians, Jews, Armenians, Estonians, and Greeks, among others). A majority of them left Georgia in search of employment. The refugees from the Abkhazia and Tskinvali regions are residing in sixty-one towns in addition to Tbilisi.

With a view to determining the usefulness of distributing national and international humanitarian assistance destined for IDPs and defining the most socially deprived layer of refugees, the CEERICS Program – repeatedly tested in various countries by the United Nations high commissioner for refugees – was also implemented in Georgia by the government.

The Ministry of Refugee Settlement faces many problems. It succeeded in settling some 124,000 refugees into hotels, vacation homes, schools and kindergartens, hospitals, etc. The total number of such sites is 1300 for the whole country. However, as a result of various cataclysms which took place in the recent seven to eight years, the above-mentioned sites of refugee settlement are presently in a sorry state. The ministry has managed to repair and restore more than eighty sites, including those which temporarily shelter 300 and more refugees. Given the difficulties connected with financing of the above-mentioned activities, the ministry approached a number of international organizations (e.g., UNHCR, and the Italian nongovernmental organization *Nuova Frontiera*) for assistance; with their support some rehabilitation activities were carried out in 1996. Work is underway to provide new dwelling space for refugees. This will enable the refugees sheltered in the private sector to move out so that the tensions arising between them and their landlords are resolved.

After the temporary settlement of the refugees, the basic problem was to find employment for them. In coordination with the Ministry of Social Security, Labor, and Employment, some jobs were found in the nonproductive sector. Thanks to the assistance of the State Ministries of Health, Education, Internal Affairs, and Security, nearly 60,000 refugees were given employment in these areas. Lands were provided for temporary use to the refugees settled in rural areas (according to Presidential Decree Number 41). Unfortunately, the number of refugees involved in commercial activities and small businesses is not known as they remain unregistered. According to the estimations of the ministry, they number around 85,000. The ministry is working closely with various international organizations that facilitate the development of small and average businesses among refugees.

Particular attention was given to the problem of educating adolescent refugees. All refugee children were sent to schools; they were provided with free books and clothes. The Ministry of Education of the autonomous Republic of Abkhazia was actively involved in this process. Refugee schools – where both the teachers and the students come from the refugee population – are given special treatment. Additionally, each refugee, with the exception of pensioners (whose problem, beginning from 1997, was solved by the law on IDPs and refugees), continues to receive monthly financial support equal to a minimum wage. It is to be noted that the 1997 state budget provides for an increase in the amount of this support.

According to the 18 October 1995 Decision Number 665 of the Cabinet of Ministers of Georgia, the families which shelter refugees are given a 50 percent reduction in public utilities charges. As far as those refugees who are settled in an organized way (in sanatoriums, guest houses, and hotels) are concerned, the state budget makes a monthly provision of 7 lari per person to pay for public utilities. This is made in addition to the assistance provided to each refugee family and is allocated from the state budget directly to the account of organizations and institutions where the refugees are settled in an organized way. Similarly, the refugees pay no fare while using the state electro-transport.

One of the most serious problems is that of health care. Among refugees, there are 14,087 mothers with many children and 7,134 single mothers raising children without a husband; 8,118 men who became invalids during the conflicts; 7,927 orphans; and 4,255 families which have lost their breadwinners. In 1996, around 30,000 free individual medical care policies were allocated for refugees – from the total of 100,000 provided by the State Ministry of Health for the population of Georgia as a whole. Similarly, the Ministry of Health allocated medicaments amounting to 130,000 lari for refugees belonging to the most deprived category. These medicaments were subsequently sent to the Ministry of Health of the autonomous Republic of Abkhazia (functioning in Tbilisi) for free distribution among refugees. It should be mentioned that in 1997 there is a plan to distribute some 60,000 policies for refugees. Accordingly, the amount of money needed to supply free medicaments to refugees will be increased.

In spite of all these measures, a great deal still remains to be done – particularly when the "Law on IDPs and Refugees" begins to function. The most important concern now is the financial security of this law, and this will be reflected in the state budget, which is a difficult task to accomplish given the fiscal circumstances of the country.

If the concept of vulnerability is to be of any real use in effective targeting, a conceptual basis and clear criteria and indicators must be defined in order to determine the categories of the most vulnerable. Vulnerability can be defined only in the concrete contexts of the country, by the mandate of a governmental agency or humanitarian organization. With this end in view, following the decree of the president and the decision of the Cabinet of Ministers, the Bureau for the Coordination of International Humanitarian Assistance was established. For the time being, fifty international organizations are functioning in Georgia, including specialized agencies of the United Nations and the European Commission's Humanitarian Office. Before the creation of the bureau, the activities of both national and international nongovernmental organizations were not coordinated, and consequently, there was often a duplication of programs. Thanks to the bureau's activities, the humanitarian assistance programs have expanded to cover the entire country with better coordination. Coordination meetings are organized frequently in which various ministries and institutions participate together with international organizations.

The international organizations functioning in Georgia are carrying out various assistance programs for unprotected strata of the population: providing foodstuffs and medicaments, and setting up projects to build social infrastructure, to rehabilitate buildings, and to increase employment. During 1995-1996, some 75,035 tons of foodstuff were distributed among 800,000 persons, 386 sites were rehabilitated, and 12,570 persons were given jobs. In 1996, humanitarian assistance entered a new phase. The international organizations embarked on the realization of development programs, which include capacity building, rehabilitation of psycho-social and social infrastructure, employment, and the creation of sources of income. This was in addition to the traditional types of assistance (which taper off gradually).

The following types of humanitarian assistance programs are being put into operation in Georgia: foodstuff and nonfoodstuff provision, free dining rooms, medical assistance and medicaments, building and reparation works. The following international humanitarian organizations are conducting building and repair activities: Nuova Frontiera, Save the Children, IRC, and OXFAM. They have repaired dwellings for orphans and the elderly, boarding schools, and have embarked on the urgent rehabilitation of downtown buildings for settling of refugees in Achara.

Projects aiming at employment in the sphere of small business were carried out by NRC, IRC, OXFAM, IOCC, "LAZARUS" WFI, and SED. Food assistance programs for the socially unprotected population (mainly lone pensioners, mothers with many children, and the disabled) were financed by the following donors: ECHO, USDA, Christian Aid/WFP/, ACT, WFP, CARITAS Germany, CARITAS Italy, ICRC, CARITAS Denmark, TSA, IFRC, ACF, UMCOR, among others. Nonfoodstuff assistance programs (mainly used clothes) were financed by the following donors: UNICEF, UNHCR, DOD, IOCC, CWS, ICRC, EMSA-USA, and IRC. The medical assistance projects were financed by ECHO, MSF, the Dutch Red Cross, MSF Holland, UNICEF, USAID, DOS, and DOD.

Table 4.10 Activities implemented under the project for the development of small business and education (World Vision/Georgia "SEED") August 1995-September 1996

Type of Activity	Quantity	Average 6-month income (in lari)	Average gain per $100 of investment	Increase in private monthly income (in %)
Service	4	1437.6 L	673.72 L	300.01 L
Cookery	43	595.55	368.25	289.51
Miscellaneous	14	630.95	604.23	268.59
Ceramics/Jewelry	4	864.7	726.93	824
Sewing/knitting	26	398.44	435.39	135.62
Handwork	13	433.41	319.84	87.4
Stock-raising	2	44.67	194.07	29.41
Total	106	562.44	431.78	222.05

Due to the fact that in the near future one can hardly expect any significant amelioration of the economic situation for the socially unprotected layers, as well as the fact that humanitarian assistance is likely to decrease, it is necessary to utilize the experience accumulated in the countries of West Europe in their charitable foundation activities. Figure 4.2 below shows the directions of humanitarian and development programs in Georgia, shedding light on the methods by which assistance programs are realized.

Figure 4.2 Directions of Georgian humanitarian and development programs

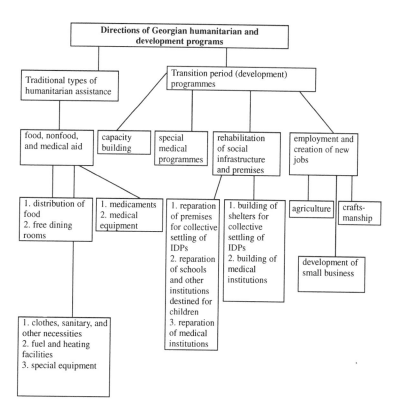

Various experts, participants of scientific conferences, and the mass media attach great importance to the negative results of social differentiation, which can ignite a "social explosion." In Georgian scientific literature, there are diverse opinions on the strata created as a result of social differentiation in the transition period. In particular, some argue that the percentage of salary in current incomes is scanty; it does not exceed 20-25 percent (comparatively, in Russia it is 44 percent). In fact, apart from the official (frequently secondary) source of income, an important part of other incomes of the population is unregistered and hidden. This, in turn, prevents the deterioration of the situation of a major part of the population.

In the transition period, changes in market relations caused changes in social relations, and, as a result of important social differentiation in the country, new social layers and groups are being created. The social structure is changing under the impact of economic reforms. The lower and higher sections of contemporary society are composed respectively of the poor layers and the elite; but it is the middle class which is most numerous. Basically, it is this middle layer that determines the socio-economic progress and acts as a guarantor of social and political stabilization. It is this class which is characterized by a high level of education and professionalism, and greater political participation.

A second sort of social structure is typical of a developing country. It can be presented in the form of a pyramid whose peak is "adorned" by the representatives of the oligarchic elite, and whose base consists of the numerically preponderant poor. Here the middle layer is represented by small and middle producers, government officials, and a comparatively small number of intellectuals. However, both by its number and economic importance, this middle group does not represent an influential political force.

The Georgian case is a unique one. As far as the education and development of society are concerned, the country corresponds to the first model; however, the transition phase has considerably altered the situation – because of the decline in income levels, the Georgian intelligentsia has been considerably impoverished. It has been worn out by political and ethnic confrontation and is virtually struggling for its physical survival.

IV. The Political Dimension of Poverty

Throughout the Soviet period, the concept and structures of "civil society" were nonexistent. Official policy disallowed such structures. Thus, NGOs and community organizations were practically prohibited, or, if they did exist, took the form of "puppet" organizations. Nor was there any participation of ordinary citizens in government and the decision-making processes. This resulted in a lack of civil society infrastructure in the form of NGOs, as well as a lack of understanding of the values relating to democracy, community, and civic responsibility and, even more importantly, a lack of expectation that these should be present. The present political system in Georgia has many of the attributes of democracy. However, most of its structures and institutions are underdeveloped. They do not compare favorably with the Western democratic perspective.

A growing number of public institutions and groups are concerned with building democracy in Georgia, but they are still in their formative stage. They lack not only material resources that are indeed very scarce, but also a clear understanding of their roles and capabilities to influence the polity and governance. Nor do they have experience in appealing to wider audiences and attracting potential supporters. Like other organizations that are the product of the transition, many of the newly emerging NGOs are smaller in size and are recent in origin. Some have become overly preoccupied with local fundraising or with finding Western partners and securing external financial support. Some pursue a hidden agenda, using social problem rhetoric merely to disguise their real activities. Most of them are active in larger towns or solely in the capital city of Tbilisi. There is little activity elsewhere.

Independence and the reality of a post-Soviet era came somewhat unexpectedly to most people. Although there has been a deep-rooted longing for independence and an attraction to the West, the real need for reform has not yet matured sufficiently to enable a social discourse to take place; nor do there exist any social groups or strata that have any clear understanding of the preferred model of development. Everybody would like to live according to Western standards, but this vague idea cannot serve as a basis for development and reform.

This situation, common to many other post-Soviet societies, was evident during the pre-election campaign, when it appeared that practically no political party had any clear ideology, program, or models, other than rather embryonic ones based mostly on intuitive social-democratic or nationalist ideologies. The same can be said of the government personnel, parliamentarians, and political elites in general; and this makes the process of reform too dependent on the personality of the leaders, external pressures, popular attitudes, and other random factors, rather than on a solid social basis and explicit group interests.

It should be mentioned that among many other factors influencing the process of development, the personality of President Shevardnadze is one of the most specific. Having returned to Georgia with few initial resources other than personal capacities, he has succeeded in becoming by far the most influential figure of the political reality in Georgia, applying his vast experience and the respect he commands from international political elites to the task of strengthening the position and international standing of his native country. The personal style of Shevardnadze is a permanent topic for discussion, as far as it influences both the pace and the direction of reform. His ability to operate effectively in reality, and to balance various conflicting powers both inside the country and on the international scene, has been a source of political stability for the country.

Political stability in the country created a propitious setting for the active realization of the objectives pursued by various parties and voluntary organizations. Almost all political parties and voluntary organizations have pretensions to protect the interests of the poor. There are more than 100 officially registered political parties. They can be classified into: (1) *leading parties,* capable of creating a particular political climate; (2) *anticipating parties,* adapting their activities to the existing situation; and (3) *backward parties,* which are under the tutelage of stronger parties. This gradation of parties is made on the basis of their activity profile, financial status, and organizational functioning. However, in general, their socio-political position is predetermined by the personality of their leader, rather than by the activities they conduct. Presently, almost all parties and voluntary organizations believe that the era of political mass meetings and demonstrations is over, and that political debates have moved from the streets to the meeting halls. The exhausted and socially depressed population is rather mistrustful with regard to the intentions of the political parties. This negative attitude of the population toward political démarches can be explained by the bitter experience of political and criminal cataclysms of 1991-1995 (ethnic conflicts, civil war, brigandage, and terrorist activities).

Both political leaders and ordinary citizens have the impression that, given the present difficult socio-economic situation, thoughtless and eyewashing political action in the country could result in a social explosion which could be used by certain political forces for political destabilization. In the opinion of population, the majority of parties and voluntary organizations conduct their activities according to their ambition and private political interests, and this cannot facilitate eradication of poverty.

The people have completely forgotten about the existence of trade unions, which are not capable of exercising any influence to protect the interests of workers; their leaders use their position for their own well-being. In spite of the fact that, at first sight, the Soviet system of unified trade unions almost disappeared and separate independent branch trade unions were established, these unions lack the necessary power and cannot influence the governing organs with a view to protecting the interests of the people. In our opinion, this can be explained by the weak authority of trade union leaders, who are hardly known even in their own branches, not to mention in the country. They conduct their activities in an outdated manner, since the mentality of trade union leaders has remained unchanged. They fight reticently against each other in order to "find their place under the sun." Needless to say, under these conditions they have no time for people. This is aggravated by the financial difficulties they face, as well as by a number of other factors.

It should be mentioned that people place more hope on the authority of the President and on his ability to settle the crisis, than on anything else. The political attitudes of the people are shaped in many respects by the opinions and the authority of their leader. A clear expression of this was seen during the parliamentary elections of 1990 when people supported the well-known nonconformist Zviad Gamsakhurdia. A similar, albeit a somewhat modified situation, was observed during the presidential and parliamentary elections of 1995: the political party named "Union of Citizens," created by Eduard Shevardnadze two years before the above-mentioned elections, gained a victory in the parliamentary elections and obtained an overwhelming majority of votes in the state parliament.

If the previous parliament lacked the necessary power to supervise the government and administration, the present situation has more or less improved, since the majority of government officials, both in the central and regional administration, are members of the Union of Citizens and supporters of President Shevardnadze. Under these conditions, the leading party should apparently face no difficulties in the realization of the pre-election program. In particular, this concerns the realization of social programs aimed at creating million of jobs, decreasing sharp differentiations in the levels of living, and providing a subsistence minimum to all people. However, the activities implemented so far lack effectiveness in that the poverty situation in the country has not changed. Eradication of poverty still remains a grave problem, since the rate of increase of salaries is slower than the rate of increase of the subsistence minimum.

The following factors have contributed to the ineffectiveness of the leading party: an abundance of careerists and a lack of common ideology; unqualified leaders and a deficit of state thinking; outdated methods of work and the lack of an innovative, creative approach. In spite of the importance that the Union of Citizens attaches to social issues, it has failed to define its political ideology due to the diversity of its members' political opinions. The majority of them support the strict monetary and liberal-democratic policy embraced by the International Monetary Fund and the World Bank. During the pre-election campaign, one of the authors of the economic program of this party, Mr. Vladimir Papava (currently the minister of economy) strongly criticized the Georgian version of "shock therapy" and proposed a synthesis version. However, in his scholarly works and articles, and particularly in the reforms he carried out, his anti-liberal policy was obvious. According to him, liberal policy is necessary for the revival of economy. At the same time, to avoid confrontation with people, a move to the left is also necessary. Thus, the flexibility of the socio-economic program of the Union of Citizens issues from the objective of its own realization. By manoeuvering to the left, it avoids possible factors of social explosion, while by manoeuvering to the right it satisfies the demands of the right wing of the party, as well as the liberal-democratic demands of the International Monetary Fund. It should be mentioned here that the party's move to the left is, in our opinion, conditional upon the President himself, who adeptly controls the situation and acts on the basis of his rich political experience and foresight. He has helped people to avoid hunger by implementing separate social activities within the limits of economic capabilities of the country.

Given its social programs, the Socialist Party can be considered as one of the parties supporting the President. It was created several months before the elections by the former vice-speaker of the state parliament, Mr. Vakhtang Rcheulishvili. Many thought that the status of socialism should have depreciated in Georgia, and that Mr. Rcheulishvili should have lost out, but he managed to create a good reputation for the party through his personal authority and single-minded policy. The party rejected Soviet socialism and opted for "European" socialism. Already before the elections, Rcheulishvili demanded on behalf of the party that the constitution of Georgia, together with other attributes, reflect the countries' social status, thus constitutionally binding the country to care about people. True his party failed to overcome a 5 percent barrier in proportional elections, but the four socialist majority deputies were joined by other like-minded nonparty majority deputies, thus creating the fraction. In contrast to the Union of Citizens, the Socialist Party clearly expressed its ideology as left-wing centrism and created, from seventeen socially oriented parties which remained outside the parliament, the left-wing centrist bloc, and afterwards, together with the Bulgarian Socialist Party, the permanent assembly of left-wing centrist parties of the Black Sea basin countries (the Union of Citizens was not included into this). This resulted in a further rise of the reputation of the Socialist Party within the country.

The program documents of the Socialist Party emphasize that "at this stage the basic objectives should be the eradication of poverty and a decrease in social tension." In this context, the party supports the realization of a well-elaborated socialist policy. True, under the present tight fiscal circumstances little can be distributed, but social policy is to make people feel that what the country has is not to be used for the enrichment of a small group of people, but is to be distributed equitably. Such an approach will contribute to social solidarity and social tolerance, as well as to the unification of the nation. Simultaneously, we will rapidly achieve the level when we will be able to provide the subsistence minimum to each person experiencing financial difficulties. Only after this will we be able to lay down a real basis for the structures of market economy. At the final stage of reforms, our society should be able to allocate approximately one-third of the gross national product for social aims. The party is rather reluctant with regard to taking separate charitable and self-advertising actions since in the end they are all ineffective. Although, given the situation and with a view to overcoming social problems, it frequently renders assistance to the most socially deprived layers – IDPs, large families, the disabled, and lone pensioners. The party, therefore, is concentrating its activities on the elaboration of large-scale socio-economic programs and their practical realization. With this end in view, it created from amongst the members of the parties united in the left-wing centrist bloc (a majority of them are scientists and specialists in separate branches of economy), the Economic Forum of Georgia to work on the creation of alternative solutions for overcoming the crisis; these find their reflection in the Program for the Sustainable and Safe Development of Georgia. This program serves as a counterbalance to the strict liberal economic policy carried out by the World Bank and International Monetary Fund. According to the deep conviction of members of the above bloc, any reform should be carried out taking into account the specificities of country's development.

By creating the left-wing centrist bloc in 1996, the Socialist Party gave a new direction to the activities of Georgia's political parties. The existence of more than 100 political parties made the political situation tense and caused the people embarrassment. The unification of the left-wing forces by Mr. Rcheulishvili paved the way for the unification of the right-wing centrist forces with the National Democratic Party. This created an excellent basis for new and purposeful political thinking in Georgia.

In comparison with strong political parties, voluntary organizations are less noticeable in the socio-political life of Georgia, although some of them have intensified their activities in the recent period. Their programs for action are more or less similar and basically include humanitarian activities. Like the political parties, activities of these organizations are also decided by their leaders in terms of the influence they have in the governing circles, as well as their contacts with humanitarian organizations abroad. They are not antagonistic toward the government. While their influence on the political parties is rather intangible, many political parties use them during the elections with a view to gaining a victory.

The nongovernmental organizations have partially taken the place of trade unions in the socio-political life of the country. The NGOs can be divided into the following categories:

1. organizations supported by certain political forces
2. organizations dealing only with humanitarian actions and not connected to the political parties
3. organizations created by political parties, with the intention of raising their reputation in the population
4. organizations functioning through the assistance of international humanitarian organizations
5. organizations which conduct charitable activities and hope either to develop into a political party or to join an already existing party

At the moment, the following nongovernmental organizations can be considered influential ones: the Demographic Society, Women of Georgia for Peace and Life, the Women's Committee of the Socialist Party, Association for the Protection of Mothers and Children, *Mandilosani*, the Olympic Committee of Invalids, and the Association for Assistance in Employment Matters. However, as mentioned above, their activities do not go beyond humanitarian actions and, therefore, they are not in a position to tangibly influence the political situation in the country.

V. Conclusion

The challenge of eradicating poverty has engaged the attention of every progressively thinking person, the government, and the voluntary and political organizations. The best way to solve this problem is to achieve synchronism and harmony in carrying out political, economic, and social activities. This is rather difficult for a post-communist country in transition. The reforms which have already been carried out and those which are still to be carried out are characterized with certain contradictions, as far as their political, economic, and social aspects are concerned.

From the political point of view, the reform process was impeded by internal and external political forces leading to ethnic conflicts and civil war. The geopolitical location of the country, and its national and religious structure were insufficiently reflected in the strategic development of Georgia. A properly formulated internal and external policy would have definitely resulted in a less tense socio-economic situation. At the same time, given the socio-economic potential of Georgia in the post-communist phase, the level of living would have definitely been higher. After the proclamation of independence, the national government did not attach due importance to the interests of neighboring and remote countries, which were part of the geopolitical location of Georgia. The state policy with regard to the interested countries was not balanced, and through their nationalistic, adventurous actions, certain political forces (both inside and outside the country) succeeded in attaining their oligarchic goals, plunging the country into a catastrophe. The existing political situation hampered foreign investments in Georgia. Only in the last years, has the consistent internal and external policy carried out by President Shevardnadze given the country a real chance to overcome the crisis.

The above-mentioned particularly concerns the expansion of not only political, but also economic integration, and the creation of a system of external economic relations which would maximally answer to the state interests. For the time being, there are three ways of forming economic integration: (1) the European Union and the Black Sea Economic Cooperation Organization (BSEC), (2) the Commonwealth of Independent States (CIS), and (3) the Caucasus. At the same time, we should not forget that the best investor is the country's population itself, which, instead of becoming involved in the national production process, migrates, due to various reasons, to the CIS and other European countries with the hope of finding gainful employment. That is why the great number of trade fairs in the country swarm with goods brought from various countries, excluding national ones. In its turn, the decline of local production is caused by faulty customs and tax policies, which make no provisions to encourage the development of national production. It is advisable for the state government to elaborate a realistic, pragmatic, and steady socioeconomic policy, which would pay particular attention to the balance of the above-mentioned variants of economic integration.

Georgia has always been the central country of the Caucasus. Georgia is in a unique position, since all the countries of the Caucasus have access to the Black Sea only via Georgia. The Caucasus has all the prerequisites to become a common socio-economic space, but if the state government fails to choose the correct approach with regard to this issue, the results can be undesirable and disastrous, both from political and socio-economic points of view. Both the BSEC and the Caucasus are to play an important role in the timely opening of the Eurasian corridor. At the same time, this region can connect North with South – Georgia can become a highly developed transit country. However, this requires thorough preparation, particularly by creating an active system of social protection for the population, so that people do not impede the utilization of the strategic location of the country for its socio-economic revival.

In this context, the approaches of the Union of Citizens and the Socialists are very interesting. The former more or less leans on the ongoing reforms, on the "ready prescriptions" of the International Monetary Fund and of the World Bank, while the latter believes that these "ready prescriptions" contributed to the growth of poverty and are likely to cause social explosion. Among others, the strategic integration policy of Georgia is brought to the forefront in the program of the Socialists, although they feel that the policy's failure will lead Georgia to the role of a "servant country," losing control over its own national economy. The trade unions are currently going through a difficult process of reform, and their activities are absolutely ineffective. The right-wing opposition parties are busy defining a strategy of relations with the Russian Federation and other CIS countries – although an important part of them (national-democrats) accept the prescriptions of the International Monetary Fund but feel that their proper realization is impeded by a lack of competence and continued Soviet thinking among members of the government.

On the whole, both scientists and politicians generally agree that the ongoing economic reform has violated the principles of social justice in the country. Due to the imperfect mechanism of the creation and distribution of national income, there is high income differentiation in the country. The active redistribution of national wealth among elites and oligarchic groups is in progress, and representatives of foreign countries take part in it secretly. In this situation, few think about the eradication of poverty, the creation of jobs, and the resolution of other social problems.

The state budget for 1997 was approved by the state parliament. It was prepared on the basis of recommendations of the International Monetary Fund and, in the opinion of the Socialists, does not take into account the principles of a socially oriented economy. In particular, it is rather strained and tends to fill the state budget with regressive taxes. Income is basically measured with value-added and excise taxes, whose portion is rather high. Neither a percentage nor an absolute amount of income taxes and profit taxes has increased. This means that the state budget is still dependent on imports and not on domestic production, which is the best way to create new jobs. In spite of the calculated subsistence minimum for the country, the law on the subsistence minimum adopted by the parliament lacks efficiency since its implementation is impeded by the low level of salaries due to the low level of production. In the opinion of experts of the Economic Forum of Georgia, when considering the sources of revenue for the state budget, priority should be given to income taxes and profit taxes paid by the population (as in all civilized countries), and not to regressive taxes representing an important source of corruption in a defective taxation system. For this, it is necessary to maximally use the law on the subsistence minimum. This would strongly contribute to the revelation of hidden incomes of the population and producers. Simultaneously, the scale of the informal economy would reduce drastically. In this case, legalization of the official level of the informal economy (35 percent) would be enough to cover the deficit of the present central budget (200 million lari), not to mention its expert assessment level (55-65 percent). This, in its turn, would be an important precondition for the socially oriented market economy. Moreover the scanty expenses allocated in the 1997 budget for active employment policy are passive in nature, since they are less than the humanitarian expenses, not to mention the organizational expenses of the employment fund.

With a view to improving the analysis of the problem of poverty and to elaborating an active policy for its eradication, research should be carried out on social groups, taking into account national and religious implications. The following gradations of poverty should be defined subject to their incomes: absolute poverty, low income, relative poverty, and subjective poverty. Simultaneously, research should include the interdependence of poverty and such factors as age, sex, level of education and formal qualification, as well as the prospects for future.

Studying the problem of poverty from this point of view is justified by the multinational composition of the population (more than 100 nationalities) and by its religious diversity. Together with Christians, Sunni and Shia Muslims, Jews, and others reside in the country. Eradication of poverty among these groups has a political importance, since socio-economic discontent can be developed by certain forces into ethnic or religious conflicts, of which Georgia has a bitter experience. This idea comes from the results of interviews with IDPs, victims of ethnic conflicts, and from experts (political scientists, sociologists, economists, etc.). According to their opinion, the basic reason Georgians and representatives of other nations migrate from the country is not religious and national oppression and discrimination, but social vulnerability, which was successfully used in the period from 1990 to 1993 by certain internal and external political forces to achieve their goals.

Appendix

Table 4.11 Summary of the balance of manpower resources, 1985-1995 (in thousands of persons)

	Years						
	1985	1990	1991	1992	1993	1994	1995
Population	5252	5418	5421	5412	5396	5372	5369
Manpower resources	3149	3176	3161	3138	3108	3064	3034
Employed in national economy	2667	2663	2518	1984	1792	1450	1730
Students	226	209	201	203	208	182	200
Unemployed	255	204	442	951	1108	1132	1104
Registered unemployed	–	–	6	105	180	65	70
Employed in material production sphere, including: ·	1872	1919	1731	1367	1201	1203	1169
Industry	521	560	497	355	303	273	254
Building	245	281	226	135	125	64	90
Agriculture	728	695	666	640	553	539	510
Timber	16	12	11	10	9	10	6
Transport and communications	134	115	103	75	57	90	90
Trade and service	186	257	227	153	153	227	219
Employed in nonmaterial sphere	795	844	787	617	591	547	561
Municipal economy	111	131	109	62	66	59	49
Science	75	73	63	42	41	34	36
Education, culture, art	277	310	290	239	223	232	240
Health and social security	167	184	186	159	156	155	160
Banks and financial institutions		12	12	12	12	11	10
State organs	68	52	48	39	49	35	35
Other		82	79	64	44	20	31

Table 4.12 Profile of the unemployed by profession and age, 1994-1995 (in percentages)

	1994	**1995**
Total registered	100	100
Specialists	31	31
Junior staff	25	26
Workers	44	43
Less than 18 years old	3	4
18 to 24 years old	22	22
25 to 29 years old	25	25
30 to 40 years old	26	27
41 to 60 years old	23	22
60 years old	1	0

Table 4.13 Distribution of the unemployed according to region, 1 September 1996 (in percentages)

Regions	**Unemployed**
Total in Georgia, including:	100
In Tbilisi	9
In Achara	1
In Imereti	39
In Samegrelo and Zemo Svaneti	15
In Guria	8
Racha-Lechkhumi and Kvemo Svaneti	1
Shida Kartli	4
Mtskheta-Mtianeti	1
Kakheti	6
Kvemo-Kartli	15
Samtskhe-Javakheti	2

Table 4.14 Migration (in thousands of persons)

	1990	1991	1992	1993	1994	1995
Immigrating to Georgia	20	17	8	13	13	1
Emigrating from Georgia	59	61	50	43	45	18
IDPs	–	–	–	296	282	289
Refugees registered in the Russian Federation	–	–	–	…	103	118

Bibliography

Archvadze, I. 1996. "On Certain Aspects of the Nonstate Redistribution of National Wealth in Georgia." In *Financial Economic Problems in Georgia in the Transition Period.*

Bureau for the Coordination of International Humanitarian Assistance. 1996. *Humanitarian and Development Programs in Georgia.*

Chavleishvili, T. 1992. "Indexation of Monetary Incomes in the Population: Foreign Experience and Its Adaptation to the Situation in Georgia." *Matsne,* no. 3.

Chikava, L. 1997. *Economic Theory in Brief.* Tbilisi.

Dershem, Larry D. 1997. *Food, Nutrition, Health, and Nonfood Vulnerability in Georgia, 1996: A Household Assessment.*

Georgian Department of Socio-Economic Information. 1997. *The Socio-Economic Situation in Georgia in 1996.* Tbilisi.

Gogodze, I. and A. Tsakadze. 1995. "Determining Indicators for the Subsistence Minimum Wage." In UNDP *Human Development Report, Georgia, 1995.*

Kahniashvili, J. 1996. *Macroeconomics.* Tbilisi.

Checkouts, I. 1996. *Labor Market Regulation Issues in Georgia.*

Meskhia, I. 1996. *Economic Reform in Georgia.* Tbilisi.

Papava, V. 1995. *From "Shock Therapy" to Social Stability.* Tbilisi.

Sulaberidze, Avtandil. 1996a. *The Orientation of Leaders of Privatized Enterprises in Georgia.* Tbilisi.

_____. 1996b. *Problems of Socio-Demographical Development in Georgia.* Tbilisi.

UNDP. 1995. *Human Development Report, Georgia.*

_____. 1996a. *Human Development Report, Georgia.*

Van de Veen, Albertien. 1996. *Southern Caucasus Mission Report,* 14 November-9 December 1995, ECHO document.

In addition to the above-mentioned sources, some information was culled from interviews with some 500 IDPs and 100 experts.

Acknowledgment

We could not have completed this study without the timely assistance of various Georgian ministries and organizations, international and national nongovernmental organizations, scientists and experts, who kindly provided us with the information used to prepare this study. For this we express our sincere gratitude. We are also thankful to the Georgian students who helped us a great deal in writing this chapter.

This study is based on previous research carried out by scientists of the Institute of Demography and Sociological Research of the Georgian Academy of Sciences, as well as through our own research, comparisons, and conclusions.

The working team was composed of the following:

1. Mr. Avtandil Sulaberidze, team leader and deputy director of the Georgian Institute of Demography and Sociological Research
2. Ms. Maia Sulaberidze, student of the Faculty of Oriental Studies at the State University of Georgia
3. Mrs. Lina Datunashvili, senior researcher at the Institute of Economy at the Georgian Academy of Sciences
4. Mr. Dimitri Gvindadze, deputy secretary-general, Georgian Commission for UNESCO

While conducting this study, we received invaluable assistance from the Georgian Ministry of Foreign Affairs, and in particular from the Secretariat of the Georgian Commission for UNESCO led by the secretary-general Dr. Peter Metreveli, and we express our deepest gratitude for this.

Chapter Five

THE RUSSIAN CASE

Social Policy Concerns

G. Pirogov and S. Pronin*

Institute for Comparative Socio-Political and Labor Studies
Russian Academy of Sciences

Introduction

Russian society is going through a series of economic and social adjustments. This process of adjustment is very painful. The sudden switch from a state-controlled economy to a market-oriented economy has been traumatic for the people. It has also caused problems for the administration, which has had to reorient itself to meet the challenges of the new situation. While a new system of labor relations is emerging, the majority of the population still subconsciously feels inclined to act in accordance with the behavior patterns of the previous system. Such an incongruity between the expected and persistent behavior patterns creates a situation of tension.

The labor skills, professional knowledge, physical and intellectual abilities that were previously downgraded or not utilized have assumed a new importance in the changed scenario. Those who are highly skilled and, therefore, have market value abroad, are adapting to the world system; several others have become disadvantaged because their skills are not internationally saleable. Such workers are getting involved in the system of secondary employment, which operates both legally and illegally. Such an adjustment to the new conditions is accompanied by the

* The authors are thankful to the director of the Institute, Professor T. Timofeev.

loss of previous social norms, creating a state of anomie. It also promotes instability in both the social life and in economic production. It is also partly responsible for the emergence of new types of poverty. Simultaneously, individual workers are innovatively searching for an adequate place in the transforming economic structure. Those who have been able to get relocated in the new system are likely to succeed in evading poverty.

The sudden transition to a market economy has caused a slump in production. This slump has mainly hit high-tech, labor-intensive industries. The highly skilled laborers working in them have been rendered unemployed with no prospects of being absorbed in other industries within the country. The fortunate among them have succeeded in finding jobs in other countries and have thus fled the country. This outflow of highly qualified specialists, "the brain drain," is almost a national tragedy. Scientists and technicians are leaving the country not so much to "cash their skills in foreign currency" as to find sustenance for their families. Wage arrears, piling up for several months, have left them with no option but to quit work in Russia and earn a living abroad. Payment conditions are particularly bad for research workers: they are seriously underpaid and their research projects are underfinanced.

It is true that Russian specialists working abroad are often underpaid by international standards. It is also recognized that not every highly skilled Russian can find a job in the international market. Yet people vie for these jobs because the wages are much higher than what they can earn in Russia, and because they feel that they are improving upon an insecure situation. Those who are not able to get permanent jobs abroad (and there are millions) are getting involved in what has come to be known as the *"shuttle trade"* – they travel to other countries to buy less expensive goods, which are of inferior quality, and bring them back into the country to trade on the retail market. Not only is the highly qualified Russian labor force being absorbed by the world market, even those engaged in disgraceful, harmful, and dirty activities, including crime, are also exploiting these opportunities. A sizeable number of Russian girls, for example, are regularly being smuggled into foreign brothels. Many young people are joining criminal gangs, which operate both in Russia and abroad. It must be said, however, that the number of such people, and particularly the number of highly skilled people who are able to find alternatives in other economies, is very small compared to those who are unable to escape the system and who are thus getting pauperized in the new economic and political milieu.

The situation in Russia needs to be thoroughly analyzed in order to develop adequate relief programs. The present paper is an attempt in this direction. Due to a lack of substantive statistical data, results of surveys and case studies have been used along with material gathered through informal interviews with experts in the field. We hope that this paper will provide the basis for further thinking and will stimulate research on the problem of poverty.

I. Measuring Poverty

To estimate the poverty profile, official statistics use the *decile coefficient* and the *poverty threshold*. The decile coefficient is the relation of the average per capita income of the poorest 10 percent of the population to that of the richest 10 percent. In 1996, the decile coefficient was about 13.5. However, it must be said that there are difficulties in identifying the poorest and the richest sections of Russia's population. The data are not very trustworthy and cannot be regarded as representative of the two groups.

The *Engels coefficient* is also widely used in Russia to measure poverty. It is based on the ratio between food expenses and the total general expenses of a family. In 1995, the average Engels coefficient was 0.35 to 0.40 for a household consisting of two parents and two children. Those families in which this ratio is higher than the average – that is, families spending more than 40 percent of their income on food – are regarded as poor.

Another yardstick used to measure poverty is *average per capita income*. Those who are near this average are the ordinary people, described as having a medium level of well-being (something similar to the Western concept of the "middle class"); those below this range constitute the poor; and those above belong to the category of the rich. Poverty is further differentiated in terms of the relative distance from the average per capita income and is characterized by indigence, poverty, and misery. Similarly, there are different categories of prosperity. Roughly speaking people can be classified into six categories: 1) the *destitute* are those whose income is one-fourth of the average per capita income; 2) the *poor* are those whose income is between 25 percent and 50 percent of the average income; 3) those whose income is between 50 and 75 percent of the average income are classified as *needy* – characterized by indigence; 4) those whose incomes range between 75 and 125 percent of the average income – that is, those who are closer to the average per capita income – are the *ordinary people*; 5) the *well-to-do* are those whose income is 150 to 200 percent of the average income; and 6) the *wealthy* are those who earn more than double the average income.

The following chart illustrates the proposed classification:

Figure 5.1   Categories of Prosperity

a b o v e average	200% and above	Affluent	Wealthy
	Between 125% and 200% of average income	Well-to-do	Well-to-do
average	Between 75% and 125% of average income	Mid-level well-being	Ordinary
b e l o w average	Between 50% and and 75%	Indigence	Needy
	Between 25% and and 50%	Poverty	Poor
	25% and below	Misery	Destitute

The poverty line is drawn at the 25 percent level: those whose income is one-fourth, or even less, of the average per capita income are the real poor.

The percentage of poor households computed both by the government and the All Russian Center for Public Opinion Studies (VCIOM) on the basis of average per capita income are given in Table 5.1. VCIOM has computed these figures using three different criteria. The first criterion is the level of the current money income corresponding to the official value of the subsistence level defined by *Goskomstat* (the Russian Federation's [RF] State Committee for Statistics) and the Ministry of the Economy: 366,000 rubles or U.S.$73.20 for one household member per month. The second criterion is a subjective estimate of the subsistence level (according to VCIOM expertise): 500,000 rubles or U.S.$100 for one household member per month. The third criterion is the subjective estimate of the threshold value of poverty: 300,000 rubles or U.S.$60 per month.

What is intriguing is the fact that VCIOM has come up with a relatively higher percentage of families living below the poverty line than the official figures, in all the three different calculations. It is also important to note that VCIOM's computation of the average per capita income has resulted in figures that are much lower than the official ones.

Subsistence minimum is a crucial indicator of the spread of poverty. Usually people whose life conditions are below the estimated scale of the subsistence minimum are considered poor. Measuring this way, the counted number of the poor is highly dependent on how the subsistence

Table 5.1 People below the poverty line in terms of average income
Official estimates and VCIOM* findings (in thousands of rubles for one
household member per month)

Source	Poverty boundaries			Average per capita income			Poor households (% age)		
	March 1994	March 1995	March 1996	March 1994	March 1995	March 1996	March 1994	March 1995	March 1996
Official data	60	219	366	115	348	662	30	30	23
VCIOM data:									
First criterion	70	200	366	83	187	354	58	69	62
Second criterion	154	323	580	83	187	354	92	91	81
Third criterion	–	–	300	–	–	354	–	–	52

*VCIOM (All Russian Center for Public Opinion Studies)

minimum is estimated, thus leaving the government officials a lot of
room to manoeuvre in order to statistically adjust the number of the
poor to the government's political needs. In Russia the Presidential *Ukaz*
(Decree) Number 210 "toward the creation of a system determining the
RF population's minimum consumer budget" was issued on 2 March
1992. According to the Ukaz, the estimation of the regional minimum
budgets was made the responsibility of regional authorities, who had to
adjust their calculations according to specific regional conditions, consumption habits, and available financial resources. However, the regional
estimates have to be coordinated with the all-Russian estimates and targets. On 11 November 1992, the RF Labor Ministry approved methodological instructions on the estimation of the subsistence minimum. The
instructions are not obligatory but only recommendations. In April 1997,
the state *Duma* (the first chamber of Russian parliament) legislated and
sent a new law on the subsistence minimum to the Council of the Federation (the second chamber of Russian parliament), along the same lines
as the former Ukaz Number 210, by which the task of estimating subsistence minimum was delegated to the regional levels. The Labor Ministry's
instructions have survived up to now. This new law, however, has not yet
come into force, and the Labor Ministry's instructions are still valid.

According to the instructions, the subsistence minimum (SM) is an
indicator of the volume and the structure of the consumption of the
most important goods and services, characterizing the minimal conditions necessary for the reproduction of the labor force. The monetary
indicator of the SM is called the subsistence minimum budget (SMB).
The SMB corresponds to the money income level securing the volume

and structure of consumption as defined in the SM. The SMB is used as the poverty line or poverty threshold.

The SM and SMB are recommended to encompass the following:

- the minimal acceptable consumption level and structure of different socio-demographic population groups;
- volumes and structures of material resources necessary to satisfy the survival needs of the population;
- minimal wages, salaries, benefits, pensions, and compensations; and
- concrete programs and measures for social protection.

The SM and the SMB can also be used to identify the population groups in most urgent need of social protection and assistance. Practically speaking, the SMB is used as an official poverty line. The computations of the SM are based on a goods and services consumer budget, the components of which are: food, nonfood items, and services. Provisions are also made for taxes and other obligatory payments. These are computed separately for children under six years, older children (between seven and fifteen), active labor force members, and pensioners. These were separately calculated for eight different geographical zones in the country.

The food basket for the subsistence minimum consists of eleven aggregate groups of food products: bread and groats products, potatoes, vegetables, fruits and berries, meat products, milk and milk products, fish, eggs, sugar and confectioneries, oil and margarine, and other items (salt, pepper, etc. are 5 percent of the total basket). The total calorie intake of the basket per day is as follows: the population average is 2236.7 kilocalories (kcals); for men aged sixteen to fifty-nine, 2720.4 kcals; for women aged sixteen to fifty-four, 2138.4 kcals; for pensioners, 1979.6 kcals; and for children, 2078.8 kcals. The nonfoods were computed as RF averages. The corresponding set was developed by the All Russian Research Institute on the Consumer Market and Marketing and the Moscow Consumers Association. The set does not include expensive durables such as refrigerators, washing machines, furniture, nor cultural and sports items.

Initially it was also recommended to include in the subsistence minimum some kinds of services: housing rents and related expenses, everyday services, transport and communication expenses. But later, due to difficulties in estimating the set of necessary nonfood goods as well as the durability of goods and consumption per person of different items, it was decided to estimate fully only the value of the food basket and to compute the rest by multiplying the previous value levels of the nonfoods and services with separately computed price indices (deflators) of these aggregate consumption groups. Afterwards a structure of the SMB was computed for reference usage (see Table 5.2). At present the Ministry of

Labor and Social Development is developing new instructions to return to computations of nonfoods and services on the basis of norms and to use the actual prices of each item instead of deflators for the whole group.

Table 5.2 The structure of the SMB for the RF and the city of Moscow, 1996 (in percentages)

Items	Structure for the Russian Federation as a whole (according to the Labor Ministry)	Structure for the city of Moscow (according to the Moscow Tripartite Commission)
Foods	68.9	60.9
Nonfoods	19.2	14.9
Services	7.3	19.6
Taxes and other obligatory payments	4.6	5.2

Source: Proceedings of the interregional conference on *The role of social partnership in the socio-economic development and regulation of socio-industrial relations,* Moscow, April 1997. The value of the SMB food basket is computed by multiplying each item in kind by the corresponding average buyer's price estimated on the basis of the household budget survey data.

A comparison of the food basket with the actual consumption in 1995 (Table 5.3) indicates that three and a half years after the start of the reforms, actual consumption was very close to the minimal norms of the subsistence basket.

Table 5.3 Normative and actual consumption of food (kg/month per person)

Items	Food basked of the SM (approved in 1992)	Actual consumption in the Third Quarter of 1995 (for a household of husband, wife, and two children under 16)
Bread and groats products	11.20	7.40
Potatoes	10.30	7.60
Vegetables	7.80	8.60
Fruits and berries	1.60	2.20
Meat products	2.30	3.10
Milk and milk products	17.90	21.80
Eggs	14.30	15.00
Fish	1.00	0.50
Sugar and confectioneries	1.70	1.80
Oil and fats	0.97	0.40

Source: (i) Monitoring of households' socio-economic potential 1996, 58; (ii) *Methodical instructions for subsistence minimum consumption.* RF Labor Ministry 1992, 10-11.

A survey carried out by the former RF Ministry of Social Protection showed that in fifty-one of the sixty-seven regions, more than 30 percent of the households had incomes under the subsistence minimum budget, including seventeen regions with 40 percent of all households being poor, fifteen regions with more than 50 percent poor households, five regions with 60 percent, three regions with 70 percent, and another three regions with more than 80 percent poor households. There were fifty-six regions in which the rate of households in extreme poverty was more than 10 percent.

The RF State Committee for Statistics *(Goskomstat)* has recently introduced two new indices to characterize poverty in a more comprehensive way. They are the *poverty gap* and *poverty acuteness*. The poverty gap is the observed household's per capita income mean deviation from the subsistence minimum budget expressed as the total of income deficits related to the total number of the observed households (see Formula 5.1). Poverty acuteness is the observed household's per capita income weighted mean deviation from the subsistence minimum budget expressed as the total of squared income deficits related to the total number of the observed households. The use of the deficits' squares provides for a greater specific weight of those households whose deficits are higher (see Formula 5.2).

Formula 5.1

$$P_{gap} = \frac{\sum_{i=1}^{N} (y - x_i)}{N}$$

Formula 5.2

$$P_{acuteness} = \frac{\sum_{i=1}^{N} (y - x_i)^2}{N}$$

where y stands for the subsistence minimum, x for the income of the i-th observed household, and N for the total number of households observed.

II. Poverty Profile

Contemporary Russian society is characterized by the phenomenon of the *new poor*. In addition to the traditionally disadvantaged groups –

such as pensioners, the disabled, and students – several wage earners have become impoverished due to severe cuts in wages and salaries, particularly in the state sector. Over the years, the difference between the minimum wage and the subsistence minimum has widened.

In the beginning of the new era of post-communist society – in December 1991, to be precise – the minimum wage fixed by the state was seven times the subsistence minimum. In 1994, it was brought down to represent only 2.3 times the subsistence minimum. And as time passed by, the minimum wage continued to slide down. It fell to as low as 10 percent of the subsistence minimum in March 1995; the situation improved slightly in 1996 when it was 14 percent of the subsistence minimum. Seen in relation to the average income, the minimum wage represented 37 percent of the average wage in December 1990; in December 1991, it went down to 18 percent; and as many as 1.7 million people were receiving these low wages in 1996, thus constituting the ranks of the poor despite being in the labor force.

But this is only one part of the story. In the state sector, not all employees suffered a similar fate. Those who form part of the so-called budgeted sphere – working in the economic ministries – have managed to protect their interests by adjusting their salaries to the changing structure of consumer prices in the same fashion as the employees in the private sector. It is common knowledge that the salaries of the government officials start at a point where the salaries of the "intellectuals," for example, end. (In May 1995, the average salary of Finance Ministry officials was more than sixty times the minimum wage!) Similarly, for the state committee dealing with property problems (*Goskomimuuscheslvo*) the salary was fixed at forty-one times the minimum wage, and for the Ministry of Economy at twenty-six times.

The intellectual class has suffered worst in the process of transition and economic reform – they are among the low paid groups. The average remuneration level of a research worker in Russia in 1994, for example, was thirty-six times lower than in the United States. The same is true of teachers and professors. In 1994-96 the negative trends became even more evident as the real wages and salaries in Russia decreased by 15 percent. Taken as a whole, the Russian system of education and vocational training (including labor force retraining) is in a very bad shape. It is now quite clear that if the present crisis in the education system continues, Russia will irretrievably lose its scientific manpower over the next two decades. In Russia's current situation of general socio-economic crisis, the deterioration of education is one of the main sources for the spread of the so-called new poverty. These "new poor" include the most valuable labor force groups, and their disastrous pauperization is evidence of a dramatic depreciation of human capital in Russia.

The salaries of the "intellectuals" (including researchers in academia) significantly lag behind those of the employees working in the production sphere. For example, the salaries of those working in health care, as well as those dealing with social protection and with physical culture and sports, are only 62 percent of those received by industrial employees; those working in education earn only 55 percent of industrial wages, and those working in culture and the arts earn only 51 percent.

A number of other factors have contributed to the steady growth of new poverty. These include a sharp deterioration of the value structure of the gross domestic product. All in all, during the years of the "reforms," the contribution of wages and salaries to the GDP has dropped to 30 percent.

The structure of monetary income in Russia has been undergoing changes. In 1992, salaries and wages constituted 69.9 percent of monetary income. This share shrunk to about 33 percent in 1996. This general slump in monetary income has been accompanied by a rising income disparity affecting the general distribution of material and nonmaterial benefits and the shifting of incomes from the bottom to the top. The decile coefficient of incomes has been constantly growing in Russia. In 1991, it was 5.3; in 1992, it was already 8.5; in 1993 the figure was 11.2, and in 1994, 15.1. According to some experts at the RF Labor Ministry, in 1995 it went down to 13.5. However, it is hard to believe that this could occur in a period when the real monetary income of the population fell by 13 percent. Besides, it should be remembered that the data are available only for law-abiding taxpayers while people earning very large incomes succeed in evading taxation.

At the same time, as far as official statistics are concerned, they fail to represent real social stratification. For a proper representation, it is necessary to take into account the ownership of estate property, securities and other assets, as well as the distribution of status in the managerial decision-making processes. On the other hand, the uppermost social strata report their income in a distorted way, hiding their real income and assets. As for the situation of the lowest strata (such as persons with no fixed abode or address, refugees, etc.), the objective assessment of their poverty is impossible.

The overall share of Russian employers' spending on human capital (including that of the state, as the biggest employer) is going down. The ratio of wages and salaries in the GNP has come down in Russia. This fact becomes especially evident when compared internationally. Furthermore, one should take into consideration still another, this time purely Russian, factor that has spurred the growth of new poverty: namely, arrears in the payment of wages and salaries. Prior to the 1996 presidential elections, the country's indebtedness totaled about 20 trillion rubles. Even before his election, the RF president promised to resolve this problem once for all. However, by November 1996 the sum owed to people as arrears for their wages and salaries already reached 43 trillion rubles. In the first quarter of 1997, wage arrears amounted to 50 trillion rubles. An increase at this rate is very alarming indeed.

The geographical distribution of poverty

The different characteristics of Russia's various regions with regard to the level and nature of their economic development and the position occupied by them in the web of the commodity and financial flows are related to the rate of the population's monetary income growth, the level of retail prices, living standards, and, consequently, the level and nature of poverty. Regions that are endowed with raw materials, that are major financial centers (like Moscow or St. Petersburg), or that are rich in agriculture (like the Stavropolsky and Krasnodarsky *krais* [areas]) have a certain economic advantage. However, the poverty-related problems of a region are not always directly dependent on its economic status. They might as well be related to priorities in the social sphere.

In terms of poverty, Russia's regions are grouped in the following way:

- regions of the Extreme North (Krainy Sever) and the territories with extreme climates;
- regions where the manufacturing industry is highly concentrated (including the old manufacturing regions);
- regions where military industrial complex (MIC) enterprises are concentrated;
- regions in deep depression (emergency regions) in which material well-being is poor and economic potential is relatively low; and
- regions hit by different catastrophes.

Sixteen of Russia's eighty-nine regions are officially considered to be emergency regions, and their situation is considered as critical in terms of employment markets. Many regions have a high ratio of dependents; this phenomenon is especially pronounced in the European part of the country where every fourth person has reached retirement age (e.g., the Novgorodskaya, Pskovskaya, Bryanskaya, Kostromskaya, Tverskaya, Tulskaya, Tambovskaya, Ryazanskaya, Kurskaya, and Voronezhskaya *oblasts* (regions). These regions also have the highest mortality rate. Therefore, urgent measures of social protection are needed to improve the security system for pensioners and to provide adequate social services. The problem of unemployment is particularly acute in Pskovskaya, Archangelskaya, Vladimirskaya, Ivanovskaya, Yaroslavskaya oblasts, and in the Ingushetia republic.

Most of the regions (especially those in the European part of Russia and to the north of the Caucasus) have to deal urgently with the problem in order to provide the necessary living conditions required to settle the large number of migrants, including the refugees. There is an influx of migrants in such regions as the Krasnodarsky and Stavropolsky krais, the Belgorodskaya, and Ulyanovskaya oblasts. The size of the migrant population in these areas is five to six times higher than the average in the Russian Federation as a whole. Therefore, it is necessary to take urgent social assistance measures in these areas, particularly to help settle the pensioners and the handicapped among the migrants. The Ulyanovskaya oblast and the Krasnodarsky krai are rated high in terms of the purchasing power of the average per capita income, implying thereby that the difference between the subsistence minimum and the average income is very small. The Chitinskaya oblast and the Tuva republic also show little difference in these two indicators; however, they are among the most backward regions of Russia because of the poor purchasing power of the ruble there.

In several Russian territories there exist essential differences as far as the purchasing power of income is concerned. For example, Moscow holds the first place in Russia as regards the purchasing power of average per capita income; however, the average purchasing power of wages and salaries received by employees in Moscow occupies between fifteenth and twentieth position. In terms of the purchasing power of the average pension, Moscow city is ranked between sixty-seventh and seventy-first. For example, as far as the same indices are concerned, the Sakhalin oblast holds correspondingly the forty-seventh, twenty-fifth and seventy-first positions among the regions of Russia.

The difference in range between the purchasing power of different kinds of income shows the difference in social status and economic position of various income groups. For example, Moscow's first place in average income, with a moderate rate for wages, shows that here the discrepancy between the wages and salaries of the employees and the income of entrepreneurs is rather large.

Some regions are characterized by a relatively low unemployment rate, on the one hand, and a tense situation in the employment market, on the other. The analysis of different regional employment markets has revealed that the situation in a number of autonomous districts (*nationalnii autonomnyi okrugs*) and republics is disastrous. In the Ingush and Karachai-Circassian republics, unemployment is as high as 75 percent. Employment problems are increasing in the regions of the Extreme

North and in some regions of Siberia and the Far East. It is to be noted that unemployment benefits corresponding to the minimum wage are received by less than half (44.9 percent) of all the unemployed. Regionally, this figure varies from 15.7 percent in the Khanty-Mansiiskii autonomnyi okrug to 92.6 percent in the Dagestan republic. In some regions (for example, the Voronezhskaya oblast) unemployment benefits in the form of minimum wage have been given to students in secondary schools, to people working in special educational centers and higher educational establishments, and to those who have not been employed for a long period of time.

Since the mid-1990s, the average period for receiving unemployment benefits has risen in a majority of the regions. This is a clear indication of the worsening of the employment situation in the country. Current legislation provides for the extension of the period of unemployment benefits in those cases when satisfactory jobs are not to be found, when persons are near retirement, or when people are sent for retraining. But such extensions are usually for not more than twelve months. The employment agencies have taken measures to alleviate the situation of those unemployed who have dependents. Such persons constitute 45.6 percent of all the unemployed receiving unemployment benefits. The average amount of the additional payment in question is equal to 75.2 thousand rubles; additional spending on dependents makes up 6.4 percent of the overall sum of unemployment benefits.

Groups most affected by poverty

The largest percentage of the poor is found among the ranks of the pensioners, and especially among those whose education is below secondary level. The number of the poor is also growing among those who make up the middle-aged and older labor force. Forty-one percent of households with children, 55 percent of single mothers with children below six years of age, and 63 percent of households headed by pensioners are poor. Poverty is more pronounced in the rural areas. Members of the poorest families rarely hold jobs in the private sector or even run a small business. Most of them receive pensions, scholarships, and other social payments. Of course, the number of poor among those who have a higher or an incomplete higher education has also grown and continues to grow. Two-thirds of the poor are employed by state-owned enterprises. The ratio of unskilled workers among the most needy is relatively high, but the poor are found both among the employed and the unemployed. However, it must be said that not all the unemployed are really poor; some of them have secondary jobs which are mostly illegal, and some of these jobs may even be criminal. Many of these jobs are in the *shuttle trade*. People in these jobs are able to earn good money, but they forget their professional skills and thus miss out on opportunities to return to productive work.

The poorest employees work mostly in the agricultural and forestry enterprises; they also work in such fields as education, science, culture, and health care. Long delays in the payment of wages and salaries cause misery to the employees in these vocations. Even those working in the economic sectors, where pay is relatively high (like coal mining and power production), are badly affected due to arrears in wages and salaries. Poverty initially spread in the so-called closed towns where MICs (military industrial complexes) were located, and in those oblasts with a predominance of light industries. But now it has also begun to spread in other regions, cities, and towns that have multiple industrial productions. This indicates the depth of Russia's crisis.

In Russia, absolute and relative poverty are developing hand in hand. Large parts of the population feel a drop in their socio-economic status with rapidly worsening living standards. In the meantime, one notices conspicuous and wasteful consumption among the very rich. The rich are growing richer and the poor poorer. A more definite picture of social stratification and polarization may be drawn by looking at the ownership of liquid assets, movable and estate properties. Whereas the average per capita income shows the stratification in the present day context and based on a single indicator, the ownership of property (liquid assets and property) is the accumulated result of a rather long process. However, the construction of such distribution profiles in contemporary Russia is fraught with many obstacles. Usual surveys tend to miss major pieces of information concerning the poorest and the richest. Under present-day Russian conditions, people are even more unwilling to reveal information about their material situation. In order to evade taxes, they supply distorted information to the income tax authorities. Official statistical information about the real income of the people is rather unreliable.

A mathematical model of socio-economic stratification developed by D. Chernavsky and G. Pirogov, however, allows us to overcome these difficulties by referring to various indirect data (prices of staple foods, durable goods, and elite commodities, as well as data on average monthly wages and salaries, and expert evaluations of profit). On the basis of these, distribution profiles of liquid assets are constructed. Examples of such profiles in the form of distribution density curves are reproduced in Figures 5.2 and 5.3. The horizontal axis refers to the volume of liquid assets (valued in thousands of U.S. dollars), and the vertical axis corresponds to the numbers of average families. The area beneath the density curves represents the total volume of liquid assets owned by households belonging to a certain interval on the horizontal axis. Since the model is of a continuous type, these areas are represented by corresponding integrals. The estimation of the liquid assets structure, as they are accumulated by the Russian population by means of the Chernavsky-Pirogov model, points out that Russia has turned itself into a bipolar society. The majority of the population (up to 70 percent of Russian households) show a low accumulation level; only 30 percent of the households fall in the category of those who have high accumulation levels. But even among them, only 0.2 percent of the households own up to 50 percent of the accumulations; and about 70 percent of accumulations are owned by just 3 percent of the households. This finding is confirmed by the estimates made by VCIOM with regard to the poverty line as it is defined in terms of income (the second criterion – 81 percent; see Table 5.3 above).

Figure 5.2   Liquid Assets Distribution

Number of Households (in thousands)

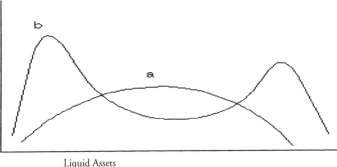

Liquid Assets

The density curves of liquid assets distribution $\rho(x)$ correspond to

a) A unimodal society with a numerous middle class; and
b) A bimodal society with numerous poor strata (the left "hump") and a small rich stratum (the right "hump"). The plateau between the "humps" represents the middle class.

Figure 5.3 Liquid Assets Distribution in Sonet and post-Soviet Russia

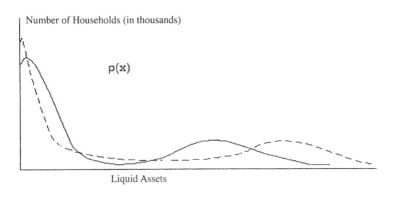

A comparison between the density curves $\rho(x)$ during Soviet and post-Soviet periods:

- the dashes line (- - -) stands for the Soviet period;
- the solid line (——) for the post-Soviet period.

The integral $\int_0^\infty \rho(x)dx$ for the Soviet period converges, for the post-Soviet it does not; the area under the curve $\rho(x)$ stretches indefinitely to right, building the "running away distribution's tail." The nature of the socio-economic structure is clearly illustrated by the curve of the density function revealing two density maxima: one in the area of the low accumulation level and the other in the high accumulation level. Additionally, the corresponding integral does not converge, and thus the distributions form "tails" to escape to the left and right, revealing the instability of the social structure itself. This distribution is called bimodal or two-humped. In a normal society (characterized by the unimodal distribution curve) there must be a middle class. But in a bipolar society there is a zone between the two "humps" where the density is instead lowered, signifying that the middle class is poorly represented in the given social structure. The degree of polarization of a bipolar society can be measured by the distance between the two maxima (or summits of the "humps"). Similarly, the relation between the "poor" and the "rich" can be measured by the areas situated under the corresponding portions of the curve. More than that, the bifurcational[1] analysis reveals

1. Mathematically, bifurcation is the heterogeneity of behavior of a mathematical object depending on a parameter in every vicinity of a chosen value of this parameter. It means that a curve whose form depends on a certain parameter may change its form or direction with arbitrary, small changes in the value of this parameter. If a curve represents a certain social niche, then the instability of the curve indicates

the stability of various social niches. It has turned out, in particular, that not a single social group of contemporary Russia (six such groups were analyzed for this purpose) has a stable social niche of its own, which suggests that there is an extreme form of marginalization in present-day Russian society.

III. The Economic Dimension of the Poverty Problem

On 11 October 1996, an Interim Emergency Commission (IEC) was established by presidential decree. The Commission is to deal with the acute problem of tax evasion. It is important to mention that because of tax evasion, only 39.3 percent of the scheduled budget revenues could be collected in the first seven months of 1996, allowing only 43.3 percent of the scheduled expenditures to be made. During this period, the tax revenues of the state treasury accounted for only 8 percent of the GDP whereas they were expected to be about 35 percent. The total amount of collection arrears reached 73 trillion rubles. The IEC suggested rigorous measures and submitted cases of defaulting enterprises to the arbitration court for insolvency litigation. This action produced some results. In October-November 1996, the revenue from taxes improved a bit, but it could not solve the budgetary crisis that is mainly due to a general decline in the Russian economy. On 17 October 1996, during a plenary session of the Russian parliament, several ministers suggested that the growth of arrears in tax collection was due to a decline in production.

This situation is aggravating poverty in two ways: 1) by augmenting the number of poor and thus widening the poverty gap; and 2) by depleting governmental resources so that social policy cannot be properly financed by the state treasury. Today in Russia the total social expenditures make up only 12 percent of the GDP. Even other East European countries are able to spend 18 to 24 percent of the GDP for this purpose. The four and a half years of reform in Russia have in fact resulted in the structural erosion of national production: there have been some investments in the fuel and power production sectors, but investments in machine building and construction sectors have drastically fallen. The high-tech potential of the defense sector is wasting away. Even worse is the situation of institutions engaged in research in the fundamental sciences.

According to official sources, by the end of 1995, the aggregate level of industrial production was only 51 percent of the 1989 level. The

---

that the social niche is also unstable – with small changes in the socio-economic conditions, people belonging to this niche may be forced to change their lifestyle and behavior patterns. In sociology this phenomenon is called marginalization.

decline was particularly acute in sectors that were producing goods for direct consumption by the people. During the first half of 1996, industrial activity further declined. The GDP was 5 percent less than in the corresponding period of the previous year. The industrial output index in June 1996 reached only 41 percent of the monthly average in 1989. The worsening of the industrial structure continued: the output in raw materials fell to a rate considerably lower than that of the manufacturing industries. The output in machine building in the first half of 1996 was down by 22 percent compared with the first half of 1995. The output of machines for civil use was only 24 percent of the 1989 level. The light industries output in the first half of 1996 fell to 20 percent of the 1995 level and to 16 percent of the 1989 level. However, some improvements were seen in the food industry (a growth rate of 5 percent).

The investment cycle is a well-known predictor of the general trend of economic activity. During 1996 the decline in investments continued. Investment activity in the first quarter of 1996 slowed down by 14 percent of the corresponding period of 1995 and was only at 17 percent of the 1989 level. In the first half of 1996 there was a further decline in investment activity: by 18 percent in the second quarter, and by 20 percent in the third.

Agriculture remains the weakest sector in Russian economy. The reform process has adversely affected it as well: the growing prices of fertilizers, chemicals, fuel, agricultural machinery and the invariably low prices of imported food products have stunted its growth. The stock of agricultural machinery is nearly depleted. The production of both machines and spare parts has been considerably reduced. There is an acute shortage of plant protection chemicals, fodder protein, fuel, and lubricants. The number of livestock is falling sharply. Production infrastructure facilities as well as rural social capital are dwindling.

The introduction of a currency rate corridor[2] negatively affected the exportability of the output of metal industries, oil chemistry, and even of raw oil. Nevertheless, it continued due to the payment crisis in domestic markets as well as to the objectives of businesses transferring capital abroad.[3] The raising of the upper limit of the currency rate corridor and the shift to the gradual lowering of the ruble rate have reversed the trend of massive dollar outflow. During the period January-August

2. Under the currency rate corridor arrangement, the free fluctuations of the currency (dollar/ruble) rate are officially allowed only in a certain interval of values limited by a lower and upper boundary.

3. The payment crisis leads to a situation in which domestic buyers constantly accumulate huge arrears of payments to domestic suppliers. Lacking cash, the producers of fuels and materials are eager to export even with losses just to have some cash flow. Another incentive to export despite losses is the possibility to hide some of the returns from tax authorities by falsely reporting cheaper prices.

1996, Russian banks brought about U.S.$21 billion in cash into the country. In this way, Russian enterprises and individuals are financing the U.S. economy.

The rate of inflation has finally begun to slow down. During the first six months of 1996 retail prices grew by only 15.5 percent, and the whole-sale prices by 14.4 percent. But there is no ground for excessive optimism. The decrease in the inflation rate can be explained not so much in terms of a financial stabilization policy as by the financial partition of the economy into two separate compartments, one of which relates to the export of raw materials and fuels and the import of consumer goods, and the other to the production for domestic markets. The first sector has achieved a near balance between money volume and money demand as determined by the turnover needs; and the other is characterized by barter transactions, payment delays, and illegal cash payments.

The method of deficit covering by means of the GKO-OFS[4] issue has blocked investment flow into the real production sector. By the beginning of August 1996, about 140 trillion rubles of GKO-OFS were in the turnover (7 percent of the GDP). Although this is not too much by Western standards, in comparison to other parameters of the Russian money market, this is an immense sum. The total volume of bank deposits made by enterprises and individuals was 170 trillion rubles. Considering the part of GKO in the hands of nonresident and non-banking institutions, it appears that about 120 trillion rubles are invested into GKOs by banks. Deducting 25 trillion rubles of obligatory legal reserves, we calculate that about 80 percent of the total savings of Russian enterprises and individuals are invested in government securities. The costs of servicing the domestic debt are thus growing rapidly. They represented a major part of the budget deficit for 1996. In an effort to support low inflation rates and to continue the financial stabilization policy, the Russian government has resorted to payment delays – both in salaries and wages, and in bills for the goods purchased from industry. Wages and salaries have remained unpaid for several months, taxes have remained uncollected, and as a consequence, money flows into social funds have virtually dried up.

By the end of 1996, another factor aggravated the economic situation. The total debt of enterprises had risen to nearly 800 trillion rubles. The payment crisis is holding the last relatively prosperous sectors of Russian economy in its iron grip: the banking system and the fuel and power production complex. The volume of arrears in credit returns and interest payments to the banks surged to 40 trillion rubles.

---

4. GKO = *gosudarstvennie kaznacheiskie obyasatelstva*, governmental treasury liabilities: OFS = *obligatsii federalnogo zaima*, federal loan bonds.

The fuel and power production sector owes the state 25 trillion rubles, but the outstanding debt of its debtors amounts to several hundred trillion rubles. Since October 1996, seemingly dormant inflation has begun to show signs of awakening at a monthly rate of 1.5 percent. The vicious cycle begins with government delays in payments and ends in tax collection arrears.

The role of the employment policy

The poverty profile of the Russian Federation is closely correlated with the employment structure. Like most other countries, Russian employment has a two-layer structure: the *core,* being made up of the more highly skilled employees; and the *periphery,* consisting of part-time and temporarily hired workers. As a result of several technological shifts, many employees have entered into a situation of uncertainty. For example, with the spread of information technologies in the service sector, some of the intermediary operations have already become redundant. The workers engaged in such operations are thus rendered jobless, or are poorly paid as they lack the skills to operate the new technology. The number of jobs requiring skills in the use of older technology has been greatly reduced. Previously regarded high-tech production branches are now degenerating. In the service sector, the relative weight of "redistributive parasitic" activities is increasing. For example, the banking and finance sector is rather weakly involved in the financing of the production sector and is mainly occupied with speculative operations and government deficit financing. A number of mediating firms have emerged only for tax evasion and price inflation. The decline in the GNP and the degradation of the country's industrial infrastructure are making it difficult for the government to take effective social policy measures to combat poverty. Therefore, in contrast to many other countries of the world, poverty in Russia has grown both in relative and in absolute terms.

An active employment policy is one of the major ways to alleviate poverty. Government employment services are taking certain anticrisis measures in the regions that have high unemployment rates as well as in those regions where unemployment levels have not yet reached the critical mark. The Employment Facilitation Regional Programs (EFRP) initiated in 1995 focus on (1) providing employment to the unemployed population; (2) preventing the growth of long-term unemployment; (3) improving cooperation with employers; (4) giving aid in money and in kind to the unemployed in extreme need; (5) improving vocational training for the unemployed; and (6) developing the organizational structure of the employment service itself. Due to a scarcity of financial resources in the employment fund, the achievements of the employment policy have been meager. For example, in the Kabardinian-Balkar republic the programs of active employment policy covered only 43 percent of the scheduled population; in the Kaluzhskaya oblast, they covered only 64 percent.

Under current critical conditions, it is rather difficult to permanently employ the jobless. Therefore, the regional employment services have tried to provide temporary employment under public works. In those regions where resources were adequate, financial aid was given to the employers to create and secure additional jobs to accommodate the unemployed. But since such regions comprised only one-third of the total number of regions, a large number of the scheduled people remained beyond reach. For example, in St. Petersburg only 1,463 additional jobs could be created instead of the scheduled 6,400 due to scarce financing. For socially disadvantaged persons, the employment services deployed a policy of job allocation.

An active vocational training policy implemented by employment services improved the competitiveness of the unemployed in the labor market and augmented their employment opportunities. An active employment policy was implemented with emphasis on capital saving. The employment services also provided aid in cash and in kind to the unemployed. The goal set for this purpose was achieved in 56.8 percent of the regions surveyed, whereas in 43.2 percent of them the goal could not be reached. Additionally, a special governmental Federal Employment Fund (FEF) was established in order to provide financial aid to the disadvantaged. Nearly 37 percent of the funds of the FEF were spent on providing material aid to the unemployed in the form of "unemployment benefits." But the ratio of this item to the total expenditure greatly varied according to region – from 3.6 percent in the city of Moscow and 5.65 percent in the Smolenskaya oblast (where the conditions of the labor market are relatively good) to 68.75 percent in the Mordovian republic and 67.34 percent in the Arkhangelskaya oblast (regions having high unemployment rates).

The second item of expenditure of the FEF was "early retirement payments" (7.99 percent). These payments are made to persons who are unable to continue to work due to their age or physical condition. Regionally, this ratio varied from 0.57 in the Murmanskaya oblast to 39.41 percent in the Kurskaya oblast. It may, however, be mentioned that an increase in the number of early retirees has affected not only the economic but also the social effectiveness of the employment program (the expenditure per capita is much greater than the alternative ways of helping the unemployed).

The third item of expenditure of the FEF was the "active employment program" representing 6.8 percent of the FEF total expenditure. Out of this allocation, 9.8 percent was channeled for job protection. This program is considered to be one preventive tool to control mass labor retrenchment. The maximum ratio of financing for these purposes was earmarked for the city of Moscow (50.07 percent), followed by the Smolenskaya (25.9 percent) and Tulskaya oblasts (24.81 percent) – all regions with relatively favorable labor market situations. On the other hand, many territories had no expenditure on this item despite high unemployment levels.

The ratio of aid given to people to start their own business amounted to 0.39 percent. This was a predominant feature in the Chelyabinskaya, Astrakhanskaya, and Rostovskaya oblasts, where this ratio reached 2.68 percent, 1.89 percent, and 1.58 percent respectively. The unemployment levels in these regions (like the Rostovskaya oblast) were relatively low or medium by Russian standards. On the other hand, in some regions (like the city of Moscow, the Leningradskaya oblast, the Nenetzkii autonomnyi okrug, the republic of Kalmykia, the Taimyrskii and Koruyakskii autonomnyi okrugs, North Osetia, and the Ingush and Chechen republics) no subventions were given to start businesses. In the framework of active employment policy, programs related to vocational training, retraining, and orientation were financed. Expenditure on this item was 6.7 percent of the total FEF. This activity was most visible in the Ryazanskaya (25.4 percent), Voronezhskaya (24.7 percent), Lipetskaya (21.5 percent), and Kaliningradskaya oblasts where the labor market situation is not so bad.

Financing "public works" constituted 2.1 percent of the total expenditure of the FEF. According to FEF official reports, the most intensive public works programs were undertaken in the Alta republic, the Evenkskii autonomnyi okrug, the Magadanskaya oblast, the Aginsk-Buryatskii autonomnyi okrug, and the Tomskaya oblast where the ratio of public work financing was correspondingly 10.8 percent, 65 percent, 7.2 percent, 6.9 percent, and 6.5 percent of the total FEF expenditure. Chicane was a special case in which the high ratio of expenditure on public works – 36.21 percent – was due to emergency rehabilitation measures. We can conclude that there have been governmental efforts to neutralize the growth of poverty by means of employment policies. These attempts, however, have not been very effective in curbing the growth of poverty.

Education and poverty eradication

There is an interdependence between the society's educational and cultural level and the spread and scale of poverty. The development of education and culture enhances labor productivity, promotes the improvement of living standards and the quality of life, and contributes to poverty eradication. Similarly a slump in living standards and mass pauperization lead to the moral and cultural degradation of the society and adversely affect the education system.

In the very beginning of the reforms, in 1992, Russia ranked fifty-two among 174 countries in terms of its Human Development Index (HDI), calculated for the UN Development Program. The index consists of weighted averages of a given country's life expectancy, its literacy rate, and income. The adult literacy rate stood at 98.7 percent, similar to all other developed countries. During the Soviet period, considerable emphasis was given to education and special vocational training. The mass pauperization of the Russian population in the post-USSR period cannot, thus, be attributed to a lack of education or professional skills; it is due to the undermining influence of the differentiated and work-related systems of wages and work motivation that existed during the Soviet period. It was hoped that reforms would boost the creative incentives of personnel and make management more efficient, but what has really occurred is a deterioration of the conditions of work for the labor force. The most creative groups in the labor force, the torchbearers of technological progress, those without whom the modernizing movement toward a post-industrial information society would be impossible, were first to be hit by this deterioration. In recent years, governmental expenditure on education and culture in Russia has steadily declined. In 1995, only 3.2 percent of the total budgetary resources of the federal and local governments were spent on education and culture, compared to 9.3 percent in Italy; 7.5 percent in France; and 6.2 percent in Japan (Russian Goskomstat 1996, 95-96).

The shadow economy in Russia: the impact of the informal sector on poverty

The phenomenon of a "shadow economy" is not new to Russia. It was present even during the former Soviet Union. But in present-day Russia, and in other CIS countries, it has grown to a gigantic scale. Its links with the criminal elements and the underworld have also enormously increased. The very first year of reform turned out to be the year of freedom for the shadow dealers and criminals. The proportion of the shadow economy to the "official" economy has increased drastically. In four years, from 1992 to 1995, the ratio of the shadow sector to the official one grew as much as four times. Some researchers are even tempted to introduce the term "shadow GDP" to distinguish it from the official GDP.

Table 5.4 The Composition of the GDP

Item	At current prices (trillion rubles)			Percent of total		
	1993	1994	1995	1993	1994	1995
Total GDP in the official sector, Including:	162.6	630.0	1659.0	100.0	100.0	100.0
goods production	81.1	258.3	675.2	49.9	41.0	40.7
services production	69.9	318.2	854.4	43.0	50.5	51.5
indirect taxes (less subvention) and import duties	11.6	53.5	128.4	7.1	8.5	7.8
Total GDP in the shadow sector, including:	44.0	246.4	750.0	100.0	100.0	100.0
goods production	24.3	96.1	171.0	55.3	39.0	22.8
services production	19.4	147.8	563.2	44.0	60.0	75.1
indirect taxes (less subventions) and import duties	0.3	2.5	15.8	0.7	1.0	2.1

Table 5.5 Ratio of the Shadow GDP to the Official GDP (in percentages)

Item	1993	1994	1995
Total GDP in the shadow sector, including:	27.1	39.1	45.2
I. goods production	30.0	37.2	25.3
II. services production	27.8	46.4	65.9
III. indirect taxes (less subventions) and import duties	2.6	4.7	1.4

The nature of shadow sector activities has radically changed during the reform period. In the pre-reform period, the shadow sector was mainly engaged in the production of scarce consumer goods. With the beginning of the reform process, the shadow economy has rapidly shifted its activities to the service sector (car servicing; repairing and reconstructing housing facilities; middlemen activities in trade; real estate dealing, including sale and purchase of apartments in large cities;

etc.). Since then, the illegal and even directly criminal dealings of the operators of the shadow economy have denigrated it. The rampant activities are unbridled smuggling, including strategic raw materials, fuel and weapons; illicit redistribution of property rights on privatized assets; illicit financial transactions, including conversion of noncash transfers into cash and capital transfers abroad; drug trafficking; bootlegging; and trafficking of human beings (mainly women and children). Racketeering and criminal security services occupy a special place in the criminal business. Whole armies of young people have emerged who criminally control the markets and make easy money through such operations. Waves of the so-called *razborkas* (gangsters' wars), often accompanied with salvos of gunfire, are raging throughout the country. The criminal business is tightly interlaced with legal or semilegal businesses. Sometimes the gangs operate under the cover of legal private security services. Private business is reinforcing its own armed security services. At present, nearly 800,000 people are believed to be engaged in this kind of activity, many of them being former military personnel or policemen. There are estimates that today in Russia nearly three million firearms are privately, mostly illicitly, owned.

These activities are causing great damage to the national economy. A system of triple taxation operates in the country, in which, beyond the governmental taxation service, criminal communities and corrupt bureaucrats are extorting money from public and private businesses. While people are able to evade taxes and thus keep the state exchequer impoverished, they cannot escape the organized crime, which collects its share without fail from everyone. At the same time, investments are almost frozen, which makes it difficult to modernize production and bring down the prices of the consumer goods. The weakening of the law enforcement machinery has led these functions to be progressively taken over by criminal elements – "godfathers" and "thieves of high authority" *(avtoritety)*. It is the small and medium businesses which suffer most from organized crime. Owners of small- and medium-sized businesses do not have adequate governmental protection and are too weak to organize their own security. However, big business too is gradually getting pressured by the criminal world. Daily murders of big businessmen are not uncommon these days. The struggle for control over large enterprises in industry, trade, finance, and banking, is continuing and growing violent, with the frequent use of explosives and firearms.

The shadow economy is both aggravating and alleviating poverty. It aggravates poverty by making the government machinery less efficient and by cheating it out of taxes, thereby preventing the government exchequer from spending on the social sector; but it alleviates the poverty of those who join the criminal gangs and thus become operators in the shadow economy. By extracting the production of really useful goods and services from the "shadow GDP" component, and adding them to the "official GDP"; and similarly, by subtracting the component which is redistributive and parasitic in nature from the "official GDI," the contribution of the shadow sector to the solution or aggravation of the poverty problem can be quantified. Such a net balance analysis in the context of the Russian Federation suggests that the shadow economy has contributed more to the aggravation of poverty than to its eradication. The following arguments support this judgment.

1. There has been a drastic growth in the shadow sector's turnover ratio with the "official GDP" (it grew from 27.1 percent in 1993 to 45.2 percent in 1995), along with the growing ratio of services in both sectors. But it can be supposed that the redistributive-parasitic component is greater in services than in goods production.
2. The growth of the shadow sector is taking place amidst the continuing decline of the official economy. This means that each unit of the real economy is more and more burdened by the redistributive-parasitic economy and is growing more heavily taxed. This process leads to the diminution of real production and is evidently among the main causes of the aggravation of mass poverty.
3. A certain stratum of persons, engaged in the shadow economy, has ever greater possibilities to extract income by one or even two orders of magnitude exceeding the income in the real economy. This leads to the influx of contraband and expensive consumer items like foreign limousines through mafia networks.
4. Finally, we have to consider that the shadow economy ruins and pushes out of its ranks numerous groups of small- and medium-business owners who are not able to resist the pressure of the racket and are left without adequate social protection. They are vulnerable to drastic changes in market conditions and suffer from the rigidity of the tax collecting administration. Their failures contribute to the growing army of the poor. These trends tend to accelerate along with the worsening of the general economic situation.

Alongside the true shadow sector there are also some kinds of "legal" economic activities which take advantage of all possible administrative loopholes to evade taxation and escape from government controls. They also resort to bribery and thus corrupt the officials. Fraud by means of financial pyramid building is also included in this category. Tax evasion undermines the financial base of the government social policy and makes it extremely difficult to implement poverty alleviation measures. Furthermore, fraud and swindling transactions have ruined millions of small investors, have eaten up the savings of the people, and have substantially augmented the ranks of the poor.

There is, however, a positive side to the development of the shadow sector in Russia. It is evident that the shadow sector also alleviates the employment problem. By expert estimates, nearly nine million people are employed full-time in the shadow economy, making up more than 12 percent of the total employment in 1995. The number of persons who are secondarily employed in it is about 36 million. Thus, total employment in the shadow sector has grown to almost 48 million people. The number of men and women having direct or indirect connection with this sector is significantly larger than this. There are estimates that 20-25 percent of the people connected with the shadow sector have relations with the criminal world. Complementary employment in the shadow sector and its criminal component are substantially changing the structure of the gross domestic expenditure (GDE).

Table 5.6 The Composition of the GDE

Item	At current prices (trillion rubles)			Percent of total		
	1993	1994	1995	1993	1994	1995
Total GDE in the official sector, including:	163	630	1659	100	100	100
final consumption	102	435	1095	63	69	66
gross capital formation	46	170	464	28	27	28
net exports	15	25	100	9	4	6
Total GDE in the shadow sector, including:	44	246	750	100	100	100
final consumption	33	183	600	72	74	80
gross capital formation	9	27	16	23	11	3
net exports (less imports) of goods and services	2	36	13	6	15	17

The composition of the "official GDE" in 1995 was as follows: final consumption (mainly private), 66 percent; gross capital formation, 28 percent; and net exports, 6 percent. In contrast, the shadow sector's GDE consisted of 80 percent consumption expenditures, 3 percent capital formation, and 17 percent net exports. We also have to accentuate the fact that the shadow sector's contribution to the state's treasury makes up only 1.4 percent of total indirect tax and revenue. It is evident that the shadow sector has managed to extract maximum profits to allow wasteful consumption by the new Russian rich. This sector is also the main channel for evading taxes and for illegally transferring resources and capitals abroad.

The distribution of wealth

During the reform period, major changes have occurred in wealth distribution. Production and nonproduction funds were removed from government control and privatized. It was supposed that large-scale privatization would facilitate the emergence of responsible owners and foster business initiative. A conception of privatization was developed according to which formal participation, not only of the staff and personnel of the enterprise, but also of the entire population was guaranteed. Staff and personnel participation was practically implemented by conceding workers and salaried persons who had the right to choose a privatization model. A majority chose the privatization model that granted significant advantages in acquiring shares to the staff and personnel. Wide participation in privatization was guaranteed by the so-called voucher system. The voucher is a kind of private of bearer check, which can be used by the recipient to buy shares in public sales and sell them in the free market.

But in reality, a redistribution of property rights occurred. The controlling blocks of shares were bought out from the personnel by a small circle of persons. The management of enterprises was seized by people who were not interested in the rights of the personnel and very often used fraudulent methods. Public sales of shares were organized in a way that did not give the small voucher-bearer any real opportunity to buy good shares. The major part of vouchers was bought out from them by the operators of the shadow economy and former managers of the state enterprises, who could then control the enterprises. The overwhelming part of enterprises was taken over by various "criminal covers" *(ugolovnaya krysha)*. The remaining state-owned enterprises were transformed into joint-stock companies with the state as the controlling block holder. Soon they were surrounded by swarms of small private firms, which very often were established for the sole purpose of pumping out profits and working capital to benefit the people in higher management. Since then, the so-called assets-stripping process has begun. Managers of large state enterprises, now transformed into joint-stock companies, have sold produced goods to these small firms at prices lower than the production costs. Investment has been underfinanced with the result that the firms continued using obsolete equipment. Sometimes stocks of raw material and valuable fixed assets were sold at symbolic prices. In such circumstances, while the production deteriorated, the management went on accumulating money and privately depositing it in the foreign banks.

In the second stage of privatization, there were mortgage auctions through which the largest and most important state enterprises were transferred to the private sector (to banking and financial institutions mainly) at a nominal cost. These mortgage auctions involved numerous law violations. In most cases, privatization did not transfer the enterprises into the hands of socially responsible owners. Therefore, those who were in control neither possessed the required professional knowledge and skills nor had the motivation to maintain productivity under the difficult conditions of the transformation period. They were simply interested in making maximal short-term profits. As a result, they rushed to inflate the prices of their products. This gave rise to monopolistic tendencies. The technological chains were ruined and industrial network systems destroyed. The general criminal atmosphere created around privatization did not allow a competitive milieu to emerge. Privatization secured neither technological modernization nor business rationality.

As a consequence, what we see today is that the majority of new owners use the income from the property they managed to acquire to finance wasteful luxury consumption and illegally transfer their capital abroad. They have built castles near Moscow, St. Petersburg, and other large cities which are called quite humbly "cottages;" they drive foreign-made luxury cars; their female companions wear expensive jewels; they live in large, private city residences; they frequent night clubs; and they even own villas abroad. Thus, the profits made by them go toward conspicuous consumption and not toward productive investment. Whatever investment they make is in the construction and improvement of their administrative buildings and offices.

It should not to be forgotten that before the reform process began, production was carried out under state management and the invested funds really belonged to the public. It is true that there was mismanagement; nevertheless, the production funds provided the means to finance public welfare facilities and to produce the goods necessary to support the disabled, the elderly, and children. They were the collectively owned assets of the Russian people, accumulated by their own efforts during their entire working lives. These funds have now gone into the hands of persons who are unable and unwilling to support guaranteed social standards.

To sum up, privatization in Russia has primarily been an illicit redistribution of wealth to the super rich which, on the one hand, has caused further impoverishment of the already poor and, on the other, has resulted in the criminalization of society. The poor have suffered manifold: from a production decline due to a change in property rights; from hampered access to public welfare facilities and social services; from the loss of a considerable number of social guarantees; and from the impossibility of replacing their worn-out and inoperative durables.

Along with the privatization and commercialization of a number of public consumption funds and utilities, new difficulties have arisen for the poor. All repair and maintenance work in privatized housing, as well as in the corresponding utility network, is now the responsibility of the owner. With the privatization of rest homes, sanatoria, and other recreational and rehabilitation institutions, the poor have the alternative of either paying the complete cost of their recreation or forgoing this privilege. Those poor who have small gardens and cottages around the big cities have to pay the full cost of the transport tariffs; older people are also unable to replace worn-out cars due to increased prices. Many people are unable to pay for their physician visits and medicines, and it is especially difficult to acquire the services of a dentist.

An estimate of the liquid assets distribution calculated with the use of the Chernavsky-Pirogov model is shown in Table 5.7. Table 5.8 represents the changes in savings concentration on the basis of VCIOM surveys. The tendency toward a concentration in the hands of limited number of households is evident. Table 5.9 shows that old-style everyday durables were acquired by a rather large number of households, but mainly before the reform period (color television sets, washing machines, cameras, audio sets, furniture). In contrast, new type of durables such as kitchen gadgets, video sets, and deep freezers are in the possession of a very small number of households, who acquired them mainly during the reform period.

IV. Social Policy Concerns

It is necessary to point out briefly the following features of the social situation in Russia in the nineties: a substantial difference has occurred between the established subsistence minimum and the average income across the country's territory; there also exist substantial regional differences in regard to poverty concentration. This problem has revealed itself in a most dramatic form in Dagestan, Buryatia, Northern Osetia, and the Chitinskaya oblast (where 43 to 68 percent of the households are facing poverty). The incomes of a third of the households studied in the Amurskaya oblast were below the subsistence minimum. This ratio was 15 to 20 percent in only fifteen territories; in eighteen territories it ranged between 5 to 10 percent, and in six territories it was less than 5 percent. Thus, poverty is spreading fast.

Poverty exerts a demoralizing influence on people. Work motivation goes down, and social and political apathy grows. Also, the danger of

Table 5.7 The socio-economic structure of contemporary Russia

Group #	Group's composition	Group's average household monthly income (in U.S.$)	Group members' ratio to total households (%)	Liquid assets		
				Household average (in U.S. $1,000)	Group's total (in U.S.$) millions	The ratio of group's assets to total assets of the whole population (%)
I.	Workers of state enterprises in manufacturing, pensioners, unemployed, low-paid public servants, peasants in collective enterprises	<100	70	0.1	3.5	2.5
II.	Medium-paid employees in private sector, well-to-do farmers, armed forces officers, mid-level government officials	100-499	20	0.3	3	2.1
III.	Highly paid workers in raw material and fuels production	500-999	5	10	25	18
IV.	High-level managers in the private sector producing for the domestic market, high-level government officials	500-999	2	10	10	7.2
V.	Businessmen in wholesale and retail trade	1000-4999	3	5	22.5	16.2
VI.	Middlemen in exports and imports, racketeers, Mafiosi	5000-29999	NA	NA	NA	NA
VII.	High-level managers in raw material and fuel production, banking and finance, the highest level of the government officials	30000 and up	0.3	500	75	54

Source: Pirogov, Chernavsky et al. 1995

NA = Not Available

manipulation of the unfortunate masses by both left-wing and right-wing adventurers looms large. The shrinking of the effective demand for local goods has aggravated the crisis and created high rates of unemployment. It has orientated the rich sections of the population toward comprador behavior leading to the export of raw materials. Entrepreneurs are deprived of any incentive to invest in manufacturing. The nation's social structure is increasingly growing polarized; the poor are getting marginalized. A large pauperized stratum has emerged. The government needs to be aware of the importance of social stability and has to pay due attention to programs for alleviating poverty. Measures to fight poverty can be divided into compensatory, shock-absorbing, and problem-oriented ones.

Table 5.8 Changes in Savings Concentration (VCIOM survey question: "Does your household have any savings?")

Answers	August 1991	March 1992	June 1993	October 1993	February 1994
Yes	66	60	25	19	17
No	30	36	71	76	78
Difficult to Answer	4	4	4	5	5

Table 5.9 Distribution of durables in Russian households (in percentages)

Item	Households without the item	Households with the item			
		Aquired a year ago		Acquired more than 5 years ago	
		Ratio to the total sample	Ratio to those with the item	Ratio to the total sample	Ratio to those with the item
Color TV sets	23.8	4.6	6.0	35.1	46.1
Washing machines	10.6	6.2	6.9	47.1	52.6
Cameras	59.4	1.7	2.8	20.4	33.7
Kitchen gadgets	89.3	2.6	24.3	2.0	18.7
Deep freezers	85.7	3.2	22.4	3.0	21.0
Audio sets	52.4	4.6	9.7	16.8	35.3
Videos	86.1	3.1	22.3	1.3	9.3
Furniture sets	41.4	3.7	6.3	29.5	50.3
Cars	76.1	1.8	7.5	13.1	56.7

Source: VCIOM 1994 survey.

As a compensatory measure, provisions should be made for payments and allowances as well as for benefits for the poorest strata, in view of general inflation increases in the cost of utilities and the basic necessities of life. Shock-absorbing measures or social safety nets – such as pensions and unemployment insurance – will have to be created. Efforts must also be made to attack the deep-rooted causes of poverty, to provide for better health care, education facilities and professional training, and to develop employment and social rehabilitation services, public works programs, and so on. These measures would make up the core of social policies.

The government circles of Russia have gradually come to understand the nature of the poverty problem and have taken some measures to neutralize it. However, all these actions have not yet been brought together to work as a coherent system. In order to achieve this, goal-oriented programs aimed at solving the key problems of economic growth must be developed; these would also ensure a more equitable distribution of income, stabilize employment, and actively combat the phenomenon of poverty.

The enormous increase of those population groups in Russia who are greatly dependent on assistance provided by the state – beggars, refugees, neglected children, and adolescents – testifies to the failure of social policy and exposes its shortcomings. In 1994, the social network was enhanced with the creation of 2,545 new institutions to implement goal-oriented programs. Some of these institutions provided social services; some were centers where one could stay during the day; some provided urgent social assistance; some provided social aid to households and children; and some acted as rehabilitation centers for adolescents without parents. Others acted as orphanages and centers providing urgent psychological aid in response to telephone calls from doss-houses.

Beginning in May 1996 some measures to improve the protection of the insufficiently provided sections have been taken. In particular, a law has been passed to increase the minimum pension by 10 percent, and the RF president has issued a decree *(Ukaz)* "on urgent measures to improve pension security for RF citizens." In January 1996, the aggregate sum of the childbirth allowance was increased by 1.5 times, and the allowance provided for childcare until a child is one and a half years old was increased twofold. Different measures have also been taken to provide social protection to other socially vulnerable categories. In a number of regions, laws have been passed (Sverdlovskaya and Kamchatskaya oblasts, the republic of Karelia, etc.) or decisions have been made by the administrative heads (in nine regions) on the subsistence minimum. A comprehensive approach for the calculation of the average per capita income has also been worked out and applied.

The payment of social allowances to the underprivileged, whose aggregate average per capita income is lower than the subsistence minimum, has been effected in sixteen territories; money payments adding to pensions and allowances for food, clothes, and fuel have been introduced in forty-one territories; benefits and compensations to pay for utilities have been provided in thirty territories. To maintain the provision of personally addressed social aid, special services are being set up; otherwise these functions are fulfilled by the centers for urgent social aid. Most regional programs for social protection are based on a complex approach to provide for the social protection of all categories of people in need. There are also special goal-oriented programs to serve the needs of certain groups. About 15 million people have received social protection under various schemes.

In Nizhny Novgorod, an operational weekly system of social indicators has been introduced which includes the price indices, the subsistence minimum by socio-demographic groups, the levels of the population's various types of incomes, the number of those receiving aid, and the ratio of the poor to the total population. In the republic of Tatarstan, poverty eradication activities were initiated in 1993 with the adoption of a program of social protection to be later fortified by a number of laws. A system was introduced to monitor the corresponding indices by eleven socio-demographic groups of the population along with a procedure for calculating the aggregate average per capita income of households. However, these measures are either regional or limited.

In 1997, the president and the government of the RF took some radical steps to accelerate the reform process. These steps consist of three main components: housing and utility services, pension system reform, and the restructuring of enterprises. Undoubtedly, these measures are instigated by the budget crisis, which erupted in the first quarter of 1997. The reform of the housing and utility services envisages the gradual abolition of governmental subventions, which hold down housing rents and utility rates. Pension reform contemplates additional employees' contributions to supplemental pension funds. The enterprise restructuring project would introduce simplified insolvency procedures for financially unsound businesses. There are grounds to fear that these measures will create additional financial burdens, especially on the poor and low-to-middle strata of the population. These strata may be most seriously hit by the rise in public utilities rates.

Government proposals to raise the upper limit of the income interval for the minimal rate of taxation (12 percent) – from 12 to 60 million rubles per year – are somewhat counterbalancing. But this is a measure clearly in favor of the middle and upper-to-middle groups. Further, these groups are not very numerous in contemporary Russia. Nevertheless, the alleviation of the income tax burden may be considered as a step in the right direction to promote effective demand as well as to lessen tax evasion. However, a policy of comprehensive legal substantiation for the conditions of paying wages and salaries, social allowances, and the genuine implementation of labor code provisions is of urgent importance. There also remains the task of developing a set of social normative-statistical indices. Yet the government income tax proposal concerns only incomes from primary jobs; the older limits on secondary jobs still remain. Thus the income tax amendments do not touch the domain of secondary and other jobs in which tax evasion continue unabated.

As to the RF Ministry of Social Protection, its plans for the future include the establishment of social protection institutes of each type in every town and even in every district of the cities before the year 2000. There has been a proposal to open 342 rehabilitation centers for disabled children, 180 institutes for psychological and pedagogical assistance, the same number of institutes for orphans, and 256 centers for persons of no fixed abode or address. However, in 1996 the Ministry of Social Protection was considered redundant and was merged with the Labor Ministry to form a new Ministry of Labor and Social Development. Thus, the contradiction between the urgency for social protection, on the one hand, and the narrowing financial and political possibilities to satisfy it, on the other, has become more pronounced.

Until recently, while making efforts to attain financial stabilization and to support "growth points," the Russian government has underestimated the need to fight poverty by means of reorienting its economic strategy and legal background. It should be noted, however, that the present-day legislation includes, as a social right, a functioning system to protect people against social risks like the loss of capacity to work, the death or loss of a family's breadwinner, maternity protection, and so on. There is a single state system to provide children's allowances and to compensate those groups that suffer in emergency situations.

The problem to be highlighted is that even today the curtailed means for social protection needs are redistributed at least twice on the way to their designated recipients. The social policy distortions connected with this factor already existed in the previous periods, but never have they manifested themselves as they do now. On the one hand, every fifth person below the poverty line has no access at all to the social support rendered by the state. Most of the needy get it in a quite unsatisfactory way. On the other hand, a major part of the social expenses is received by those who are not really needy. Social policy must be an instrument to bridge the income gap as well as to equalize life chances as they are distributed among representatives of various social strata and groups. It should not serve the opposite goal, for example, of promoting income differentiation or consolidating the privileges of this or that propertied stratum. Russian social policy should be a very serious tool with which to reinforce the social sphere and bridge the abyss of alienation between those in power and the people at large, and to facilitate the socio-economic and political stabilization of the whole of society.

There are several contradictions in the government policy. For example, in 1995 the federal budget provided 42 trillion rubles to be used for health care, which meant 23 thousand rubles per month for every citizen of Russia. At the same time, the same budget allotted 4 million rubles per month to every patient at the government medical centers. In 1996, this monstrous disproportion increased even more. The federal budget for 1997 increased spending on health care for the president's administrative department and the Foreign Ministry by 2.2 times while the increase for the ordinary people was only 1.5 times. The same is true of wages and salaries. It is noteworthy that the problem in question became much more pronounced after the Supreme Soviet was done away with at the end of 1993 and the new parliament became constitutionally much weaker. As a result, the spending on a single employee in the central government skyrocketed from 200 thousand rubles per month in 1993 to 2.2 million rubles in 1994. But this is not the final point of the redistribution process. Following their own selfish interests, lower level officials are actively participating in the redistribution of money which has been spared by those above and which, in accordance with the primary allocation, was supposed to reach the weak social strata.

A dramatic piece of evidence illustrating the point in question is the activity of the Government Population Employment Fund (GFZN) which, in contrast to other government extrabudgetary public welfare funds, is not an autonomous financial establishment as much as it is part of the federal employment service, which covers its operating expenses. This service is actually using the money it gets at its own discretion. Only two responsibilities from the fourteen given to the Fund are regulated by instructions in conformity with the law and follow the established norms of financial control. A lot of opportunities to distribute the fund's money in the interests of the administration exist. For example, in 1993 only 6 percent of GFZN money was spent to pay unemployment benefits. Added to this, the average amount of those benefits made up only 11.3 percent of the average wage. At the same time, the employment service spent 27.2 percent of the fund's income on its own functioning. The amount spent on the fund's operating needs, the overhaul of its premises, and the purchases of various equipment items required twice as much money as the unemployment benefits. The money spent by GFZN to support the development of private businesses was 2.5 times more than it used to pay for the same benefits. In 1993, 42.5 percent of GFZN income was not spent at all, creating a balance at the beginning of 1994. In brief, there are a lot of very complicated problems to solve in order to increase the effectiveness of the institutional system.

V. Protest Movements and Trade Unions

The problem of poverty is not only a socio-economic phenomenon; it has its political consequences too. This problem enters political life along the following three lines:

1. as an element of the government's socio-economic policy reflecting the attitude of the social elite to the phenomenon of poverty and forming one or another mechanism to neutralize the consequences of poverty which are detrimental to the elite;
2. as an element of mass consciousness reflecting the ability of the people to adjust to the changing situation (of mass poverty) and periodically influencing the population's electoral behavior; and
3. as an institutional factor which accumulates the attitudes of different strata, political parties, nongovernmental organizations and movements toward the problem of social inequality and mass poverty.

By the end of 1996, when social contradictions became more pronounced in Russia in the form of mass strikes, hunger strikes, and protest marches, bringing together many millions of people (as manifested, for example, during the mass actions on 5 November 1996), local and central governments began to take some measures to neutralize them. Opinion polls regularly conducted by VCIOM, Goskomstat, and the analytical surveys carried out by various research institutes have tried to demonstrate the trend in attitudes of people regarding the growing phenomenon of poverty. The data obtained through these channels show that at the end of the fifth year of the reforms, people began to lose their patience and tolerance in view of the continuous lowering of their living standards. And there is a growing number of those who think that pauperization has reached its peak and has become "unbearable."

The influence of organized political opposition on the present-day ruling structures, as it is represented by such political parties as the CPRF (Communist Party of the Russian Federation), the corresponding blocs at the state Duma, the Federation Council (second chamber of the Russian parliament), and so on is also on the rise. The Russian trade union movement is gradually becoming stronger. In contemporary Russia, where other institutions of civil society are still in their infancy, the trade unions are striving to play the surrogate role of such institutions by representing the interests of the working masses. The disastrous socio-economic situation involving tens of millions of employees has undoubtedly encouraged such a trend. It should also be noted that during the preparatory process for the Copenhagen World Summit for Social Development many nongovernmental organizations in Russia – the trade unions in particular – assigned top priority to the problem of poverty eradication.

Creative market forces coupled with Western assistance can hardly raise Russia and other former USSR republics to the level of the well-being characteristic of the most developed market economies of the West. Poverty has become the genetic label of the so-called transitional economy. The number of those whose income was below the subsistence minimum level ranged between 28.9 million to 50.4 million people. (For comparison, the number of those employed was only 73 million people). Today the falling standard of living is the major focus of the trade unions' attention. This fact manifests itself in their initiatives to motivate the Russian government, in the Federal Assembly, and in the Russian president's effort to change the course of reforms from a neo-liberal monetarist kind to a more democratic one. For a number of years, the efforts of the trade unions and of the nongovernmental organizations have concentrated on securing the right to decent work and decent payment. The chronic arrears of earned money are among the reasons for growing poverty in Russia. In 1996, trade unions actively exerted pressure on employers, including the government, by use of legal means, in the form of strikes, protests, and other collective actions, as well as through persistent attempts to solve the most acute problems through dialogue, social partnerships, and tripartite negotiations.

The International Decade for the Eradication of Poverty (1997-2006), declared by the United Nations, is regarded in Russia and other CIS countries as a timely initiative. By bringing together more than 100 million trade union members grouped within the CIS trade union centers, the General Confederation of Trade Unions has come forward with a declaration "For the Abolition of Poverty" and called for people's active participation in the Decade. It has also declared that "an economy characterized by absolute poverty cannot be effective." The escalation of poverty caused mainly by arrears in wages and salaries motivated many working people in Russia to step forward with an all-Russian protest action which involved about 15 million employees.

The protest actions were conducted through the initiative of the working people and in accordance with their demands. They are regarded as an important development in the mounting campaign to fight poverty and misery. On the eve of the All-Russian Protest Action Day, the Independent Trade Unions Federation of Russia (ITUFR) issued a special appeal to the working people. By supporting the ILO's position, it stressed that "poverty is not only an insult to the human dignity of those who are its victims, but it is also a threat to the rest of the population."

In the first quarter of 1997, wage arrears already amounted to nearly 50 trillion rubles; together with pension arrears, they stood at almost 70 trillion rubles.[5] The Russian trade unions organized a mass protest action on 27 March 1997 with some 20 million participants. This protest movement received unprecedented support from the international labor movement. A fact-finding mission of the International Confederation of Free Trade Unions (ICFTU), headed by Secretary-General Bill Jordan, visited Moscow in March 1997. The leadership of ICFTU sent a letter to President Yeltsin expressing its concern over the prevailing situation of nonpayment of arrears in wages and pensions. The ICFTU leaders considered the wage arrears as a gross violation of human rights, and particularly, of ILO Convention Number 95, which had been ratified by Russia. The ICFTU leadership has requested that President Yeltsin: 1) as the first step, improve the situation by settling wage arrears of government employees; 2) introduce legal sanctions in the case of wage arrears and secure enforcement procedures; and 3) ratify ILO Convention Number 173, concerning employees' claims for protection in employers' insolvency cases and Number 158, concerning the legal aspects of employment termination. ICFTU considers that wage arrears in Russia set a dangerous precedent, which may be used by multinationals to exert pressures on labor in other countries. ICFTU is also emphasizing that the wage arrears problem is directly related to a more general trend of "market globalization of the international economy" accompanied with disastrous consequences for national economies and social guarantees. The ICFTU position on the wage arrears situation in Russia was supported by American, British, French, German, Spanish, Canadian, and other trade union organizations.

VI. Conclusion

The current phase of transition from a command economy to a market-oriented economy in Russia is characterized by a series of "adjustments," three of which are important in the context of our present analysis of poverty.

1. An adjustment in the system of labor relations. Changes being introduced in the system of labor relations are taking time to

---

5.   It must be mentioned that as of 1 July 1997 the government settled all pension arrears.

gain acceptability. A majority of the labor force is finding it difficult to adjust to the new system and feels attached to the old pattern of behavior, which is counterproductive in the new milieu. The incongruity between the expected and persistent behavior patterns has resulted in a situation of tension.

2. An adjustment in the area of resource mobilization. Labor skills, professional knowledge, physical and intellectual abilities that were not properly utilized or appreciated in the preceding system are now considered valuable and are receiving recognition. Thus, some of the previously valued skills have become obsolete and people possessing new and higher skills are in greater demand both nationally and internationally. This has caused a migration of talent abroad, on the one hand, and the creation of a system of secondary employment, both legal and illegal, within the country, on the other. Those whose skills are now being devalued, and therefore they have lost their jobs, have entered the category of the "new poor." This has led to a state of anomie promoting instability in both social life and economic production.

3. A search for adequate placement in the new structure. The changing situation has encouraged motivated people to look for alternative positions in the new system to escape unemployment and resultant poverty. Such people attempt to adjust through reorientation and retraining, or training in the new skills.

All three forms of adjustments – responses to the emerging situation with a view to accommodating in the changing environment – are occurring simultaneously in Russian society. Ideally, it is the third kind of adjustment that is needed to make a successful transition, ensuring that there is no flight of trained manpower and no swelling of the ranks of the unemployed. Even as a temporary phenomenon, the occurrence of poverty during transition is a cause for worry and calls for concerted action on the part of the government to eradicate it by ameliorating the situation of the poor and ensuring that no more people will be added to the ranks of the poor. Unfortunately, this is not happening, with the result that poverty has become more pronounced and more widespread. It has caused polarization and marginalization in Russian society and spurred moral degradation among its people.

Russia's social structure was bimodal even prior to the reforms, but it was stable and the polarization was not so sharply expressed. The equilibrium between the "masses" and the "elite" was maintained by means of command-administrative (central planning) methods, price regulation, and an access to the public welfare funds. This equilibrium has been upset by the reform process. The diminishing demand for goods by the people (with a virtual absence of the middle class) has caused a production crisis, leading to a sharp slump in investment. The capital accumulated by the country's rich elite is not being invested in the country. It is taken out of the country for investment abroad or is used by them for wasteful consumption (such as purchasing expensive imported goods). In sum, since 1996 the general economic situation in Russia has continued to deteriorate. There are only two ways to escape the poverty trap: 1) through a radical change of the reforming vector, and 2) by accepting temporary additional costs in order to increase the country's cultural and educational potential for the sake of long-term gains in technological progress necessary for economic growth.

The analysis of the phenomenon of poverty in Russia presented in this chapter brings us to the conclusion that poverty, and economic and political reforms are closely correlated. The inequality of distribution of income and property among the Russian population's major groups are basically conditioned by the economy's critical situation as well as by the type of society emerging under the unlimited implementation of extreme liberal policies. Economic depression curtails both individual consumption and public welfare funds. The political structures, while acquiring certain democratic aspects, have so far been incapable of controlling the fair distribution of the nation's wealth and stimulating its economic growth. Under these conditions, the strengthening of the social vector of reform, including the introduction of a human factor, is of key importance. It is indeed the social factor – of which the program for poverty eradication forms the core – which is capable of strengthening the processes of economic and political democratization. The programs mapped out by the government at present, as well as its decisions and programs to do away with wage arrears, to restructure the coal industry, to protect the monoproduction-oriented closed towns of the former MICs, and to stimulate small businesses through tax incentives could promote employment, stimulate an increase in wages and salaries in real terms, and establish a balance between the subsistence minimum, incomes, and labor productivity.

In February 1997, the Russian government approved a program of social reforms for the period of 1996-2000. During the first stage (1996-1997), due to resource constraints, the scheduled measures were limited to a stabilization of living standards, a gradual reduction of poverty, diminishing the income gap between social groups, and preventing mass unemployment. However, the most important of the measures should be the settlement of wages, salaries, pensions, and benefits arrears and the prevention of the emergence of such arrears in the future; and the prevention of large-scale firings in regions with a critical situation in the labor market. In the second stage (1998-2000), when the long expected economic growth is to resume, and material and financial possibilities for boosting social expenditure should emerge, preconditions for the real growth of the population's money income, mass poverty eradication, and an optimal employment level could be created. The implementation of a comprehensive program for the creation and protection of jobs should begin. An increase in the guaranteed minimum wage level and old age employees' pensions to the subsistence minimum is also scheduled. Large-scale social reforms would solve the problem of reinforcing social protection and the social servicing of veterans, disabled, elderly people, children, and other categories of disadvantaged sections not capable of active work, as well as socially weak groups.

However, other measures of government policies are in strong contradiction to poverty eradication goals. The reform of housing rents and public utilities is putting a rather heavy burden on the lower income groups of the population. This may lead to the further depletion of public welfare funds, affecting those designated for recreational facilities for children and adults first. The restructuring of enterprises could result in massive new unemployment. Thus it remains to be seen which trend of government policy will win the upper hand.

But it is also evident that the problem in question can be solved only if the course of the reforms is corrected. In this light, the present social programs of the government may be considered insufficient. They are contradictory in nature and are formulated in rather general terms with little room for the explanation of practical measures. They are too much oriented to spontaneous market forces and, in turn, neglectful of active policy, particularly concerning the initiation of economic growth. The permanent financial difficulties of the government also leave little room for the consistent implementation of the mapped-out social programs. Whether these difficulties can be overcome in the absence of real economic growth is seriously doubtful. To conclude, the basis of poverty eradication lies in the combination of economic growth and an adequate income policy.

Industry-specific regional programs will have to be developed to fight poverty; this would require interdisciplinary research. Cross-cultural comparisons of such programs, as they are designed and applied in Russia, in the other CIS countries, as well as in the countries of Eastern Europe, will be useful in this regard. To coordinate research work in the field of poverty in Russia and to maintain necessary links with the international organizations dealing with the problem in question, it would be ideal to set up a special center for poverty studies in the framework of the Russian Academy of Sciences.

Based on our analysis, some additional suggestions are offered below to help eradicate poverty in Russia more effectively.

- Controlling deterioration of investment activity and the decline in the volume of production, which has resulted in the deterioration of jobs
- Checking large-scale firings (not only in official emergency regions)
- Creating better conditions for development and augmenting employment in alternative, nongovernmental sectors of the economy
- Securing selective support and protection for persons who have lost their employment or are likely to loose it; and providing complementary aid for employment to people who have serious difficulties getting jobs
- Providing tax allowances for those enterprises that are creating new jobs or securing old ones
- Alleviating the consequences of long-term unemployment with vocational training and retraining, and providing facilities for the life-long education of the labor force
- Maintaining more stringent control to prevent illegal capital outflow
- Introducing an active government housing policy
- Introducing income policy with heavier taxation for higher income groups
- Giving priority to economic growth instead of monetary equilibrium policies
- Maintaining rigorous government control over wage and salary payments to force employers to renounce wage and salary arrears
- Establishing a nationwide people's saving system, using both governmental and nongovernmental banking and finance institutions, including pension funds
- Reestablishing a semigovernmental public welfare system (together with trade unions and large corporations)
- Establishing a credit system specialized for all agricultural producers, including private farmers as well as collective enterprises
- Giving support to the trade unions
- Imposing heavier taxes on the excessive consumption of luxury items
- Eradicating the racket pressures on small- and medium-sized businesses
- Carrying out a careful and gradual restructuring of enterprises with a view to forestalling the danger of massive unemployment growth

Under the circumstances characteristic of contemporary Russia, the problem of poverty can be solved only if the conceptual approaches to the social, economic, and political reforms under way are modernized and if these approaches are implemented in a more or less synchronized way.

Bibliography

In English

UNDP. 1995. *Human Development Report. Russian Federation.* New York.

The World Bank. 1995. *Poverty in Russia: An Assessment* (Report N14110-RU).

Bartoli, H. 1991. "Progress and Poverty: Concepts and Dialectics in Different Countries." *Poverty, Progress and Development,* ed. P.M. Henry. UNESCO.

Braithwaite, J. 1995. "The Old and New Poor in Russia." *Poverty in Russia during the Transition,* ed. Jeni Klugman. The World Bank.

Oyen E., Miller S., Samad S. 1996. *Poverty. A Global Review. Handbook on International Poverty Research.* : Scandinavia University Press, Cambridge: UNESCO.

Tanguiane, S. 1994. *Literacy and Illiteracy in the Computer Age.* Paris: UNESCO.

Timofeev, T. 1994."The employment problems in Russia and in the CIS (a comparative view)." Paper for an international colloquium. Paris.

In Russian

International congress. 1997. "Economic reforms in Russia: a new stage." "Human relations: social policy and social partnership." Moscow.

RF Labour ministry. 1992. "Methodical instructions for subsistence minimum computation." Moscow.

Timofeev, T. 1990. "Some problems of industrial relations and social policies." Moscow.

_____. 1996. "Russian Federation social reforms programme for 1996-2000: A draft." Moscow.

Bogomolov, D. 1996. "Reforms as seen by American and Russian scholars." Russian economic magazine, Fund for economic literacy. Moscow.

Interregional conference. 1997. "The role of social partnership in the socio-economic development and regulation of socio-industrial relations." Proceedings. Moscow.

Russian Federation. 1995. "National Report to the World Summit for Social Development."

Aganbegian, A. 1996. "Depression and stagnation does not equal stabilisation." Business World 29.10. Moscow.

Baikova, A., Zhilin, U. 1994. "Transformation processes in Russia and CIS problems. Shifts in social structure." "Forum" almanac. Moscow.

Burlachkov, V. 1996. *Price and income policies under market transformation of the economy.* Academy of labour and social relations. Moscow.

Chernavskii, D., Chernavskaya, O., Pirogov, G. 1993. "A social stratification model." Physical institute of Russian Academy of Sciences. Moscow.

Chernavskii, D., Suslakov, B., et al. 1995. "Socio-economic structure of the society." *Legislation and the Economy.* Moscow.

Chernina, N. 1994. "Poverty as a social phenomenon of Russian society." *Sociological Studies.* Moscow.

Dmitriev, M. 1996. "Financing of social programmes: social expenditure policy in contemporary Russia." *Questions of the Economy.* Moscow.

Dubson, B., Rydvanov, N. 1992. "Some aspects of employment and unemployment in CIS countries." *The new Commonwealth: principles and perspectives,* ed. T. Timofee. Moscow.

Kagarlitski, B. 1995. *The corporate model and the social conflict.* Institute for comparative Socio-Political and Labour studies. Moscow.

Khramtsov, A. 1995. *Social policies in a transitional society.* Institute for comparative Socio-Political and Labour studies. Moscow.

Perevedentsev, V. 1990. "Youth and the socio-demographic problems." The Science. Moscow.

_____. 1996. "On population's migration: social consequences." "Forum" almanac. Moscow.

Pirogov, G. (ed) 1992. "Social safety nets." The Science. Moscow.

Pirogov, G. 1992. "The concept of social shock absorbers." *Mechanisms of social safety nets.* The Science. Moscow.

———. 1997. "A serious factor of mass discontent." *Wage arrears and the dynamics of mass protest.* Institute for comparative Socio-Political and Labour studies. Moscow.

Pirogov, G., Fedorov, S. 1992. "A framework for a new social policy." *Reforming processes: tendencies and problems.* Institute for comparative Socio-Political and Labour studies. Moscow.

Poduzov, A. 1996. "Poverty measurements." *Forecast problems:* NN4-5. Moscow.

Pronin, S. 1994. "The conflict and the trade-off." "Forum" almanac. Moscow.

Pronin, S., Stolpovskii, B. 1994. *Industrial democracy problems and Russian reforms in the 90s.* Institute for comparative Socio-Political and Labour studies. Moscow.

Sytchyeva, V. 1996. "Poverty measurements." *Social studies.* Moscow.

———. 1995. "Property inequality problems in Russia." *Social studies.* Moscow.

Yaroshenko, S. 1994. "Poverty's subculture problems." Moscow.

Zaslavskaya, T. 1996. "Where does Russia go? Social transformation of post-Soviet space." InterPrax. Moscow.

Zaslavskaya, T., Arutunian, L. 1994. "Where does Russia go? Social development alternatives." InterPrax. Moscow.

Zaslavskaya, T., Ryvkina, R. 1991. "Sociology of economic life." The Science. Novosibirsk.

Zherebin, V., Rimashevskaya, N., et al. 1994. "Poverty: viewed by scholars." Moscow.

Zubova, L. 1996. "Poverty and wealth images. Criteria and scales of poverty." Information report of VCIOM monitoring: No. 4. Moscow.

Chapter Six

MONGOLIA

In the Grip of Poverty

Tsogt Nyamsuren
Ministry of External Relations of Mongolia

Introduction

At the end of the 1980s the world entered a new era. After the collapse of the Soviet Union and the communist system, the world was no longer divided by Cold War borders. It is now acknowledged that socialism, once practiced by the countries of the Eastern bloc, was not able to solve cultural, social, economic, political, and ecological problems. Moreover, it will take several decades to repair the damages caused by totalitarian socialism. However, the failure of socialism confronts us with an historic challenge. People expect instant changes in their lifestyle to compensate for years of oppression and privation. In a climate of such high expectations, one forgets that the transition from a socialist society to a market-oriented economy is not an easy road. There are difficulties all along the way, and the process is lengthy. It is too much to expect immediate rewards. The transition process requires not only a change in the structure of the economy but also in the system of the polity. Social transformation involves the creation of a democratic polity and a system of social justice for all. The democratic order can become stable only when the economic, social, and legal systems are just and fair. It cannot survive without the rule of law. It will be even less viable in the absence of an unfair economic and social order.

The process of transition is made difficult by the phenomenon of poverty. Not only are there groups of people who live in abject poverty, the country as a whole is rated poor by all international standards. In the Mongolian case, therefore, a multipronged attack on poverty is needed to improve the country's economy so that the country is removed from the list of poor countries, and to alleviate and eradicate the poverty of its people. To solve the problem of poverty in a country such as Mongolia, the first requirement is to change its power structure in such a way as to redistribute, and thus utilize, economic and productive power for the larger interest of society. It will take a great deal of political conviction and persuasion to directly connect economic development with productivity, social responsibility, and social justice. The countries of the world will have to realize that we all depend on one another for support and help. Coordination of policies and joint decision making at the global level is required if we wish to move a little closer to the aim of securing a life of dignity for humankind now and in the future.

I. Mongolia: Transition to a Market-Oriented Economy

Mongolia is a landlocked country, located in the center of Asia, sandwiched between the Russian Federation and the People's Republic of China. It has a harsh continental climate. It covers a territory of 1,565 square kilometers, consisting of mountains, plateaus, and desert. It is a small country of only 2.3 million people, 600,000 of whom live in Ulan Bator, the capital city. A high percentage of its population (54.7 percent) lives in urban areas; only 45.3 percent of the population is rural. Ninety-five percent of the population are of Mongol-speaking origin; the remaining 5 percent are Kazaks, living mostly in the far western part of the country.

Mongolia is a unitary state consisting of twenty-one provinces known as *aimags* and a capital city. The country now has a multiparty system of government and the parliament is known as the State Great *Hural*. The country regained its independence with the victory of the National Liberation Movement in 1911 and the Popular People's Revolution in 1921. Thereafter, a period of renaissance and prosperity followed. With the collapse of the communist regime in 1990, many changes have taken place in the political, economic, and social life of the society. During the last seventy years of independence, the country experienced agro-industrial development: significant strides were made in the production of agricultural raw materials, livestock farming, processing industries, in the excavation of mineral resources, in energy plants, transportation, communication, and construction.

Mongolia has followed a centralized and planned economy since the 1940s. Under that system, there was encouragement neither for the private sector, nor for competition. Economic freedom did not exist. Arbitrarily fixed prices and tariffs had a negative impact on the effective use of financial and human resources, leading the economy to a stalemate.

In the early 1990s Mongolia chose to undertake the democratization of its political system and the transition to a market economy. This was legally guaranteed by the new constitution of Mongolia, adopted in 1992. Currently, the country is experiencing a difficult transitional period: the government is implementing an economic structural reform program with the support of international financial and development institutions. The structural reform measures are aimed at (1) establishing the legal bases for a market-oriented economy, (2) carrying out a coordinated financial, monetary, and credit policy, (3) preventing the danger of unlimited inflation, (4) introducing and establishing a liberalized price and exchange rate system, (5) intensifying the property privatization process, and (6) curbing the decline of the economy and stabilizing its development.

Some signs of stabilization and positive improvements can be noticed in the national economy. For the first time in four years the GDP registered some growth in 1994. Following the complete liberalization of the hard currency exchange rate, the *tugrik*[1] (Mongolian currency) was stabilized and made convertible on the domestic market. As of 1994, the private sector was already in a position to produce more than half of the GDP. Over 80 percent of the properties earmarked for privatization have already been privatized and 90 percent of livestock has been transferred to private owners.

One big factor for the nation's development is the liberalization of base prices such as gasoline and electricity. Following the parliamentary elections in September 1996, the new government was formed by the "Democratic Union," which is a coalition of the Mongolian National Democratic Party and the Mongolian Social Democratic Party. For the first time in the history of the nation, power was shifted from one side to another. The new government decided to liberalize base prices as part of the "shock therapy" to develop the national economy, which was then on the brink of collapse, despite minor improvements in the recent times. However, as a result, the people living in poverty were badly hurt and immediate steps had to be taken to address to their problems.

The government of Mongolia regards its people as having a high potential for creative and intellectual work. Hence "human resources" are at the core of its development policy. Although the economy is experiencing a tough transitional period, 17.6 percent of the national centralized budget is earmarked for education, about 10 percent for health, and 11.8 percent for social security.

1. U.S.$1 equals 851 tugriks.

The process of economic reform and structural adjustment operates in the face of rising unemployment, growing poverty, and an emerging disparity in the living standards of the population. These changes in the national economy have had a strong impact on the status of women and children. The government is acutely aware of the cloud of poverty which hangs over the nation. It has approved policies on poverty alleviation and has initiated different activities toward eradicating poverty. However, it would be hard to overcome this barrier without proper economic management.

Several months have passed since the new government took over following the parliamentary elections. In the past, the government has evaluated the real socio-economic situation, and, on the basis of that, has defined its action plan and begun to implement priority measures with resolute determination.

II. Mongolia's Poverty Profile

The economic context

Until 1990, Mongolia was a classic example of a centrally planned economy. By historical standards, and compared to the other countries of the communist bloc, Mongolia did relatively well under the old system, largely due to its low initial level of development. It was transformed from an essentially pastoral agriculture economy into a relatively industrialized one with reasonably good social indicators, and it accumulated a fund of human capital unparalleled in low-income countries.

However, the outcome was, as in all Centrally Planned Economies (CPEs), a severely distorted, inefficient industrial base integrated with the CMEA[2] system and not viable in normal competitive market conditions. In Mongolia's case, the economy developed an extreme dependence on imports and on financial assistance from the former USSR. Imports reached 58 percent of the GDP, almost 80 percent of which came from the Soviet Union; annual external financing amounted to over 30 percent of the GDP. The collapse of the CMEA system and the halt of capital flow from the Soviet Union in 1990 left Mongolia in a very difficult situation. Disruptions in traditional trading relations and in the supply of critical imports strongly contributed to the economy's worsening situation. Imports mainly consisting of petroleum products, machinery, equipment, spare parts, and basic goods decreased by half by the end of 1990, and, in 1993, continued to fall to just a quarter of their 1989 level. Exports fell by 40 percent in 1990 and continued to

---

2. CEMA stands for Council for Mutual Economic Aid.

decline until 1993. The GDP fell by 2 percent in 1990 and by almost 10 percent in 1991; it further fell by 7.6 percent in 1992, and by 1.3 percent in 1994.

For the past seven years Mongolians have been branded as "lazy." In one sense it is true – for many years they lived in a state in which everything was readily made available to them without any effort. People received free education and medical care. The government sent people abroad to study for free, and when they came back a job was there for them – and the salary was not bad either. When a person had trouble with his or her job, he or she was sent to another post or was just ignored. The lifestyle was guaranteed: all children went to school and received an education; the word "unemployed" was unheard of. Everyone lived a similar life so nobody lacked anything, that is, no one felt deprived in comparison with others. If a given item was not available to one person, it was not available to anyone. No one was poor, and no one was rich: "poverty" did not exist.

However, times have changed. In 1989, the people revolted against the socialist state; they wanted to lead a different type of life. Dramatic changes began to take place as the waves of a market economy swept through the country. Money and wealth became everyone's dream. Trade and business came to be the main source of livelihood. Everyone got involved into some kind of trade, such as buying socks and shirts from China and selling them in Mongolia and Russia. People seemed to like their new lifestyle. But again, the times changed; some were luckier than the others. The lucky ones succeeded in making enough money to enlarge their businesses, but a majority was left with nothing – no money, no job, and no guarantee for livelihood. Many were left wandering on the streets; even the children were so anxious to earn money that they dropped out of schools and ran away from their families to live on the streets. For them, the "$" sign was more important than mathematics and science. As their parents searched for easy ways to get money, they left their children in the lurch to become beggars and pick pockets. Desperate adults began to sell everything they owned – their clothes, their entire wardrobes, even their houses. Only one thing mattered for them now, "wealth" or a bottle of vodka! The people became "lazy" because they lost interest in their low-paying jobs.

The country which was not accustomed to "poverty" has, thus, become a country of the poor. People are not only economically poor, they have also become mentally poor. Money has moved Mongolia into poverty. But again things are changing as transition progresses. "Education," in this changing scenario, has become a major value. The ambition for wealth is still there, but the rat race is slowing down. People have become aware of the importance of education and feel that without a good education they will not be able to compete in the world of the market economy. But the damage has been done – already a stratum of poor has formed and many children have dropped out of school to become street children.

Keeping fixed prices and tariffs for electricity, energy, and oil production has financially deteriorated fuel and energy institutions and made them heavily indebted. Evaluating the situation, the government had no option other than to liberalize basic prices and tariffs in order to facilitate the improvement of fuel and energy institutions' financial situation and to ensure fair market competition. It was a difficult decision to make, but it was the best hope, and the decision was the right one to reduce the budget burden and lead to economic recovery. The first months were hard on the people, especially those who were already poor, and those who lived just above the poverty line. Prices of foodstuff and consumer items rose when prices were liberalized, but in a short period of time they stabilized again.

One of the vital components of economic reform, the privatization process has slowed down, with negative consequences. The inflation rate almost reached 50 percent in 1996 and kept moving upwards. GDP growth was around 3 percent in 1996. The farming, mining, fuel, energy, and some other economic sectors were not able to achieve their planned targets. The 30 percent decline in the price of copper and the 20 percent decline in the price of cashmere wool in the world market had a negative impact on the national budget, causing a further deficit. As for the foreign trade turnover, it was over 1 billion U.S. dollars, which showed a small improvement. Imports exceeded exports. There is currently a deficit of around 70 million U.S. dollars in the overall foreign trade balance. It is also clear that the present unfair attitude toward state ownership, an increasing tendency for tax evasion, and loose discipline and irresponsible behavior have led to the further worsening of an already difficult economic situation.

In past years, the government did not have a proper policy on banking and credit. In fact, this laid the foundations of unemployment and poverty. Interest on loans continues to be sky high, which detracts people from venturing into big industry; the only course left for them is small trade, for which they can afford to take loans and pay them back quickly. The 1996 budget deficit exceeded 30 billion tugriks, which constitutes 5.7 percent of the GDP.

Poverty is a fact of life in Mongolia. A person whose living standard is below the subsistence level, is considered poor. The living standard is a systematic concept covering the population's consumption in respect to the overall social and economic development of a country and its pattern of consumption. According to the international definition, the criteria based on the above concept is called the *poverty line.* By 1996, around 100,000 households were categorized as poor, 43.2 percent of which lived in Ulan Bator. Out of all poor households, 21 percent were female-headed, 6.6 percent were headed by single parents, 45.2 percent had between two and five members, and 13.9 percent had eight or more members. According to the age structure, 47.9 percent of poor house-hold members were under sixteen years of age, 11 percent were elderly (pensioners), and 26.8 percent were unemployed.

Due to a decrease in overall living standards, it became imperative to develop a multidirected poverty alleviation policy for the population's living subsistence, health improvement, education, and social security, with special emphasis on vulnerable groups, such as children of poor households, the elderly, pensioners, and female-headed households.

Table 6.1 The Extent of Poverty in Mongolia

	Number (in thousands)	Percentage of the poor	Percent in Deep poverty	Percent in Serious poverty
Urban	478	38.5	12.2	5.7
Ulan Bator	214	35.1	10.4	4.5
Rural	350	33.1	8.9	3.6
Nationwide	828	36.3	10.9	4.8

In June 1995, within the framework of the Poverty Alleviation Program, the State Statistical Office of Mongolia, jointly with the World Bank, conducted the Living Standard Measurement Survey. Its main objectives were to determine that poverty was one of the main factors of the social crisis, to determine the extent of poverty, its causes and consequences, to estimate the minimum living subsistence level for the nation and for the various regions, and to find ways to eradicate poverty.

In accordance with the 1991 government decree, the minimum living subsistence level was defined for the first time in Mongolia. Since then it has been revised nine times. Such revisions were necessary due to rising inflation rates. Since 1991, the State Statistical Office has estimated the minimum subsistence level on the basis of the consumer basket and according to the consumer price index.

What is the *consumer basket?* The cost of the consumer basket is computed on the basis of the regular Household Budget Surveys carried out by the State Statistical Office. The basket is comprised of the basic necessary commodities and services. The population's consumption pattern is subdivided into eight groups. A total of 508 primary necessary commodities and services were selected for inclusion in the consumer basket; these were evaluated at current prices. Individual consumption was defined on the basis of the norms and standards set up by the State Planning Committee and by the decrees and rules passed in the 1970s and 1980s by other relevant ministries. Since 1992, the pricing of the commodities and services selected in the consumer basket has been done on the basis of the market prices of the particular region and city under consideration, and the minimum living subsistence level is adjusted accordingly.

The commodities and services selected in the consumer basket were classified into the following groups:

1. Foodstuffs
2. Clothing and footwear
3. Housing and utilities
4. Household items
5. Medical and hygiene items
6. Transportation and communication
7. Cultural items
8. Miscellaneous

There are differences in the structure of consumer baskets for the urban and rural population groups, and for men and women.

Consumer price. Since 1993, in addition to the computation of the consumer basket, the minimum subsistence level has also been determined using consumer prices from the (household) survey and market prices for various commodities and services.

In view of the base price liberalization in September 1996 and changes in the consumption pattern of the population, we will consider the revised, unofficial subsistence minimum based on the results of the consumer price survey for October 1996, without changing the consumer basket structure. The regular Household Budget Survey conducted by the State Statistical Office used the following indicators to determine the minimum living subsistence level: the average consumption of a household member, monthly monetary and total income, structure of the monthly monetary and total expenditure. Table 6.2 shows data on the approved subsistence minimum in 1995 and 1996.

For minimum subsistence living level estimates, the lowest price of goods and services, and the long durability of some consumption goods are taken into account. However, in rural areas, consumption goods are regarded as less durable. For computation, in addition to the cost of nonfoodstuffs and services, results of the Household Budget Survey carried out by the State Statistical Office (for the first nine months) were used.

Table 6.2 Population Consumption Patterns (in tugriks)

	Urban			Rural		
	1995	October	1996	1995	October	1996
		by price index	by basket		by price index	by basket
Foodstuffs	5979.7	9028.8	7321	4781.4		6900
Clothing, footwear	914.3	1323.8	1226	983.8		1473
Housing, utilities	533.8	976.2	1788	108.6		593
Household items	301.9	394.9	570	366.3		726
Medical, hygiene items	182.8	251.2	241	503.7		263
Cultural items	87.5	143.1	574	156.2		458
Transportation, communication	574		406			597
Miscellaneous		291	273			390
Total:	8000	12,400	12,399	6900	11,399.5	11,400

The expenditure on different consumption items for October 1996, used for the estimation of the minimum living subsistence level, are shown below:

1. *Foodstuff expenses.* According to the September results of the Household Budget Survey, daily foodstuff calorie intake by the member of a household below minimum living subsistence level was 1206.6 calories in urban areas, and 1640 calories in rural areas. These figures are only 66.1 and 94.3 percent of the standard calorie intake respectively of household members living below the minimum subsistence level. The low figure of daily calorie intake (1206.6) in the urban area shows how poverty is worsening in the urban population. For an adequate supply of food, 11,412 tugriks are needed in urban areas, and 8,382 tugriks in rural areas. If we compare data on consumption with the adjusted data on the minimum subsistence level according to changes in the price of commodities and services, we find that the consumption level is only 64 to 82 percent of the expected level of food consumption. The revised October 1996 data, based on the Consumer Price Survey, show that consumption expenses per capita in the urban areas have gone up from 8000 tugriks in 1995 to 12,400 tugriks; and in the rural areas, from 6900 tugriks to 11,400 tugriks. But these figures of actual expenditure still fall short of the minimum requirement of 16,490 tugriks in the urban areas and 12,882 tugriks in the rural areas.

2. *Clothing and footwear expenses.* These were computed on the assumption that households below the minimum subsistence level

are unable to purchase ready-made clothes and footwear. They are thus using cheaper materials to make them. The principle of the lowest market prices was also applied to this category.

3. *Housing and fuel expenses.* For this category, a different approach was applied because of the regional variations. For urban centers, the expenses related to housing, fuel, and electricity were taken from the Household Budget Survey data; but for rural areas it was assumed that none of these expenses are incurred since the rural population uses natural resources such as water and fuel without having to pay for them. In order to generate annual data to estimate housing expenses for the minimum subsistence level, it is assumed that poor people generally live in *ger* (a traditional tent dwelling). The latest estimation shows that a household living in a two-room apartment in a city has to spend 1,784 tugriks for rent; the same amount is paid for the use of electricity, fuel, and water by a *ger* household (1,788 tugriks). For a house in a rural area, the comparable expenses are 593 tugriks. Thus, urban housing expenses are three times that of rural ones.

4. *Expenses on household items.* For this category, basic estimates were made, using the average number of household members and their commonly used items, such as dressing tables, bookcases, etc. In some cases, the age structure of household members was considered.

5. *Expenses on medical hygiene items.* For this category, the age structure of the household members is an important criterion. However, the level of consumption for medical and hygiene items is assumed to be similar in both urban and rural areas.

6. *Expenses on cultural items.* This category includes the supplies needed for school-going children; for a newspaper subscription, and for minimum expenses for stationery.

Table 6.3 Poverty Assessment (in tugriks)

Items	Urban	Rural
Foodstuffs	7321	6900
Clothing and footwear	1226	1473
Housing – fuel and electricity	1788	593
Household items	570	726
Medical care	241	263
Cultural expenses	574	458
Transportation and communication	406	597
Miscellaneous	274	390
Total	12,400	11,400

As a consequence of the economic crisis and the continued failure of production, the living conditions of the people – especially, those of the most vulnerable groups – have dramatically deteriorated, and poverty and unemployment have become social problems. Current poverty in Mongolia is mainly a result of the economic crisis and restructuring. The number of unemployed people actively seeking jobs and registered at labor bureaus reached 55,200 as of December 1996, showing an increase of 10,900 as compared to December 1995. In previous years, the labor force increased by 3 percent, but there was no corresponding increase in the number of jobs. In fact, there has been a decline in the number of employees in the state-funded institutions and state-owned industrial enterprises.

When we talk about people who are not engaged in organized labor, we mean those who were registered as unemployed during the census. It is clear that many of them are engaged in some activities, either in the informal sector, in small trading businesses, or in petty services. Last year (1996), the Labor Department conducted a survey on unemployment and poverty covering 146,100 unemployed people. It found that 72,200 of them (49.4 percent) were working in the informal sector.

In 1991, Labor Coordination Agencies (LCAs) were set up at national and local levels to register those people who were actively seeking work, and to assist them in getting permanent or temporary employment. The number of the registered unemployed continues to change. In October 1996, these agencies registered 53,000 people; this is 6.5 percent of the economically active population. However, not many people register with the LCAs for the following reasons:

- The absence of a proper labor market and the comparatively low image and role of labor coordinating agencies.
- People who are actively seeking work do not approach LCAs because they do not provide an unemployment allowance and financial support. There are also restricted prospects for finding employment.
- By the end of 1995, in accordance with a government decision, all LCA registration books were revised and some corrections were made by artificially decreasing the number of unemployed people. As a result of this "organized" work, the unemployment rate has declined from 8.7 percent in 1995 to 5.4 percent in 1996.

The following are the major contributing factors to unemployment:

- Layoffs occurred in connection with structural adjustments and privatization. For example, in 1990 about 95.5 percent of those employed were engaged in the public sector; this percentage fell to just 27.7 in 1995, representing a loss of 249,000 jobs in the public sector during 1991-1995. This is linked with a sharp decline in production in state-owned industrial enterprises and the privatization of 474 public industrial enterprises.

- During the past few years, the coordinating system for the planning and distribution of cadres has become ineffective, and the method of preparing professional cadres has not been carried out in line with the structural reform strategy and the population employment policy. Because of these shortcomings, at least 50 to 60 percent of working age youth could not find employment either in educational institutions or in the job market.

- 75,900 children graduated from the eighth and tenth grades of the general education schools in 1996, at least 38,700 of whom have joined the ranks of the unemployed. The introduction of an education fee in vocational training has also influenced the growth of unemployment.

- Massive layoffs have also resulted from the shortage of foreign investment during the first years of the transition. Additionally, many industrial enterprises halted their operation or could not operate at full capacity due to the shortage of fuel, petroleum, and raw materials.

- The "laziness" of the people has also contributed to unemployment, as was mentioned earlier . There are signs that unemployment will continue to increase in the near future. The following are possible contributing factors:

  - With the liberalization of prices, the economic situation of industrial enterprises and economic entities will further deteriorate, demanding structural adjustment which will then result in further layoffs.

  - With the improvement of labor statistics, there will be a better enumeration of the unemployed, and therefore the figures will be slightly higher. The number of people registered as unemployed is likely to increase with the introduction of the unemployed allowance on 1 January 1997, as this may serve as an incentive for people to register with the labor coordinating agencies.

  - The number of unemployed people will increase if we add those who graduated from vocational training schools and those who have lost their market competitiveness in the private sector.

There is an indication of possible renewed layoffs in state-funded organizations as part of the structural adjustment program, particularly in the education and health sectors. The possible termination of pensions for those 103,000 people who were retired early should also be considered. If this possibility occurs then at least 50 percent of these people will join the ranks of the unemployed.

The number of unemployed people has thus reached almost 217,000, although only 53,000 have registered themselves with the labor exchanges as they are actively seeking jobs; these represent 6.5 percent of the economically active population and 4.9 percent of the labor resource. Growing unemployment is one of the major concerns of Mongolia.

Poverty is reflected not only in low income and a deterioration of the population's living standards, but also in several negative consequences, such as the deterioration of people's health due to malnutrition, a decline in morals, the disintegration of family structures, and a rising crime rate. More particularly, there has been a decline in educational and cultural achievements. The intellectual bankruptcy of the people, the rising number of school dropouts, and the increase in the number of street children are the most worrying aspects of the poverty phenomenon.

The problems faced by the vulnerable groups of the population will now be briefly discussed.

Street children

The socio-economic crisis of the 1990s gave rise to poverty, and as a consequence, many children ran away from home and joined the ranks of the street dwellers. The following are some of the reasons for this:

1. Family poverty (the basic needs of children cannot be met by families living in abject poverty)
2. Family conflicts (conflicts between fathers and mothers, lack of morals, family abuses)
3. Disruption of the moral and educational systems (children drop out from schools and are influenced by bad elements)
4. Limited access to public services

Street children can be divided into three different categories or groups along the general pattern followed in other countries on the basis of (1) the cause for leaving home, (2) their lifestyle, and (3) their upbringing. Thus, there are children (1) who work on the streets during the daytime but keep close contact with their families; (2) who have occasional contacts with their family but who generally spend a considerable period of time as homeless in streets; and (3) who have lost all contact with their family, and who lead a permanent life of homelessness.

Until 1994, there was no concrete policy to help street children. There was neither any information on their number, conditions, location, and needs nor any mechanism to extend help to them. To remedy this, a small project was launched with assistance from UNICEF, to evaluate the situation of street children, to prevent children from taking to the streets, and to help those who had become homeless. Within the framework of the project, "Assistance for Homeless Street Children," attempts have been made to devise ways of helping them.

An attempt has been made during the last two years to produce an integrated study reviewing the situation nationwide. According to the study, it is estimated that there are around 2,700 homeless or street children all over the country (although it should be noted that a study cannot cover everyone). Eighty percent of those who were studied live in *aimags,* provinces, and urban settlements along the main railway line. The main reason that children leave home is poverty in their family, which leads their parents to push them to the streets. Although there is a new law "On the Protection of Children's Rights," parents refuse to abide by it.

Aged and disabled people

During the past thirty years, the population of Mongolia has increased by 93.1 percent, with 1.1 million additional persons; the number of the aged has increased by 19.8 percent (263,000 people) during the same period. While the percentage of the elderly dropped from 11.1 to 6.9, their actual number has increased. By 1996, there were 158,600 aged people in Mongolia; of these, 37 percent were male and 63 percent female. Thus, there is a much higher percentage of aged women in Mongolia.

The constitution of Mongolia states that "every Mongolian citizen has the right to receive financial and material aid in the occasion of old age, loss of work capability, during prenatal and postnatal periods, and in other circumstances defined by the law." This provision of the constitution provides a legal foundation for the care of elderly people. Accordingly, men who have worked for twenty years and have reached the age of sixty, and women who are fifty-five and over are entitled to receive a pension. Under this provision, 125,600 people are currently receiving pension; these constitute 79.2 percent of the entire elderly population in the country. Pensions are the main source of their livelihood; the average monthly pension is equivalent to 32.1 percent (in some cases, 26.8 percent) of the average monthly wage, which is 1500 tugriks higher than the present minimum living standard level. However, considering the present low level of salaries and the increasing price of consumer goods and services, pensions are not sufficient to meet the essential needs of a normal life. There are also 8,400 aged people who do not qualify for social care pensions. They are those whose income is above the officially set minimum income level. The rest, 15.5 percent of the aged, are currently engaged in some kind of working activities for which they receive wages.

People with physical and mental disabilities from birth, including the blind, hard of hearing, those with speech impairments, and the victims of accidents are considered to be disabled. There are over 40,000 disabled people in Mongolia; 14,400 of them are mentally retarded and 8,700 are under the age of sixteen. Ninety-three percent or 37,300 get some type of allowance from the government.

Women

Although women's status is comparatively high in this country, more and more women are suffering from negative social consequences like poverty and unemployment. Women are often the victims of poverty because they are believed to lack economic potential and are, therefore, given low priority in the labor market. According to 1996 statistics, the employment rate for women is 10 percent lower than for men, and more than half of the registered unemployed seeking work are women. Other contributing factors are women's limited access to credit and economic resources, their inability to upgrade their education, to obtain vocational training, to administer property, and their very low representation at the decision making level.

Currently, many new catchwords, such as household economy, household budget, household manufacturing, and female-headed households have become common in everyday life. In this transition period, these new catchwords usually bear very distinctive prefix of "poor." "Female-headed household" and "poverty" in particular have become synonymous.

Although poverty affects the entire family, women in the family often suffer the most. This situation is linked to the traditional role of women in family affairs. The situation is particularly difficult for those women who head their households. The increase in the number of female-headed households is due to the rise in the number of divorces, nonregistered marriages, and unwed mothers. There are also women who have to assume the responsibility of heading the household because their husbands are either chronically ill, disabled, or alcoholic.

The largest number of female-headed households (at least 1.4 to 4.8 percent higher than the national average) are in the Umno-Gobi, Gobi-Altai, Bayanhongor, Huvsugal, and Dornod aimags. At present, almost half of these female-headed households (46.1 percent) are living in poor conditions. Out of all poor families, 22.5 percent are female-headed households. The greatest concentration is in the Bulgan aimag where 87 percent of the female-headed households are poor. In the Dornod aimag, this percentage is 71.9; in Tuv, it is 69.6; and in the Bayanhongor aimag, it is 58.8.

About 62 percent of these female-headed households are in the cities and the rest (38 percent) are in rural areas. As for the capital city Ulan

Bator, about 9.1 percent of all households are female-headed, 39.4 percent of which are poor. They constitute 29.5 percent of the poor households in the city. This proportion is 7 percent higher than the national average, indicating a higher percentage of poverty in the city. At least 30.6 percent of poor families have four or more children below fifteen years of age. According to one survey, there are 186,600 children belonging to poor families, 46 percent of whom live in the cities. Many of these women do not have any regular source of income. Others receive a pension or allowances which are not sufficient to cover their expenses, even for essential needs. There are many women who cannot pay for their apartments, fuel, children's nursery, vocational and higher education fees, clothing for their children, and stationery.

III. Poverty Eradication: Policies and Actions

The Copenhagen Declaration and Program of Action together comprise a new social contract at the global level. As the former secretary-general of the United Nations, Dr. Boutros-Boutros Ghali, rightly underlined in his Address to the World Summit for Social Development:

> The social problems, which once could be confined within borders, now spread across the world, once considered to be the exclusive responsibility of national governments, they are now of global scale and require global attention .... True and lasting success in putting the Copenhagen agreements into action will require a coalition of all actors, working together towards the same objectives. Governments will need to act in partnership with experts, parliamentarians, grass-roots and religious organizations, trade unions, business and non-governmental organizations, harnessing their talent and enthusiasm. Together we must continue our collective efforts to help shape a better common future for all nations, communities and people.

Since the Summit, a national committee headed by a cabinet minister responsible for social policy has been entrusted with a renewed mandate to ensure nationwide coordination of the Summit follow-up. In 1994, the Government of Mongolia adopted a "Poverty Alleviation Program" (NPAP) in view of the urgent need to develop and implement a strategy for the eradication of poverty, a relatively new phenomenon in Mongolia. Many social problems have become acute, and some new ones have emerged as Mongolia has been making the transition from a centralized planning and state-subsidized social system to a market economy with its own social safety arrangements. The NPAP's overall aim is to reduce the number of people in poverty from 26 percent to 10 percent by the year 2000. It focuses on strengthening the institutional capacities of the government, at both central and local levels, for policy management and poverty monitoring; on promoting human resource development by providing better access to health and education opportunities; and on alleviating rural poverty by developing and strengthening the basic social safety net. Special emphasis is placed on income generation and the promotion of employment opportunities among small herders and the livestock sector in general. To raise the income of the rural poor, the NPAP has planned to restructure the rural economy through market development and the upgrading of basic infrastructure, targeting the poorest households for special credit and welfare schemes; and promoting small-scale rural industries in agro-processing and non-farming activities.

The implementation of this program is decentralized, with most activities directly carried out at the local and grassroots levels, by the local governments or by nongovernmental organizations and cooperatives. To ensure the coordination of NPAP activities at the national level, a Poverty Alleviation Committee, composed of representatives of sectorial ministries and relevant NGOs, has been set up.

One of the objectives of the National Poverty Alleviation Program is to increase support for and further develop the poverty alleviation fund and poverty alleviation activities. Activities include:

1. training the secretaries of Poverty Alleviation Councils at the lower levels of administration;
2. appointing and training social trainers in each aimag and in Ulan Bator who are responsible for ensuring full community participation at the local level by training and facilitating local development activities;
3. the NGO Training of Trainers Program, to help enhance their role as implementers and facilitators of local community activities; and
4. the launching of the National UNV Program, which will include recruiting ten community activities and skills trainers.

The government of Mongolia, in collaboration with relevant NGOs, is currently developing a strategy to address the issue of street children. A comprehensive program will be developed which will provide support and maintenance services for the children while at the same time discouraging them from moving to the streets.

There are currently over forty organizations, including government agencies and national and international NGOs, which are involved in poverty alleviation activities in Mongolia. The NPAP is preparing a mechanism to ensure the coordination of all poverty alleviation activities, to avoid a duplication of efforts, and to enhance the effectiveness of all activities. Support will also be provided to partners by opening up access to the Poverty Alleviation Councils and involving relevant parties in training programs. Poverty Eradication Week, which took place between 17-24 October 1996, helped raise awareness of specific poverty issues in Mongolia among the general public, NGOs, and government organizations.

The new government of Mongolia has promised to pursue a policy allocating 20 percent of its budget and 20 percent of all foreign aid and assistance to social development activities, adopting the 20/20 formula proposed at the Summit. At the same time, it will create the conditions so that everyone can complete education and training, and it will ensure that those engaged in productive labor receive sufficient social guarantees to meet their health and other requirements. The government intends to meet these ends by the year 2000.

The government considers that the best way to raise the living standards of the population and to reduce poverty is to increase employment opportunities. Therefore it plans to pursue an active policy of human resource development. The minimum living standards (poverty line) will be swiftly reviewed and revised in the light of price and tariff changes. Subsequent measures aimed at raising the salaries of state and government employees, as well as those of workers at state-financed organizations, will be implemented so that their salaries are sufficient to meet the required living standards level.

In order to improve social protection measures in accordance with the market relations requirements and to guarantee the right of citizens to health insurance, pension and benefits, a set of new laws on social protection have been drafted and submitted to the parliament. At the end of 1996, the parliament adopted these laws. These will facilitate the accumulation of reliable financial resources for a social security network. Social insurance is a social protection activity in which, by collecting certain amounts of money from employers and employees, a social fund is set up to finance health requirements, pensions, and benefits for those who have met the conditions set by the insurance law.

There is a pressing need for the government to set up an independent social assistance system and to have a focal point for the coordination of the activities carried out throughout the country. The government will also spend aid received from foreign countries and international organizations in a coherent manner, to mobilize economic entities and NGOs in this endeavor.

There is a need to refine the methodology for defining poverty by income parameters. While determining poverty status by income, additional indicators should be used. These could be the number of capable persons in a household; individual's determination to get employment;

health status; the main capital of the household; the number of cattle it owns; whether it has a protector with sufficient income, etc. The government intends to carry out tangible work in this regard in the near future and plans to constitute a more effective form of assistance, to set up government-funded polyclinics for the poor, to open dormitories for the poor in urban areas, as well as to provide one-time assistance in fuel and other materials during the winter season.

Before 1990, over twenty public organizations functioned under one-party leadership and governance in Mongolia. From this fact it is clear that nongovernmental organizations did not exist in Mongolia before 1990. Thanks to the democratization process, so far about 300 public organizations have been registered with the Ministry of Justice. They now carry out their activities within the constitutional framework but independent of any political party or the government. They are funded by their members' fees, contributions from individuals or organizations, and by revenue gained from their own activities. The public organizations operating now regulate their activity according to statutes adopted in meetings of their members and supporters.

NGOs have only recently come into existence in Mongolia and they are still at the very initial stages of their development. Many NGOs in Mongolia are concentrating on, and organizing public efforts for, protecting the interests of working people and the unemployed in specific areas. They are teaching them to be self-sufficient in the market economy environment. Some other NGOs are trying to create conditions for public participation in the government policy formulation process by promoting public activism, developing closer relations between the government and the people, and striving to ensure that public views and opinions reach law-making bodies and institutions.

The Mongolian Red Cross is expanding its relations with the International Federation of Red Cross and Red Crescent Societies and other similar foreign organizations. It has received aid from them in the form of food products, various types of clothing, medicine and injections, medical equipment, and appliances; and it delivers these to the rural poor and those affected by natural disasters. Assistance is also provided in cash. The Mongolian Veterans Association has created a pensioners partnership which engages able-bodied people in production and services in order to aid vulnerable groups. The Mongolian Women's Federation, in collaboration with UNIFEM, has implemented a project for improving women's lives and health. From June 1993 onwards, the branches of this project in Ulan Bator and Darhan interviewed women interested in running small businesses and gave them three to six month soft loans. And as a result, nearly sixty sole proprietorship concerns have been set up and about 600 women have gained employment. Clothes, bars of soap, and sewing machines received from philanthropic and non-governmental organizations in Japan, the Republic of Korea, and Germany were distributed as a grant to female-headed households with many children and no income. Some of these items were provided to set up a revolving fund to help needy women, thus creating conditions to increase women's income and create employment.

The work initiated and carried out by the NGOs demonstrates that distributing gifts to the poor during the present transition period is not considered effective as it makes them more consumption oriented. Instead, it is better to form small groups on a voluntary basis to conduct various training activities in order to enable family members who can work to gain professional skills and run small businesses. Taking measures to provide them with soft loans and leasing them equipment is also helpful.

Poverty is one of the major problems which should be solved despite all of the difficulties of transition. Poverty alleviation has not only economic significance but is also crucial politically and socially. Though there are many ways to combat it, job creation is the best way. Provisions such as clothes, food, and money for the poor are only gestures of charity. They are goodwill actions, but that is not the rational way to improve living standards. Promoting employment is the most effective means to reduce poverty.

As the prevailing poverty and unemployment are an outcome of economic and social policy, the government is paying utmost attention to these problems. Consistent with the framework of macro-policy to accelerate the transition to a market economy, measures are being taken to create a new structure of social safety nets. Though all efforts are aimed at increasing the population's guaranteed level of living every half year, the final results are not satisfactory due to difficulties in the economy, foreign exchange constraints, and a shortage of financial resources.

The government is, however, taking several measures to improve the level of employment and to decrease the unemployment rate. Through the central and local labor bureaus 18,700 people were provided with jobs in 1995 and another 4,300 people in the first quarter of 1996. Three thousand, two hundred people were provided with short-term training, after which they were able to gain employment. Revolving concessional loans of 20.9 million tugriks from the "Employment Promotion Fund" were provided to low-income residents in six aimags and eight districts. As a result, 200 new jobs were created. Additionally, the government is implementing the Technical Assistance for the Commonwealth of Independent States and Mongolia (TACIS) project in collaboration with the European Union to improve employment policy in accordance with the market economy requirements. It is also establishing capable agencies to deal with employment issues at the national level, improving labor statistics, and renewing tariffs to match international standards.

The following activities have been carried out within the framework of this project:

- Draft laws on the promotion of employment and proposals on the structural adjustment and organizational reform of central and local institutions, designed to implement labor market policy, have been formulated.
- By the resolution of the State Great Hural, the central agency for employment issues, the "Agency for Labor Coordination," has been established.

In order to facilitate the creation of additional jobs for women and poor people in the private sector, the Asian Development Bank provided a soft term loan of 3 million U.S. dollars to promote employment for low-income people in Ulan Bator. It will result in the creation of 10,000 new jobs. As of today, a loan worth 1.4 million U.S. dollars has been given to 274 economic entities. The first part of the project is being implemented in Ulan Bator.

With some commodity assistance from the U.S., a Fund has been established to support small- and medium-sized enterprises and household industries. This is an efficient form of alleviating poverty which will help create jobs for the poor, train them, and make their livelihoods sustainable.

In addition to the creation of conditions to provide jobs to all those who can work, there is an acute need to help those who are not able to work. Some measures are already being taken to help the disabled poor. These include setting up "care centers" in Ulan Bator and in some aimag centers which can provide these people with food, clothing, and specialized jobs.

The government understands its responsibility, and is focusing on the creation and increase of funds, using all its capacities in order to implement the national program and to improve the living standards of the population. Poverty alleviation, the improvement of national management capacity, and the development of the industrial infrastructure are the "three milestones" of the government's policy and plan of action. In order to achieve these three basic objectives, the people should bear the major part of the burden and responsibility. For this purpose, we should mobilize all our financial and capital resources, coordinate the work, and ensure the efficient use of resources.

During this difficult time of transition and due to resource constraints, the government of Mongolia is having difficulties implementing the above program alone. Therefore, assistance and support is desperately needed, from donor countries and international organizations, to overcome the barrier of poverty – a big restraint on development. The government will have to pay special attention to the creation of mechanisms for the rational utilization of loans and aid intended for poverty alleviation. This will require decentralization (to generate self-reliance) and joint efforts through the exchange of information, consultation, and coordination of the activities.

The government considers halting economic decline and providing a means for encouraging production to be the most important conditions for poverty alleviation. The realization of this goal will, first of all, depend on how production is increased. Recovery of production will not only restrain economic decline, it will also create the basis for sustainable growth and create an environment for poverty alleviation. In carrying out its policies on production recovery, the government is pursuing the main principle that a favorable environment should be created for all entities in any sector (private or public) engaged in production, by using classical methods of market economy relations which will lead to a full recovery of the country's economy and build a basis for sustainable development. With the simultaneous recovery of production and the halting of economic decline, employment will rise and the production and supply of commodities will be increased. In order to overcome transition period difficulties within a short period of time, assistance from donor countries and international organizations plays an important role, and the government believes that this support will not only continue but will be further expanded.

Rural poverty alleviation

Mongolia's rural economy and society have been, and still are, dominated by livestock herding. During the 1950-1990 period, the countryside was organized through collectives (*negdels*) and state farms, which had wide-ranging responsibilities, not just for the organization of production and marketing, but also for social provision and the social safety net. For example, they provided for the elderly and supported maternity hostels. Traditional forms of organization and resource use survived to some extent during the socialist period. When the dismantling of the state apparatus started in 1990, the negdels evolved into a variety of institutional forms, and some traditional institutions have re-emerged.

While the reforms now taking place in Mongolia have created new opportunities, they have also created serious problems in rural areas, including an increase and intensification of poverty. The dissolution of the negdels has removed one of the key rural institutions, and has created major dislocations in production, marketing, and social provisioning. Private sector institutions have been created and have started to function, although they are still weak. Land tenure reforms are being enacted, and there is an opportunity for the development of a land tenure policy to protect the rights and access of poor and female-headed households. The liberalization of livestock marketing has had mixed results and the current situation is confused. The marketing situation and the terms of trade facing livestock producers have deteriorated markedly, and marketed livestock numbers have fallen substantially. The poorer rural households, in particular, have suffered because of the decline in food availability and lack of food security. Rural poverty has emerged on a large scale and current responses seem to be inadequate.

Taking the inflation level into account, the government is increasing the wages and salaries of state employees, and the pensions and allowances of the citizens, as much as possible. During the last two years, civil servant wages have been increased by 7.6 times and the pensions for the elderly and disabled were increased 5.2 and 6.6 times respectively. The social protection pension has been increased by 11.5 times. Increases in per capita income are based not only on recovering/compensating price and tariff rate growth, but also on the principle of smoothly raising the living standard of the population.

Within the framework of the National Poverty Alleviation Program, the government and the local administration are engaged in the implementation of projects and programs targeted at the vulnerable sections of the population. These include implementing activities in aimags designed to provide vocational training to disabled adults, to cover the needs of mentally retarded and disabled children in schools and kindergartens, and to supply them with necessary training materials. Projects that are designed to provide temporary and/or permanent employment and to generate income resources for unemployed people in accordance with the specific conditions of the region are also being implemented. However, it is true that previously adopted legislation regarding social care could not be implemented with the existing budget resources. Currently, almost 20 percent of the population receives some kind of allowance from the state budget and the social insurance fund. This is a great burden on an already fragile economy.

The government is not taking any measures to increase salaries and pensions or to make cash reimbursements to civil servants and the vulnerable sections of the society in view of the liberalization of the base prices and tariffs, as that would further increase budget expenditure and encourage artificial price hikes. However, it is looking at the possibility of increasing the real income of civil servants and employees of the state budget institutions – for example, giving them responsibility for at least

80 percent of their social and health insurance which is being deducted from their pay. It is also proposing to finance the cost of high education of one child per officer. The government is also focusing on the stabilization of the macroeconomy and the creation of a favorable environment to facilitate further economic growth. It does not, however, intend to ignore the issues related to the social protection of the population. In November 1996, the State Great Hural approved the government's Plan of Action. Additionally, the State Great Hural recently approved the directive for 1997 socio-economic development and the budget.

The government attaches exceptional importance to the realization of an active investment policy in order to ensure further economic growth. During the coming three and a half years, 20-25 percent of the GDP will be allocated for investment. In addition to that, special importance will be given to the effective and efficient utilization of foreign loans and grants, the bulk of which will be diverted to the electricity, energy, fuel, transportation, and communication sectors, and to the development of infrastructure. Common sense tells us that with the improvement of infrastructure, the national economy will stand in improving stead, and more jobs will be created along this lengthy but right process.

The goal in 1997 is to ensure 5.8 percent GDP growth through the rapid development of the agriculture (farming, livestock breeding), mining (copper, gold, coal, oil, uranium), fuel, energy, and construction sectors. The government also intends to pursue a policy designed to increase supply in order to meet the market demand to ensure comparatively stable prices and tariffs, and to arrest the annual inflation rate at 35 percent. The government aims to ensure a positive current budget by increasing budget revenue and limiting financial expenditure, facilitating the reduction of the budget deficit to 3.9 percent of the GDP. Measures will be taken to expand the base for revenue through amendments to the package taxation law.

The state is also intensifying the privatization process in order to assure tangible structural adjustment. Steps are being taken to take inventory of state properties and to identify those which will be transferred to private parties or to the local authorities. As a result of privatization, the state budget is assured of an allocation of 20 billion tugriks in 1997. With the aim of introducing structural changes to social insurance and the social care system, necessary amendments, alterations, and changes will made to the package of laws which will regulate these relations as of 1998. The intention is also to get rid of the "feed me" mentality, to revive social production, and to create an environment for early pension earners to find gainful employment so as to improve their living standards, guided by the principle of enabling every able person to contribute to the growth of the economy while acting independently. We also have to take measures to stop early retirement which involves the payment of pension without work.

The government also deems that the introduction of a five-day work-week is an important factor for the social issues of the civil servants and employees of the state-funded organizations. It is contemplating the creation of a system to ensure that genuinely needy people benefit from state social care and assistance programs.

In addition, it has been proposed that in 1997 a total of 6.9 billion tugriks, twice more than the previous year, be spent on social care activities for the vulnerable section of the population. These funds will be utilized to provide a concessionary price for house rent, telephone, fair-priced coal and wood for the most vulnerable households, and for assisting the disabled by providing discount fare for their travel, accommodation at sanatoria, medical treatment, and similar other measures. Priority will be given to mobilizing additional resources for the improvement of the living conditions of the most vulnerable section of the population.

Table 6.4 shows the expenditure on social protection (as a percent of GDP).

Table 6.4 Percentage of GDP Spent on Social Protection (1991-1995)

Expenditure	1991	1992	1993	1994	1995
Wages	9.8	6.8	4.7	6.1	6.3
Subsidies	9.8	3.8	2.1	2.1	1.2
Social security	12.3	6.2	7.3	4.8	5.4
Education	10.1	6.9	4.6	6.8	6.4
Health	5.5	4.0	4.0	4.8	4.6

Actions for special groups

For *Street Children*, mostly preventive work is carried out, centered on the family. However, more effort is needed to support the family, to discourage child labor, and to provide children with opportunities to continue attending school while they work to supplement the family income. Research in this direction is continuing and some organizations, like the "Association of Youngsters in Business," are supporting the children. Groundwork has been done to protect and assist these children as well as to prepare them for adult life. The centers rendering social services to street children are working with this project. Such centers have been established in Ulan Bator, Darkhan Uul, Orkhon, and in the Selenge provinces. There is a need to focus aimag centers on providing children with opportunities to master professional skills and find a vocational orientation. There are also programs designed to give the children education, offer them legal support (such as restoring their violated rights), and properly socialize them. Special education is needed for those children who are prone to commit crimes. This idea was reflected in a presidential decree in 1995 and in a resolution of the State Great Hural in 1996. However, so far nothing concrete has been worked out.

In the "national plan of action for the development of children up until the year 2000," the objective of ensuring that "street children who live without the care of parents or custodians and without housing and other essentials are returned to normal living conditions" was spelled out. UNICEF is planning to give financial and technical assistance to street children in its program for 1997-2001.

It is difficult to determine the exact number of street children today. The National Center for Children and the General Police Department are working to determine the reasons why children take to the streets, to keep a close watch on children whose rights are violated, and to help them return home. The prime minister of Mongolia has spoken out on behalf of the children suffering in the streets, many charities have been set up to help these children, but still there is no improvement in the situation.

According to the people who work at the above-mentioned activities, children do not seem to care about all the support offered to them, choosing the "freedom" of streets over the shelter of the care centers. When the police succeed in tracing the addresses of children and try to return them to their respective homes, the parents often do not want them back. They believe their children have a better chance at survival on the streets, and that they would starve at home. For this reason, the children often give false addresses. In 1996, one concerned office registered 2,238 children, of which only 600 were regular visitors to the office. In Ulan Bator 25-50 children are brought to this office each day and are sent to care centers. While researching this paper, this author had a chance to visit one of the care centers where some of the children were kept in lockup so that they could not return to the streets in the cold weather. When the room door was opened for me the children screamed "Teacher, we want to go back to the streets." I tried to find out whether they were treated badly, but this wasn't the case; they had everything at the center: televisions, video games, and the like. And yet, the children generally only came there when they were sick or tired of staying out, or when they needed clothes or other items for their daily use. And then they run back to the streets. It is a hard task to return street children to the right track. A special kind of educational curriculum is needed for the further development of these children.

As for *the Aged and the Disabled,* the government takes care of their health and food. It bears the expenses for their health insurance and domestic travel in connection with medical treatment. The cost of sanatoria for war veterans is also the responsibility of the government. As part of the privatization program, the elderly are allowed to inherit state-owned apartments free of charge. For those living in ger, the cost of wood and coal required to keep them warm is also borne by the government. The elderly are also entitled to obtain loans to construct their own private apartments or to improve the conditions of their housing. They are exempted from city bus fares. Special assistance is provided to them to obtain some private property. Due to privatization, at present over 90 percent of the livestock is in private ownership. Of the aged, 49.9 percent are living in rural areas and have benefited from privatization. Regular care and protection is provided to those older persons who have no one to look after them and who are incapable of leading an independent life. They are given free lunches, clothing, etc.

Despite all this care and attention from the government, it would be fair to say that poverty has impacted the elders. This is related to the people's attitude toward old age. Respecting elders was one of the notable characteristics of our traditional society and culture. But with the changing times, respect toward them has diminished greatly. They have become a "profitless fragment" of the society. When the economic burden fell on the public, it became impossible for many to worry about the aged because they had other pressing problems. As support for the elderly decreased, our grandparents and parents, turned poor. It would not be incorrect to say that most of the elderly people in our society live in poor conditions, with no one to take care of them.

The government is implementing the following measures to ensure the social security of the disabled:

- Pensions for the disabled are granted to those who paid pension insurance for three of their last five working years, before becoming disabled.
- The victims of industrial accidents who have lost their capability to work for long periods of time, or permanently, receive disability pensions regardless of whether they have paid pension insurance or not.
- According to the Social Security Law, those who have completely lost their capability to work, those who are handicapped by birth, those who fell victim to a disability before the age of sixteen, and those who are blind, deaf, or mentally retarded are entitled to receive social care allowances.

Labor codes and health insurance laws provide special provisions to ensure social guarantees for the disabled. There are special tax concessions for employed disabled people. Also, the incomes of economic entities that produce equipment for the disabled are tax exempt. The government has made necessary reimbursements six times in connection with the introduction of the floating exchange rate, the liberalization of the rice business, and the growth of the inflation rate. As a result of these measures, the size of pensions for the disabled increased by 17 times.

A draft proposal to increase reimbursements to those disabled people who began receiving allowances before 1 January 1995 was submitted to a cabinet meeting discussion, and the following laws were formulated:

- a law on minimum wage,
- a law on immigrant workers and the export of labor,
- a law on labor security,
- an amendment to the employment law, and
- a law on the creation of workplaces for disabled people.

One way in which to ensure social guarantees for the disabled is through state assistance and concessionary services, similar to the services for the aged. The disabled also enjoy special privileges, such as free city transportation and the right to live in care centers if they do not have a caretaker.

There is one special vocational training school and three small production units operated by disabled people in Ulan Bator and about ten more small sections and units in the local regions employing over 500 disabled people.

Special attention is paid to the rehabilitation of disabled people, to their access to vocational training, and to the improvement of their living conditions. For example, education for disabled people has been regulated at the state policy level. There are several special training centers and about 140 special classes, groups, and schools for disabled, blind, and mentally retarded children, nationwide. The government is taking measures to prevent disability, to improve working conditions, labor security, and medical services. The state helps the disabled to participate at national and international cultural and sporting events. These activities have been widely supported by economic entities and individuals.

Several steps have been taken to help the poor *Women*. Way back in 1988, the Mongolian Women's Committee, then representing women at the decision making level, initiated a "Care" tour and set up an "Affection Foundation" to help poor female-headed households with many children and orphans. They helped enroll more than 700 children in kindergartens and nurseries, and also admitted some mothers in sanatoria for treatment. In 1990, the Mongolian government provided the Affection Foundation with 3 million tugriks from the state budget.

Through this foundation, female-headed households from the Gobi desert region were able to acquire livestock.

In order to facilitate the implementation of the decision of the Fourth World Conference on Women, held in 1995 in Beijing, the Mongolian government approved a "National Program for the Empowerment of Women." In its chapter on "Women and Poverty," the program publication stated that poverty among women would be reduced by 50 percent by the year 2000 (Government of Mongolia 1995a).

The Government of Mongolia has reached an agreement with the Asian Development Bank for a loan of 3 million U.S. dollars to implement the MON/1920 project designed to increase job opportunities. With the assistance of Japan, and in collaboration with the World Bank, twenty-four small-scale projects were designed to generate income in Ulan Bator and eight other provinces. Within the framework of these projects, 700 people, including female-headed families with low income have been provided with permanent or temporary employment. During 1993-1995, about 4000 women found employment through central and local brokers.

In collaboration with UNIFEM, UNFPA, and ILO, and also with the embassies of Australia and the Netherlands, the Mongolian Women's Association has created a network for the welfare of the female-headed households. Through TACIS (Technical Assistance for the Commonwealth of Independent States), as well as in cooperation with the relevant institutions of Japan, it is carrying out a project to generate additional income for women to promote family well-being.

In 1996, 8 million tugriks were allocated from the state budget to provide school uniforms for orphans and children from extremely poor families, including female-headed families. UNDP created a Women's Development Fund in March 1996 with a contribution of U.S.$700,000. This fund was organized within the framework of the National Poverty Alleviation Program. The government spent 69.8 million tugriks to maintain maternity rest homes, and 3911.1 million tugriks on health insurance fees for the vulnerable sections of society.

The UNESCO-funded project "the informal education of cattle-breeding women in Gobi aimags," 510/MON/10, is being successfully implemented in five Gobi aimags, covering 15,000 women. The next stage of the project is under way.

The following are actions that could be initiated to eradicate poverty among female-headed households and street children:

- Introduce some social protection measures designed to address social, cultural, and economic issues related to the increasing cost of raising children. Formulate and implement projects and concrete programs designed to support families – to facilitate their stability and to help the increasing number of female-headed households.

- Implement the goals advanced by the "State Policy on Population," adopted by the State Great Hural in 1996 to promote family welfare and stability in all the general guidelines on socio-economic development and in the annual national and local budgets.
- Ensure the close linkage between the goals advanced by the National Poverty Alleviation Program in regard to women and the other national programs in the fields of food, health, and education.
- Carry out surveys during the 1999 census on single mothers and fathers raising their children.
- Help poor women who head households to survive through the sponsorship of wealthy and capable people (encourage the movement to help the needy).
- Provide a small amount of soft loans (100,000 tugriks), considering the possibility of quick repayment, and regulate their proper usage.
- Attach priority importance to providing shelter to poor female-headed households, while preventing a concentration of poor in one locality.
- Take special measures on behalf of street children and focus on their education and health protection.
- Set up a number of consulting centers in urban and rural areas and provide legal and health consultations.

The time and necessity have come more than ever for the private sector to step up its development. The government is trying to support businesses as best as it can so that they can share the burden of social care. One of the main goals of economic policy today is to rebuild and restructure domestic industry. Private companies have established many new types of services such as hotels and restaurants, and have they entered the mining industry. They have given jobs to many unemployed and their salary scales are better than those of the government.

The creation of a proper legal environment for private sector investment is essential. The current laws on foreign investment need to be revised to create this environment and make investment a reality. The relevant institutions are also formulating draft proposals to promote small- and medium-sized industries and to develop savings and loan cooperatives.

Conclusion

Today everyone agrees that poverty is not a new, post-communist phenomenon. Prior to 1911, and even after the advent of the socialist regime, poverty was very present in Mongolia. However, until 1990 we continued to pretend that we were all rich and that poverty did not exist. We used to boast that the poor resided only in America, and that poverty was a non-communist phenomenon. But with the collapse of communism, we came face to face with reality and became aware of the appalling poverty conditions in our country.

Poverty is a reality in Mongolia. There are poor communities which lack the necessities of life. Moreover, there is a prevailing mentality about poverty which is very frightening. We now realize that people living in poverty, and in a poor society, lack intellectual prowess, technical skills, and the knowledge to properly manage and develop their lives; and so they remain underdeveloped. Poverty is increased by a lack of private property and a stable income source. During the socialist regime, the government was the sole source of income for all citizens, but with the continuous decline in domestic industry, many were rendered underpaid and unemployed. In addition, the policies pursued by the government were totally counter to the welfare of the people. The banking system was inadequate and the interest rates were too high; all this discouraged the private sector from investing in industry. Most small entrepreneurs took the safer route of trade in order to make quick profits and repay their loans. This resulted in a price hike in consumption goods on the market. And so the burden fell on the pockets of poor consumers. Prices increased to such a degree that even a generally well-paid civil servant could not afford to buy a pair of shoes with his or her monthly salary. Poverty and unemployment have affected both the morale and the morality of the people. The rising incidences of theft, burglary, corruption, deception, juvenile delinquency, and prostitution are other consequences of this disturbing phenomenon.

Sadly enough, poverty is not the worst part of the unfair system. What is worst is the loss of social and ethical values. Mongolia is a nation rich with historic traditions, where "the truth triumphs." However, in recent years, it has become a society in which "money and power triumph." The new government has promised to reform and restructure all its "bad habits." This can be done only when the government, first of all, directs its policies toward the development of domestic industry. The monetary, financial, and credit systems need radical restructuring, as do investment and tariff policies. Secondly, the people should be enabled to acquire and own property. Land and housing privatization must be properly encouraged and favorable conditions must be created for investment, both domestic and foreign. Third, the current National Poverty Alleviation Program should be implemented in earnest to eradicate poverty.

Following the experience of other countries in which social funds have been set up to deal with the "social costs of adjustment," Mongolia should also set up such a fund. Such a fund could be seen as a strong temporary financing entity, which would manage loans efficiently and promptly while ensuring accountability and transparency. Thus, the right institutional framework combined with appropriate procedures could provide the government with additional capacity to manage a significant amount of resources for the poor.

Since the NPAP is designed to address poverty through macro-social policies, as well as through concrete short-term activities, it is important to prioritize the various activities in order to properly allocate funds. For the long-term macro-policies, funds in the initial phases would be needed only for purposes of technical assistance. The short-term activities are those needed for immediate intervention to provide relief from poverty. In other words, long-range policies should focus on creating conditions to prevent poverty, while short-range policies should focus on uplifting the poor.

Since the present government lacks implementing capacity, as does any other developing country, the creation of independent funds appears logical. Nevertheless, if a lack of implementation is an issue in Mongolia, it might be more desirable to create a single fund with four programs, instead of four different funds. The objectives of the social fund might include employment generation through well-targeted credit plans, infrastructure rehabilitation, and support for well-targeted social services.

All of the above-mentioned activities must be strictly managed and regulated. Auditing will need to be well organized, for instance with a unit in charge of overseeing all financial operations. External auditing to oversee unit allocations and expenditures could also be contracted out. All the necessary legal services will be needed to assist in legal aspects. Technical assistance will also be needed in order to run the activities precisely and expeditiously. And finally, an information network will be vital for the fund's activities.

Bibliography

Ardyn Erkh newspaper. 1996. "Poverty Why?" 10 December, no. 1433.

ESCAP. 1996. *Report of the Committee on Poverty Alleviation through Economic Growth and Social Development on Its Third Session.* Bangkok, 16-18 October. E/ESCAP/CPA (3) Rep.

Enkhsaihan, H.E. Mr. M. 1996. Statement by the Prime Minister of Mongolia at the general debate of the fifty-first session of the United Nations General Assembly, 4 October 1996.

Far Eastern Economic Review, 9 April 1992.

Government of Mongolia. 1993. *National Program of Action for the Development of Children in the 1990s.* Ulan Bator.

_____. 1994. *National Poverty Alleviation Program.* Ulan Bator, June 1994.

_____. 1995a. *Mongolian National Report for the Fourth World Conference on Women,* Beijing, China, 4-15 September 1995.

_____. 1995b. *Implementation Status of the Mid-Decade Goals of the National Program of Action for the Development of Children in the 1990s,* National Report, Ulan Bator, November 1995.

_____. 1996a. *The National Program of Action for the Advancement of Women.* Ulan Bator, June 1996.

_____. 1996b. *Report of Activities and Priority External Assistance Requirements.* Poverty Alleviation Program Office, February 1996.

Oyunsuren, D. 1996. "Street children and their fortunes." *Government News,* 23 November 1996, no. 267.

Permanent Representative and Ambassador of Mongolia. 1996. "Implementation of the Outcome of the World Summit for Social Development." Statement to the fifty-first session of the United Nations General Assembly, 4 October 1996.

Thesing, Josef, ed. 1995. *For Democracy and Social Justice.* Konrad Adnauer Stiftung.

United Nations. 1994. *Programme of Action Adopted at the United Nations International Conference on Population and Development.* Cairo, 5-13 September 1994.

_____. 1995. *The Copenhagen Declaration and Program of Action.* World Summit for Social Development, United Nations, New York, 6-12 March 1995.

UNDP. 1995. *Policy Papers Commissioned by UNDP for the World Summit for Social Development,* nos. 1-10.

_____. *Human Development Report* (for 1994,1995, and 1996).

UNRISD. 1995. *After the Social Summit: Implementing the Program of Action,* Geneva, September 1995.

The author expresses her grateful thanks to the following persons for giving their time for interviews.

J. Batsaikhan, instructor at the children's care center of the Bayan Gol district, 16 January 1997

Officer D. Dorjpalam, General Police Department's children's address-determining office, 16 January 1997

Sonom, Aagii, Tamir, children at the care center, 16 January 1997

T. Lhagva, national committee chairman of the National Poverty Alleviation Program, 12 January 1997

N. Gerelsuren, president of the Mongolian Women's Association, 24 January 1997

S. Onon, coordinator of the National Poverty Alleviation Program, 26 and 28 January 1997

.